IMPROVING IRELAND?

Improving Ireland?

*Projectors, prophets and profiteers,
1641–1786*

TOBY BARNARD

FOUR COURTS PRESS

Set in 10.5 pt on 14 pt Minion for
FOUR COURTS PRESS LTD
7 Malpas Street, Dublin 8, Ireland
e-mail: info@fourcourtspress.ie
http://www.fourcourtspress.ie
and in North America for
FOUR COURTS PRESS
c/o ISBS, 920 N.E. 58th Avenue, Suite 300, Portland, OR 97213.

© Toby Barnard 2008

A catalogue record for this title
is available from the British Library.

ISBN 978-1-84682-055-7

All rights reserved. No part of this publication may be reproduced, stored in or introduced into a retrieval system, or transmitted, in any form or by any means (electronic, mechanical, photocopying, recording or otherwise), without the prior written permission of both the copyright owner and publisher of this book.

Printed in England
by MPG Books, Bodmin, Cornwall.

Contents

	LIST OF ILLUSTRATIONS	7
	ABBREVIATIONS	9
	PREFACE	11
1	The cult and cultures of improvement	13
2	Sir William Petty, Irish landowner and improver	41
3	Interests in Ireland: Richard Lawrence as improver	73
4	Improving Ireland's past	89
5	Improvement, imagination and antiquarianism in mid-eighteenth-century Ireland: the earls of Egmont and Lohort Castle, County Cork	120
6	The worlds of an improving Galway squire: Robert French of Monivea, 1716–79	143
7	Ireland improved?	167
	INDEX	185

Illustrations

appear between pages 96 and 97.

1. Poor Clare nun and Franciscan friar from John Stevens, *Monasticon Hibernicum*, 1722
2. The coat of arms of John, duke of Montague, from Geoffrey Keating, *The general history of Ireland*, 1723
3. The coat of arms of William King, archbishop of Dublin, from Geoffrey Keating, *The general history of Ireland*, 1723
4. Engraving after a drawing by Jonas Blaymires of Limerick cathedral from Walter Harris (ed.), *The works of Sir James Ware*, 1746
5. Jonas Blaymires, drawing of the west end of St Patrick's Cathedral, Dublin, *c.*1737
6. Engraved portrait of Charles Smith, apothecary and historian, *c.*1750
7. Watercolour view from Burton House, County Cork, 1737
8. Kanturk Castle, County Cork, engraving, *c.*1740
9. Liscarroll Castle, County Cork, engraving, *c.*1740
10. W.H. Toms, engraving of Lohort Castle, *c.*1738
11. Lohort Castle, County Cork, watercolour, *c.*1840
12. Charles Hay, unexecuted garden design for Lohort, County Cork, 1742–3
13. Charles Hay, unexecuted garden design for Lohort, County Cork, 1742–3
14. Pair of chairs painted with armorials of earl and countess of Egmont, 1756
15. Plan of Cecilstown, County Cork, 1748
16. Engraving after Jonathan Fisher, the canal between the lakes of Killarney, 1770

Abbreviations

Barnard, *Ascents and descents*	T.C. Barnard, *Irish Protestant ascents and descents, 1641–1770* (Dublin, 2004)
Barnard, *New anatomy*	T.C. Barnard, *A new anatomy of Ireland: the Irish Protestants, 1641–1770* (New Haven and London, 2003)
Barnard, *Making the grand figure*	T.C. Barnard, *Making the grand figure: lives and possessions in Ireland, 1641–1770* (New Haven and London, 2004)
BL	British Library, London
Bodleian	Bodleian Library, Oxford
CRO	County Record Office
CSP, Dom; Ireland	*Calendar of State Papers, Domestic; Ireland*
ECI	*Eighteenth-Century Ireland*
EHR	*English Historical Review*
HIP	E.M. Johnston-Liik, *History of the Irish parliament, 1692–1800*, 6 vols (Belfast, 2002)
HMC	Historic Manuscripts Commission
Hoppen, *Common scientist*	K.T. Hoppen, *The common scientist in the seventeenth century: a study of the Dublin Philosophical Society, 1683–1708* (London, 1970)
IADS	*Irish Architectural and Decorative Studies*
IESH	*Irish Economic and Social History*
IHS	*Irish Historical Studies*
JRL	John Rylands Library, Manchester
JRSAI	*Journal of the Royal Society of Antiquaries of Ireland*
NA	National Archives, Dublin
NLI	National Library of Ireland, Dublin
Oxford DNB	*Oxford dictionary of national biography*
PRIA	*Proceedings of the Royal Irish Academy*

PRONI	Public Record Office of Northern Ireland, Belfast
Smith, *Cork*	Charles Smith, *The antient and present state of the county and city of Cork*, 2 vols (2nd edition, Dublin, 1774)
TCD	Trinity College Dublin
TNA	The National Archives, Kew
UL	University Library

Preface

THESE ESSAYS EXPLORE THE IDEAS and practices of improvement. They focus on seventeenth- and eighteenth-century Ireland. They have no pretensions to offer a comprehensive account of the cults and cultures of improvement, even in Ireland. Instead they look at specific episodes. Some were collective endeavours; others, the effort of an individual. As several of the improvers studied below found, long engagement with matters of improvement was sometimes disillusioning. In addition, activists on occasion believed that closer study of the past should be included in their programme. Such antiquarian investigations aimed not just to warn and to avoid earlier mistakes, but to recover lost wisdom which could help fashion a better Ireland. Accordingly, the essays explore varying emphases on past, present and future.

There is no wish to overthrow the familiar narrative of Irish society and economy transformed between 1641 and the 1780s. Parts of Ireland changed dramatically during this time. They prospered, were pacified, appeared placid, and were connected by thicker meshes with Britain, continental Europe, North America, the West Indies, even the Orient. Change occurred and was celebrated. The celebrants strove to measure it. Maps and surveys, both national and local, aspired to – and sometimes achieved – greater accuracy. So, too, did censuses and the recording of exports and imports.

Aspirations to objectivity were accompanied by changes in the ways in which Ireland was viewed and imagined. These shifts reflected obvious and visible alterations. Yet, they also owed much to changed ways of looking and reacting, which, in their turn, arose from broader cultural and intellectual developments. Frequently these influences came from outside Ireland: rationalism, enlightenment, romanticism, antiquarianism. One effect was to awaken appreciation rather than provoke condemnation of what was distinctive about the island. At the same time, the customary, hermetic and apparently unchanging survived in numerous places and minds.

The accounts that follow report the diversity, the setbacks and the oddities, as well as the undoubted achievements, of the zealous improvers. Maybe the quirks bulk too large. Since some of the studies rest on evidence that has attracted other investigators, the measured evaluations of the latter supply correctives. Despite Irish touchiness about the ownership of fields, when I have trespassed into what others may regard as theirs I have encountered nothing but friendliness and helpfulness. I am grateful to the many who have set me right and, more vitally, set me thinking and re-thinking. Among those who have written on topics treated here I thank particularly Tony Aspromourgos, Mervyn Busteed, Denis Cronin, Adam Fox, Eoin Magennis, Ted Greer McCormick and Andrew Sneddon. Again I owe much to the conversation, knowledge and hospitality of many. Notable among them are Bernadette Cunningham, Alison Fitzgerald, Desmond Fitzgerald (the Knight of Glin), David Fleming, Raymond Gillespie, David and Deirdre Hayton, Peter Harbison, Marie-Louise Legg, John Loughman, Anthony Malcomson and Edward McParland.

The first essay builds on one contributed to a conference connected with the Hartlib project at Sheffield University: M. Greengrass, M. Leslie and T. Raylor (eds), *Samuel Hartlib and universal reformation*. The account of Robert French was published originally in R. Gillespie and G. Moran (eds), *Galway: history and society*. Earlier versions of the Petty and Lawrence essays appeared in *Festchriften* for, respectively, Hugh Trevor-Roper and Aidan Clarke. I recall gratefully the zest with which Hugh opened, conducted and concluded a successful campaign for me to read the sources then in private ownership which underpin that essay. Aidan and Mary Clarke initiated me into the Dublin of the 1960s, now as remote in spirit as the 1760s. Since then Derry Falvey has enabled me to relate my wayward enthusiasms to specific locales in Munster. From the earliest to the most recent of the engagements reported here, Anthony O'Connor has joined me in hunting for Sir William Petty's iron and in dallying with the ladies of Lohort, thereby mitigating the austerities of research. And, yet again, all at Four Courts – especially Michael Adams, Martin Fanning and Anthony Tierney – practise a truly eighteenth-century approach to publishing and printing, for which this author is profoundly grateful.

CHAPTER ONE

The cult and cultures of improvement

IMPROVEMENT FUNCTIONED LIKE A CREED. Devotees tended to be conquerors and colonizers. An article of their faith was the superiority of their culture: they and their ways epitomized civility. Believing this, adherents had a mission to spread their beliefs and practices. Others, presently inferior, would benefit – materially and morally – from being improved.

Less friendly assessments see the doctrine as a device to justify either one race or one confession subjugating another. Annexation and occupation could be defended as necessary to implant a better culture and religion. The doctrine of improvement proved convenient in the treatment of Ireland. Invaders and would-be rulers insisted that English, Scottish and (after 1603) British ways improved on those of the indigenes. Written laws, leases and contracts would replace the apparently unstable and arbitrary arrangements of the native Irish. Clear administrative procedures and uniform courts would enforce them. Agricultural methods had to be altered; manufactures introduced; trade would displace barter; orderly towns would take the place of makeshift settlements. Dress, housing, diet, even language were not immune from the reformations. Then religion was tossed into this volatile brew: first, Roman rather than Celtic practices were to be promoted; then, Protestantism in place of Catholicism.

In Ireland, the English state inaugurated and oversaw the improvements. Urgent anxieties over security lay behind the initial English (or Norman) entanglement in the later twelfth century. The state decided to annexe and subordinate Ireland. Quickly ideology appeared to back the endeavours.[1] What might be interpreted simply as dynastic or national aggrandisement was represented differently. Subjugation was to be achieved through Irish assimilation to English – or Scots or British – habits, and (from the 1530s) to Protestantism. Benefits would accrue not just to the conquerors and colonists but to the subjected. When they were turned into loyal subjects of the English monarch – also king or queen of Ireland – they would be rewarded with peace, plenty and prosperity. Moreover, as Protestants, their eternal as well as earthly lives would be guaranteed.

---

1 J. Gillingham, 'Images of Ireland, 1170–1600: the origins of English imperialism', *History Today*, 37/2 (1987), pp 16–22; idem, 'The English invasion of Ireland' in B. Bradshaw, A. Hadfield and W. Maley (eds), *Representing Ireland: literature and the origins of conflict, 1534–1660* (Cambridge, 1993), pp 24–42.

Progress was disappointingly slow. The objective of an anglicized and docile Ireland eluded successive monarchs from Henry II to Henry VIII. Increasingly the task was delegated to others. Yet, the state never altogether extracted itself from the work. It set the framework, and offered incentives for groups or individuals to undertake the settling and development of Ireland. Legal and financial lures were employed. A series of confiscations transferred much land from the old, generally Irish and Catholic, owners to newcomers. The latter acquired the forfeitures at massively discounted prices. The grants contained formal requirements to improve the properties. The materials and styles of building were specified. So too were how the holdings should be peopled, stocked and cultivated. The aim was to turn the settlements into replicas of English originals.

By the seventeenth century, observers divided between optimists and pessimists. The gloomy, unconvinced that Ireland could ever be much improved, dwelt on the unchanging and intractable elements. Reports also told of wide divergences throughout the island. Dublin, the contiguous area of the Pale, the ports and regions intensively colonized in more recent times – notably parts of Ulster and Munster – offered reassurance that Ireland was indeed altering. In contrast, remoter places, when penetrated, looked impervious to improvement. A few intrepid travellers recounted what they had themselves encountered. More common were the sedentary, who repeated myths and legends. One visitor commented, 'Ireland hath ever been accounted a land of wonders, tho the greatest wonder seems to be that such incredible stories should be told and so firmly believed as they are by the Irish to this day.'[2] Both strangers and locals projected their own, sometimes bizarre presuppositions onto accounts of Ireland.

Even the hopeful admitted that improvements progressed more slowly than expected. The sluggishness was explained variously. Bleak determinists denied that the aboriginals were by nature capable of full social, economic and cultural development. Accordingly, they should either be supplanted by or exchanged for more malleable stock, imported from Britain and continental Europe. Other observers concluded that much of Ireland was held back by inhabitants who, through remoteness, primitivism and confession, had yet to adopt habits conducive to civility and prosperity. Thinking of this sort also encouraged the introduction of immigrants, who might act as a leaven. The newcomers would foster industry, social and civic activism and bring religious enlightenment. Fresh settlers were introduced throughout the seventeenth century. Their fail-

---

2 Thomas Denton, *A perambulation of Cumberland, 1687–1688*, ed. A.J.L. Winchester, Surtees Society, ccvii (2003), p. 515.

ure to bring the predicted transformation posed awkward questions. One response was not just to continue the existing strategy, but to intensify and accelerate it. More immigrants were needed and they should be helped more. Critics contended that the government, both in Dublin and (more commonly) in London, so far from giving the promised assistance, hindered the improvers. However, by the 1640s, as the island dissolved into warfare, the recently settled were confronted with embarrassments. The Protestant settlers had amassed much property and power but were negligent and selfish. Yet, Protestants in Ireland preferred to blame anyone except themselves – government, the Catholic majority, foreign powers, the geography of Ireland – for the disappointments. Nevertheless, the thoughtful conceded that the conquerors' claims to superiority needed to be demonstrated as well as asserted. The demonstration took the form of a practical patriotism, in which collective and individual drives to improve bulked large.

Introspection produced worrying conclusions. Too many of the new proprietors, it was alleged, enjoyed their recent acquisitions with no thought for others or for the future. So self-indulgence, luxury, negligence and absenteeism were criticized. Much in the critique derived from scripture, with the clergy loud in the denunciations of the sinners who retarded or ignored the duty of exploiting what God had created and Providence had given to them. Secular arguments, often intertwining with the religious, stressed civic and social responsibilities. Property-owners must remember that they had obligations towards the property-less.

Those who subscribed to the idea that external factors caused the disappointments acted to rectify the situation. They lobbied to modify or reverse the misconceived government measures. Such political campaigns were protracted and seldom totally successful. In the interim, individuals showed their credentials by innovating on their properties. These activists were a minority. Furthermore, useful as such private initiatives were, their impact on trade and farming was slow. In order to popularize improvements, collective action was required. To this end, groups were formed. During the 1650s, they were loose and informal. In the 1680s the efforts took on sharper definition with the establishment of the Dublin Philosophical Society. It proved short-lived, but it was followed by other organizations dedicated variously to reforming manners, founding Protestant schools, nursing the sick, relieving the poor and promoting agricultural and technological change. The societies became the focus of civic activism and patriotic endeavour. Fashion recommended a polite culture enthusiastic about material and moral betterment. In 1761, Edward Willes, a judge from England, toured Ireland. He observed that support for improvement was now *de rigueur* among the members of the grand jury – the elite of the county – even in the remoter regions.³ Few openly dissented from the credo. To that extent, attitudes had been altered. Whether they resulted in effective action is less clear.

II

Property conferred responsibilities. By the end of the seventeenth century, the dramatic and engineered reduction in the number of Catholic landlords left Protestants with the leading role as improvers. The new incumbents, keen to see off detractors, wished to show that they monopolized the doctrine and practice of improvement. This was not so. Catholics, where occasionally they did retain large acreages, as in Kerry with the Brownes, Viscounts Kenmare, or (on a smaller scale) Charles O'Conor in County Roscommon, ran regimes little different from those of energetic Protestant improvers.⁴ Despite what apologists for the Protestant interest maintained, ideology counted for less than rapacity or necessity in recommending improvements.

Any holder of Irish lands encountered frustrations and failures that might then prompt innovation and experiment. Those hitherto unfamiliar with Ireland, promised by the alluring brochures a status and income much higher than they could enjoy in Britain, were frequently disillusioned. Irish lands, other than in the low prices, did not meet extravagant expectations. Of necessity, owners, while grumbling at official unhelpfulness, schemed to increase the yield and value of their estates. They welcomed a creed that equated their self-interested actions with public spiritedness. As well as handing enhanced rentals to heirs, they were fashioning a prospering and peaceful Ireland, even perhaps a Protestant one. The Irish were being inured to useful labour. Tenants, faced with higher rents, sought the means to pay them. Some landlords introduced employments, such as textile-making, extractive and metallurgical industries, even fishing, or new crops – notably flax – which enabled tenants to diversify and so supplement their meagre earnings. In time, the volumes of inland trade and exports, as well as in the returns from land, grew. Improvers preened themselves.⁵

---

3 J. Kelly (ed.), *The letters of Lord Chief Baron Edward Willes to the earl of Warwick, 1757–62* (Aberystwyth, 1990), p. 95.   4 L.M. Cullen, *The emergence of modern Ireland* (London, 1981), p. 76; E. MacLysaght (ed.), *The Kenmare manuscripts* (Dublin, 1942), pp 179–246.   5 L.M. Cullen, *Anglo-Irish trade, 1660–1800* (Manchester, 1968); R. Gillespie, *The transformation of the Irish economy, 1550–1700*, 2nd edition (Dublin, 1998).

How far planned campaigns contributed to the changing situation will be discussed in the studies that follow. Some consequences had not been prophesied. Where Catholics had the scope, they behaved like any attentive landowner, treating property as a trust of which they were merely temporary custodians. The attachment of the long-established regardless of confession to improvement was demonstrated strikingly in a treatise of the 1690s. Written probably by a Catholic Plunkett from County Meath, it elaborated the familiar theme. Such were the constraints on Catholics, now mostly dispossessed, that the tract was not published at the time.[6] Instead, it was the Protestant victors who evangelized through print.[7] Where Catholics managed to hold onto lands, they were as keen as their Protestant neighbours to experiment with new techniques and crops, as the examples of Lord Kenmare and O'Conor of Belanagare suggested. Further confirmation of Catholic interest in innovations is provided by Patrick Darcy, conspicuous throughout the 1640s as a defender of Catholic rights. He emerged in a less familiar guise after the restoration of Charles II in 1660. Darcy detailed how the fisheries in and around his native Galway might be developed. The failure to realize the full potential of Ireland's waters would obsess a succession of Protestant improvers throughout the next century.[8]

More commonly by the close of the seventeenth century, Catholics occupied and farmed substantial tracts as tenants. Many adopted frugal habits. Thereby they met the high rents. In addition, discretion was less likely than ostentation to attract either the envy of Protestant neighbours or official reprisals.[9] Reticence did not altogether shield Catholics from hostility. Because they were debarred from taking leases longer than thirty-one years, they were discouraged from investing in and improving farms. It was suspected that they turned instead to the towns. Catholics, not just in numbers but in their share of trade, were thought to dominate most boroughs and ports outside Ulster. Even in Dublin, by the middle of the eighteenth century, the balance in numbers was tilting decisively in the Catholics' favour. Received wisdom insisted that the indigenous Irish led nomadic existences and never founded towns. Their remarkable adaptation to urban life – an unexpected trend – unsettled Protestants.[10]

---

6 'The improvement of Ireland', ed. P. Kelly, *Analecta Hibernica*, 35 (1992), pp 47–84. **7** R. Molesworth, *Some considerations for the promoting of agriculture, and employing the poor* (Dublin, 1723); [G. Rye], *Considerations on agriculture* (Dublin, 1730). **8** P. Darcy to unknown, 6 Nov. 1660, TNA, 30/24/50, 4. **9** K. Whelan, 'An underground gentry? Catholic middlemen in eighteenth-century Ireland', *ECI*, 10 (1995), pp 9–66, reprinted in Whelan, *The tree of liberty: radicalism, Catholicism and the construction of Irish identity, 1760–1830* (Cork, 1996), pp 3–58. **10** D. Dickson, 'Catholics and trade in eighteenth-century Ireland: an old debate revisited' in T.P. Power and K. Whelan (eds), *Endurance and emergence: Catholics in Ireland in the eighteenth century* (Dublin, 1990), pp 85–100; P. Fagan, *Catholics in a Protestant country* (Dublin, 1998).

Theories of improvement as economic and political conditions, within Ireland itself, in Britain, Europe and indeed in the wider world changed. By the eighteenth century, secular arguments, associated with enlightenment and the physiocrats, were strengthening, but did not swamp the religious ones. Constants remained: notably the blend of utility, materialism and morality. The particular combinations of these classic elements are examined in the studies that follow. By way of preliminary, it is useful to look more closely at the advocacy and implementation of improvement that attended the dramatic redistribution of Irish property during the 1650s.

III

The aftermath of each war in sixteenth- and seventeenth-century Ireland was a propitious moment to redouble efforts to tame the indigenes and bring the island definitively within the English ambit. Rebels lost their lands. The reliable replaced them. New owners were expected to accelerate change. Loose knots of clerics, administrators and lawyers keen on 'reform' have been identified among those making and implementing policy in Ireland from the 1530s onwards. Each was influenced by intellectual currents: the revived teachings of Aristotle; fresh applications of Augustinian pessimism; Erasmus's writings; Machiavelli's ruthlessness; an updating of civic humanism; the authoritarianism of a strengthened state.[11] The 1650s offered fertile ground for the projectors and prophets. The many implicated in the uprising of the previous decade lost their lands. Ireland, likened to clay on the potter's wheel or a blank paper, could be remade. Either Utopia or the New Jerusalem looked imminent. Revolution in England and Scotland, with the king tried and publicly executed in 1649, aroused apocalyptic fervour among a minority. Some visionaries included Ireland in their brighter future. More immediately, Ireland posed a danger to the sickly English Commonwealth. First the rebellious island had to be subjugated; then a mixture of traditional and novel policies could be applied.

Advice on how best to handle a reconquered Ireland contained less poetry than had been offered by Spenser at the end of the sixteenth century; less law than was advocated by Sir John Davies in the reign of James VI and I. Millenarianism had sprung up in unlikely interstices as Europe cracked apart in confessional and dynastic warfare of the early seventeenth century. Some

---

[11] From a voluminous literature, B. Bradshaw, 'Sword, word and strategy in the Reformation in Ireland', *Historical Journal*, 21 (1978), pp 475–502; C. Brady, 'England's defence and Ireland's reform: the dilemma of Irish viceroys, 1541–1641' in B. Bradshaw and J. Morrill (eds), *The British problem, c.1534–1707* (Basingstoke, 1996), pp 89–117; N. Canny, *Making Ireland British, 1580–1650* (Oxford, 2001), pp 1–58.

uprooted by Catholic advances fled first to the United Provinces, then to England and a few eventually to Ireland. The refugees, guided by the Book of Revelation and other scriptural texts, prepared for the reign of the Saints on earth and the second coming of Christ. Protestantism, since the 1520s splintered into contending theological systems and denominations, must first be reunited. Next the material and moral regeneration of humankind was to be hastened. The zealots found a congenial environment in England, where, after Charles I's execution, a better world waited to be fashioned.[12]

At first sight, the relevance of Ireland to this grandiose scheme looked obscure. After 1649 it presented a depressingly familiar scene. Returned to English control, but devastated and depopulated, it awaited the restoration of the basics of cultivation, trade and government. The magnitude of the tasks invited innovation. Familiar measures had not prevented the uprising of 1641 and protracted war thereafter. In the 1650s, lands had first to be redistributed. Some 8,500,000 acres were allocated to a motley group of nearly 35,000 soldiers and investors. But before these proprietors could be settled, the forfeitures must be surveyed. Taxing work, it required the talented. Nor was it the only task to draw the ambitious and able to Ireland. In the past, careers and fortunes had been made in the western kingdom. Idealists were attracted by the chance to serve in the front line where Protestantism battled against Catholicism, civility against barbarism, reason against superstition, England against Ireland. During the 1640s, under the guidance of fluent expositors from central Europe, notably Jan Comenius and Samuel Hartlib, there developed a loosely linked group eager to apply novel remedies to economic inertia and spiritual torpor. Reformers in England, as well as being inspired and organized by Hartlib, learnt from the writings of Francis Bacon. Under these tutors, observation and experiment, not the unthinking reiteration of custom, became the touchstones.

The amalgam of idealism, utility and careerism appealed to those unimpressed by the traditional nostrums. Even before 1649 a few in Ireland had contact with Hartlib. In particular, bishops of the Church of Ireland saw applications in the programme to the hapless task of winning over the Irish to Protestantism. However, by 1647, these clerics had either fled to Britain or lost all direct power in Ireland.[13] It fell to collaborators with the republican order to spread the experimental and utilitarian philosophy. Hartlib's followers in

[12] M. Greengrass, M. Leslie and T. Raylor (eds), *Samuel Hartlib and universal reformation* (Cambridge, 1994); G.H. Turnbull, *Hartlib, Comenius and Dury* (London, 1947); C. Webster, *The great instauration: science, medicine and reform, 1626–1660* (London, 1975). [13] E. Boran, ' "Propagating religion and endeavouring the reformation of the whole world": Irish bishops and the Hartlib circle in the mid-seventeenth century' in V. Carey and U. Lotz-Heumann (eds), *Taking sides? Colonial and confessional* mentalités *in early modern Ireland* (Dublin, 2003), pp 165–84.

Ireland formed a scrappy coalition. Members, while sharing a method, quarrelled over politics and religion. Furthermore, strong personalities jarred. Most prominent were Benjamin Worsley and William Petty, both close to the Dublin government and vital to the land settlement. The indefatigable Hartlib asked his contacts in Ireland to forward projects dear to his heart. Conspicuous among them was the completion of a detailed natural history of Ireland. Government had long shared the belief that only by knowing fully about the resources could they be exploited properly. For this reason, it wanted the island surveyed and mapped and the owners (both new and older) and surviving inhabitants to be counted. Such information was a prerequisite for future exploitation and effective taxation. A further motive for exact enquiries was religious. The terrain and its peoples told of the wonder of creation. Therefore, precise descriptions were extolled as a form of worship.

Worsley and Petty were employed in the more mundane labour of planning and executing ambitious surveys. Later Petty would publish maps of the Irish counties of unparalleled accuracy and analyses of the island. Until these circulated from the 1670s, the interested depended on *Irelands naturall history* published in 1652. It belonged to a propagandist tradition reaching back into the sixteenth century and earlier. Like its predecessors, the account described the distinctive features of Ireland, and particularly those that were untapped. The book was at once topical and partisan. It celebrated what had so far been done to realize the potential of Ireland and bemoaned how much had been destroyed by the insurgent Irish during the 1640s. It was a tribute to a group of settlers whose achievements were in danger of being overlooked by an unsympathetic government. The compilations also aimed to persuade fresh immigrants to try Irish life.

Irelands naturall history was written by the brothers Boate, originally from Holland. One, Arnold, had served in Ireland as a state physician, until he sailed away in 1644. He remembered a pre-lapsarian world before Catholic rebellion. The *History* was completed by the second brother, Gerard Boate. The Boates and their book owed much to the outlook of beleaguered European Protestantism, especially that of Hartlib and his circle. The volume was prefaced by one of Hartlib's associates, John Dury. *Irelands naturall history* has been hailed for its new precision in describing the island. For some passages, the Boates utilized their own observations; in others, they relied on hearsay. In the second respect, the Boates did the bidding of the group with which they had ideological affinities. Powerful Protestants, settling into the pleasures of property and position in Ireland, were suddenly uprooted in the 1640s. Shocked by abrupt deracination, exile, with its privations and humiliations, inclined them towards the attitudes and – perhaps – the company of other refugees. Some Irish Protestant émigrés found comfort in the explanations and projects of Hartlib and his auxiliaries. Scripture, especially as interpreted by fellow sufferers, admonished, consoled and exhorted. Activity not passive resignation was counselled. The exiles intrigued for the recovery of Ireland and their own reinstatement as its owners and rulers. Print was one means through which the case could be communicated. Quickly and effectively, the group imposed its version of Irish events in and immediately after 1641 on impressionable readers outside Ireland.

The Protestant exiles, settling into a long campaign for restitution, laboured to influence the policies of the contesting king and Westminster parliament. As they composed pamphlets, propaganda successes came before the military ones. The weightiest contribution came from Sir John Temple. In 1646, when it was still uncertain who would win the war in Ireland, Temple's *Irish rebellion* was published (in London). Temple's history was believed because he was Master of the Rolls in Ireland and therefore official custodian of judicial records. His chronicle, a horror story, was stuffed with apparently true accounts of atrocities extracted from the legal depositions lately gathered in Ireland. Temple's *Irish rebellion* emanated from a group eager to see action to return Ireland to its expelled Protestant proprietors. It systematized and extended scrappier accounts. Its appeal endured for the remainder of the seventeenth and throughout the eighteenth centuries. In propagating an Irish Protestant legend, its role can be likened to that of John Foxe's *Acts and monuments*, Crespin's *Livre des martyres*, or Goulart's *Mémoires*. Temple's immediate aim, largely achieved, was to urge the seizure of the insurgents' lands, once they had been defeated, and to speed that defeat by despatching an expeditionary force from England.

The Boates' *Ireland's naturall history* belonged to the next phase of the Irish Protestants' campaign: the resettlement. By the time it was published in 1652, the reconquest for which Temple and his associates had intrigued was largely accomplished. The Boates' book was intended as a manifesto for the new world about to be created. The raw materials in Ireland were itemized. In common with Temple's *History*, it was an apologia for the earlier Protestant planters. An apologia was certainly needed. England had repossessed Ireland only through the efforts of a huge army commanded by Oliver Cromwell. The English regime, having borne the heavy expense of the campaign, was unimpressed by the contribution of the settlers. Far from forming a bulwark for the English and Protestant interests in Ireland, it seemed that they had been so corrupted by local ways that they could neither withstand the rebellion nor alone defeat the rebels. In the coming redistribution, to be finalized by the English parliament and the military, there would be little place for those earlier settlers who had survived and wished now to return. Instead, uncorrupted soldiers and civilians fresh from England, Scotland and Wales would take over the forfeited properties.

Ireland's naturall history was designed as a manual for whoever turned up on the island. In his introduction, Dury, another of the fugitives from resurgent Catholicism in continental Europe, shamelessly courted Ireland's new rulers – the English republicans. Dury cast them as the agents of Ireland's spiritual, moral and physical redemption. The text itself, composed by the two Boates, relied heavily on the Irish Protestants kicking their heels in war-time London. Sir William Parsons, his son Richard, and the bishop of Dromore, Theophilus Buckworth, moping in the fens, had happily helped. Schooled by such informants, the Boates saw Ireland through Irish Protestants' eyes and shared the insights with a larger readership. The dominant theme was the English as 'the introducers of all good things in Ireland'.[14]

By 1652, this assertion was to be read as a timely defence of the 'old' Protestants – those established there before 1641. The Boates, to prove their case, described Protestant achievements, including examples of proto-industrialization. Most striking were the iron-workings developed by two families, whose great stakes in Ireland promised to keep them at the forefront in the post-war reconstruction: the Cootes and Boyles. Making iron had served as an apparently profitable way to strip Irish assets. It hardly required the Boates' glowing descriptions to persuade others into the business. However, the publicity for the Cootes and Boyles may have tempted the impressionable into foolhardy ventures: foolhardy since they seldom brought large profits, although there could be indirect ones.

The first earl of Cork had died in 1643 when it was still unclear whether or not the recent plantations, from which he had done sensationally well, would survive. Cork had joined those who lobbied energetically for England to suppress the rebellion and to make it the pretext for further confiscations of Catholic-owned property. His children, some of them living intermittently in England, assisted the campaign alongside other refugees such as the Parsons and Temple. Sons also fought (and one died) in the war in Ireland. In London, Cork's offspring, the Boyles, gravitated to circles, assertively Protestant but speculative and inquisitive, in which those uprooted by religious strife in central Europe – such as Hartlib – were prominent. Through 'The Invisible College', they promoted Comenius's and Hartlib's programme of Protestant reunion and proselytism, of religious revival, moral regeneration and physical improvement.

14 G. Boate, *Irelands naturall history* (London, 1652), sig. [A7v], pp 59, 114, 123–4, 130, 144, 148, 159.

Some of the projects were clouded by apocalyptic expectancy; others converged with the methodology and practices of Francis Bacon.[15] Hartlib and Comenius enabled the disoriented refugees from Ireland to see their experiences as an element in a larger scene of Protestant desolation. At the same time, the exiles were comforted by predictions of ultimate deliverance and of a future in which the interrupted initiatives of the earlier century would be resumed and perfected. Out of these groups had come first Temple's cautionary history and now the Boates' prospectus.

IV

The Boates' reliance on the partisan testimony of the Boyles and their associates showed in the magnification of what had been achieved before and lost after 1641. It was stated, for example, that Cork had made an astonishing £100,000 and that Coote had earned a 40 per cent return from their iron manufactures. Coote's works, located near Mountrath in the midlands, were said to have employed 2,500 or 2,600. His efforts, 'building, planting, hedging and the like', were repaid by a spectacular rise in the value of his estate. Textile works were certainly operating under Coote's sponsorship, but other contemporary evidence does not confirm the Boates' claims.[16] The Boates further subscribed to a tradition, embodied in the writings of other defenders of the English and Protestants, such as Sir John Davies and Sir James Ware, that the native Irish were lazy and malapert. The indigenes lacked the skill to work stone, extract ores or fashion metals. Backwardness was also tellingly demonstrated in the Irish incapacity to found towns. Moreover, the Irish resented the intrusion and innovations of the skilled immigrants. The recent warfare had been marked by episodes of particular ferocity and almost ritualized violence, intended 'quite to extinguish the memory of them [the settlers], and of all the civility and good things by them introduced amongst the wild nation'.[17]

Irelands naturall history was suffused with the enquiring spirit approved by Bacon and Hartlib. Opening the cabinets of nature showed the awesome achievements of God and so constituted a form of devotion. It also presaged the fuller use of latent resources. Before the Boates' compilation, Ireland had been described perfunctorily and partially. Thanks to their helpers, the brothers

---

15 Webster, *The great instauration.*   **16** Boate, *Irelands naturall history,* pp 97–8, 134–7; TCD, MS 833, f. 223.   **17** Boate, *Irelands naturall history,* pp 72, 89; J. Davies, *A discoverie of the true causes* (London, 1612), pp 168–82; J. Temple, *The Irish rebellion,* 2 parts (London, 1646), i, sig. b[1], pp 14–16, 40–1, 83–5; ii, p. 41; J. Ware, *De Hibernia & antiquitatibus eius, disquisitiones* (London, 1654), pp 94–6.

bulked out the earlier guides. Yet, despite the additional materials, the *Naturall history* was defective and, already by 1652, out of date. Its boast about the rarity of plague in Ireland, for example, was a particularly poignant example of hubris. After 1650 an epidemic spread rapidly and killed more than the preceding war. Victims included the commander who had replaced Oliver Cromwell, his son-in-law, Henry Ireton. The resulting depopulation long stunted the regeneration planned by the Cromwellians and Hartlib's followers.[18]

Omissions from *Irelands naturall history* were unavoidable. The published text was a fragment: one of four intended sections. To finish it accordingly became an objective of Hartlib. Questionnaires were sent to his contacts in Ireland: Robert Child, William Petty, Miles Symner, Robert Wood and Benjamin Worsley.[19] Their presence raised hopes that Ireland would be refashioned and that lessons from the Irish experience could then be applied elsewhere.[20] Moreover, the methods favoured by Hartlib and his followers, such as the standardized format for reporting, promised to systematize what hitherto had been desultory and haphazard. The approach would be followed by later enquirers, such as Robert Plot in Restoration England and in the Ireland of the 1680s, 1690s and 1730s.[21] In addition, the circulation of interrogatories and the pooling of information indicated Hartlib's faith in collaboration as the key to unlock secrets. It inaugurated moves to collect, collate and apply knowledge which would recur, in Ireland no less than in England. The small and factious group of the Interregnum was succeeded by the formal societies of William Molyneux, Samuel Madden, Arthur Dobbs and Walter Harris. Each – hardly less factious but larger than the Cromwellian coterie – aimed to gather and disseminate data and so close the gap between Ireland's untapped and actual wealth.[22]

The *Naturall history*, owing to its silences and heavy emphases, entrenched notions that would have been better questioned. It assumed, conventionally enough, that energetic cooperation or the interventions of the state could correct the material and spiritual malaise in Ireland. The transformations would come through both human exertions and the liberation of hidden and divine

---

18 M. Symner, answers to Hartlib's interrogatories, Sheffield UL, Hartlib Papers, 62/45; L.M. Cullen, 'Population trends in seventeenth-century Ireland', *Economic and Social Review*, 6 (1974–5), pp 149–65; P. Lenihan, 'War and population, 1649–52', *IESH*, xiv (1997), pp 1–21; Hull (ed.), *Economic writings of Sir William Petty*, ii, p. 609. **19** For the individual members: T.C. Barnard, 'Miles Symner and the new learning in seventeenth-century Ireland', *JRSAI*, cii (1972), pp 129–42; C. Webster, 'Benjamin Worsley: engineering for universal reform from the Invisible College to the Navigation Act' in Greengrass, Leslie and Raylor (eds), *Samuel Hartlib and universal reformation*, pp 213–35. **20** T.C. Barnard, 'The Hartlib circle and the origins of the Dublin Philosophical Society', *IHS*, xix (1974), pp 56–71. **21** S. Piggott, *William Stukeley* (London, 1985) pp 22–3. **22** Barnard, 'The Hartlib circle', pp 56–71; Hoppen, *The common scientist*; E. Magennis, '"A land of milk and honey": the Physico-Historical Society, improvement and the surveys of mid-eighteenth-century Ireland', *PRIA*, 102, section C (2002), pp 199–217; and below, pp 89–119.

powers. The Boates, beguiled by and indebted to the brash Irish Protestants, and with a penchant for the dramatic, lingered lovingly over the costly and memorable, such as glass-works, iron foundries and mines. At best the impact of these ventures on the enrichment of Ireland was ambiguous. Entrepreneurs proudly advertised the schemes as 'commonwealth work', since they employed many, supplemented tenants' agricultural earnings, implanted arcane skills, inculcated a work ethic and cleared the woods and bogs where the unruly Irish traditionally sheltered. However, such activities did not typify those – mainly in textiles and farming – that employed most and slowly improved the lot of the generality of the population.[23] The untypical attracted attention and indeed applause, thanks to the willingness first of the Boates and later of organizations like the Dublin Society to publicize them. The innovators were flattered. They needed some reward for their outlay. The manufactures seldom yielded steady profits, although they could turn assets, notably timber and water, into welcome cash.[24]

The danger in the Boates' account of the scale and profitability of Coote's and Cork's enterprises was to entice the credulous into similar undertakings. Lord Cork, to be sure, had derived an estimated £95,000 from his iron foundries between 1607 and 1643: close to the £100,000 recorded by the Boates. His profit, in contrast, totalled a less startling £25,000. This was small beer when set beside an annual rental approaching £20,000. Boate said nothing about the incidentals that persuaded Cork and others to persevere. It was convenient to have money paid in England by the purchasers of the iron. The owner and tenants enjoyed ready supplies for domestic and defensive requirements. Then, too, the income of some tenants was boosted. Yet, colonies of industrial workers were never as big as Boate boasted when he described the Cootes' at Mountrath. Large-scale enterprises rarely employed more than 400. Furthermore, specialists had to be imported to man the works. In time, they might instruct the locals, but in general the latter performed only unskilled tasks. Nor was the predicted discipline of labour always evident. Burly artificers, isolated at remote sites, tended more to pugilism than pacifism.

The delusive allure of the deposits suspected to lie entombed in Ireland continued. Groups were organized to fund prospecting. Experts conducted searches and tests. Mines were sunk and foundries, furnaces and kilns con-

---

23 S.J. Connolly, *Religion, law and power: the making of Protestant Ireland, 1660–1760* (Oxford, 1992), pp 41–59; W.H. Crawford, *The impact of the domestic linen industry in Ulster* (Belfast, 2005); Cullen, *The emergence of modern Ireland*, pp 25–108; D. Dickson, *New foundations: Ireland, 1660–1800* (Dublin, 1987), pp 96–127; Gillespie, *Transformation of the Irish economy*. **24** T.C. Barnard, 'An Anglo-Irish industrial venture: iron-making at Enniscorthy', *PRIA*, lxxxv, sect C (1985), pp 101–44; idem, 'Sir William Petty as Kerry ironmaster', ibid., lxxxii, sect C (1982), pp 1–32; T.O. Ranger, 'The career of Richard Boyle, first earl of Cork, in Ireland, 1588–1643', unpublished D.Phil. thesis, Oxford University (1959), pp 127–71, 264–9.

structed. Proprietors persisted in their investments because extra money might be earned or they were assured that, with persistence, they would soon be enriched. In addition, bold entrepreneurs were fêted, thereby adding lustre to personal reputations. Even without the Boates' propaganda, the adventurous and desperate were likely to try what seemed to succeed elsewhere. Credulity, curiosity and cupidity rather than close study of texts like *Irelands naturall history* drove many landowners. Except for the occasional lucky estate, such as the Wandesfordes' at Castlecomer with its coal deposits, the staples of farming and textiles brought the steadiest returns. Conventional occupations were not entirely ignored by the Boates, but they were not accorded the same prominence as the exceptional instances of proto-industrialization.

Previous writers, urging a new beginning in Ireland, denigrated those already there. Similarly, *Irelands naturall history*, published in the immediate aftermath of a bitter war, was unlikely to treat the defeated generously. Indeed, the vanquished Irish, authors of their own misfortunes in Temple's *Irish rebellion*, were cast by the Boates as an obstacle to a peaceful and prosperous Ireland. Accordingly, they are dismissed as among 'the most barbarous nations of the earth'. It is no surprise that the Boates saw no merit in the world of the Old Irish. Only a few living on the spot appreciated that some of the practices which, viewed from afar, seemed barbaric, worked well.[25] Equally troublesome for commentators of the 1650s was how to treat the earliest waves of settlers from England and Wales. These planters, labelled as 'Old English', were generally thought to have shed most of the admirable English (or Welsh) attributes as they lapsed into Irish ways. Proof came from the events of the 1640s when differences in culture, outlook and origins had counted less than the Catholicism that most Old English shared with the Old Irish. They united to fight under the banner of the Confederation of Kilkenny. Henceforward, the Old English, seen as enemies of England, were allowed little credit for what they had done towards the improvement of Ireland. Yet, members of the Old English élite, so long as they owned substantial property, behaved like grandees throughout Britain and continental Europe.[26] The Old English, forced into an adventitious pact with other Irish Catholics during the 1640s, strove thereafter to distance themselves through their styles of living from their erstwhile asso-

---

[25] V. Gookin, *The great case of transplantation in Ireland discussed* (London, 1655), p. 17. [26] T.C. Barnard, 'Gardening, diet and improvement in late seventeenth-century Ireland', *Journal of Garden History*, x (1990), pp 71–85, reprinted in Barnard, *Ascents and descents*, pp 208–34; B. Ó Dálaigh, 'A comparative study of the wills of the first and fourth earls of Thomond', *North Munster Antiquarian Journal*, 34 (1992), pp 48–63; J. Ohlmeyer, *Civil war and restoration in the three Stuart kingdoms: the career of Randal MacDonnell, marquis of Antrim, 1609–1683* (Cambridge, 1993), pp 1–76.

ciates. Above all, they wished to refute the calumnies about disloyalty and degeneracy and prove to sceptics that they were the best upholders of the English interest in Ireland.[27]

The fact that some of the keenest exponents of improvement in Ireland were Catholic Old English contradicted an assumption fundamental to the English approach. Where they could, the Old English introduced useful and elegant novelties. Darcy, as has been noted, publicized a cause that Protestants regularly espoused. And, it was one from this sophisticated and cosmopolitan world rather than from an uncouth Protestant squire who wrote (around 1698) the first systematic treatise on improving Ireland's trade and agriculture.[28] Nevertheless, as the Old English share of land contracted, so too did opportunities to engage in improvements.

V

The Boates' silence about the achievements of the Old English hinted at the gestation of their tract among the impoverished and embittered Protestant refugees. The authors' reliance on this group accentuated another imbalance in the work: its concentration on Leinster and Ulster. Arnold Boate, on his tours of duty as government physician, travelled chiefly through those provinces. In them also lay the estates of his informants, the Parsons and Bishop Buckworth. If, as has been argued, the stronger regional diversification of Irish agriculture occurred only late in century (paradoxically when the national economy was better integrated), then examples taken overwhelmingly from Ulster and Leinster need not have invalidated the messages.[29] In actuality, the diversity within Ireland was great. Differences in ecology and climate were deepened by patterns of settlement. In the earlier part of the seventeenth century, the plantations of Ulster and Munster

---

[27] A. Clarke, 'Colonial identity in early modern Ireland' in T.W. Moody (ed.), *Nationality and the pursuit of national independence: Historical Studies*, xi (Belfast, 1978), pp 57–71; A. Creighton, 'The Remonstrance of December 1661 and Catholic politics in Restoration Ireland', *IHS*, xxxiv (2004), pp 16–41. [28] Barnard, *Ascents and descents*, pp 208–34; J. Byrne, *War and peace: the survival of the Talbots of Malahide* (Dublin, 1997); 'The Improvement of Ireland, c.1698', ed. Kelly; H. O'Sullivan, *John Bellew: a seventeenth-century man of many parts* (Dublin, 2000); W.J. Smyth, 'Property, patronage and population: reconstructing the human geography of mid-seventeenth-century County Tipperary' in T. McGrath and W. Nolan (eds), *Tipperary: history and society* (Dublin, 1985), pp 108–9, 118–21. [29] Cullen, *The emergence of modern Ireland*, pp 83–108; Dickson, *New foundations*, pp 96–127; D. Dickson, *Old world colony* (Cork, 2005), pp 215–46; R. Gillespie, 'Continuity and change: Ulster in the seventeenth century' in C. Brady et al. (eds), *Ulster: an illustrated history* (London, 1989), pp 104–32; R. Gillespie, 'Lords and commons in seventeenth-century Mayo' in R. Gillespie and G. Moran (eds), *'A various country': essays in Mayo history* (Westport, 1987), pp 44–66.

widened the divergences both between those two planted provinces and between them and regions less touched by fresh settlement.[30]

The *Naturall history* tells little of Munster, other than to marvel, perhaps with an unwonted note of asperity, at Lord Cork's activities.[31] It may be that the Boates, in smoothing out any notion of significant local quirks, merely reflected the exiles' attachment to a loose but inclusive concept of an English and Protestant Ireland rather than to specific locales. If so, the view was a product of exile. Regional and parochial loyalties were subsumed in the loose but compelling concept of a Protestant Ireland. Not until the 1680s did strong local allegiances appear among settlers, usually from the most densely populated and prosperous regions. This feeling, focussing on mansions, estates, kinship, clientage and political organization, was registered and probably fostered by the first attempts to write county histories.[32] Even so, it remains odd that Munster featured so little in the *Naturall history* when the province was dominated by the lineage of Boyles, the family so active in London in backing Hartlib's projects.[33]

The Boates' distortions reflect their sources. A closer look at the experiences of Parsons and other assistants does something to clarify the biases. Sir William Parsons, a self-promoting expert on – albeit contemptuous of – the Irish and their ways, was appointed one of Ireland's governors in the vacuum that followed Strafford's recall in 1640. In that capacity, Parsons had to respond to the rising. Soon he fell out with the newly commissioned viceroy, Ormond, over whether or not to negotiate with the insurgents. The dissentient Parsons was dismissed from the Irish council and quickly scuttled to England. There, in worsening penury, he accepted doles from the Westminster parliament, plotted revenge with other exiles and renewed his acquaintance with Boate. Parsons' attitudes, never friendly towards the Catholic Irish, hardened as he raked through the clinker of his hopes and fortune.[34] Such was the dislocation that he

[30] N. Canny, 'The Irish background to Penn's experiment' in R.S. Dunn and M.M. Dunn (eds), *The world of William Penn* (Philadelphia, 1986), pp 139–56; W.H. Crawford, 'Landlord-tenant relations in Ulster, 1609–1820', *IESH*, 2 (1975), pp 6–11; R. Gillespie, *Colonial Ulster* (Cork, 1985); R. Gillespie, 'The transformation of the borderlands, 1600–1700' in R. Gillespie and H. O'Sullivan (eds), *The borderlands: essays in the history of the Ulster–Leinster border* (Belfast, 1989), pp 75–92; M. MacCarthy-Morrogh, *The Munster plantation: English migration to southern Ireland 1583–1641* (Oxford, 1986); P.S. Robinson, *The plantation of Ulster* (Belfast, 1984). [31] Boate, *Irelands naturall history*, pp 122, 137. [32] T.C. Barnard, 'The political, material and mental culture of the Cork settlers, c.1650–1700' in P. O'Flanagan and N.G. Buttimer (eds), *Cork: history and society* (Dublin, 1993), pp 309–65, reprinted in Barnard, *Ascents and descents*, pp 35–83; Hoppen, *The common scientist*; J. Walton (ed.), 'Two descriptions of County Waterford in the 1680s, ii. Sir Richard Cox's account', *Decies*, 36 (1987), pp 26–31. [33] Barnard, 'The Hartlib circle', pp 70–1; M. Hunter, *Robert Boyle 1627–1691: scrupulosity and science* (Woodbridge, 2000); M. Oster, 'The scholar and craftsman revisited: Robert Boyle as aristocrat and artisan', *Annals of Science*, 49 (1992), pp 255–76; Webster, 'Invisible college', pp 19–42. [34] BL, Egerton MS 80, f. 20; ibid., Harleian MS 3292, ff 26–31; Bodleian, Rawlinson MS A 258, f. 37; *CSP Ireland, 1647–60*, pp 726, 728, 766, 767, 771, 775; HMC,

did not know whether a colleague in Dublin was alive or dead. Similarly, Boate had not heard whether Bishop Spottiswood's 'pretty little village' on the shores of Lough Erne had survived.³⁵ Parsons, settling his affairs before the fate of Protestant Ireland was clear, bequeathed lands seized by the rebels in the hope that, within the next twenty-one years, 'there will be such quietness in Ireland by the blessing of God' as to allow their repossession. Parsons died in 1649, before he could re-enter the promised land which he had described lovingly to the Boates in London. Through *Irelands naturall history* something of Parsons's outlook and priorities was kept alive.³⁶

Within early seventeenth-century Ireland, the Parsons tribe had proliferated. Cadets settled in the Irish midlands at what was soon renamed Parsonstown (later Birr). Glass-making was started nearby in the 1620s and would be noticed approvingly by the Boates. Indeed, the township of Parsonstown exemplified much that the Hartlibians treasured. Protestants were attracted as tenants; the superior English modes of construction, with stone chimneys, and English breeds of cattle and sheep were introduced; industries and regular markets were sponsored; a school was opened; and morals were regulated.³⁷ Even before 1641, the idyll had been disturbed. Technical difficulties closed the glass-house; Irish Catholics lived alongside the newcomers; the school was moved elsewhere. Later, the godly discipline was subverted by the minister.³⁸ The owner of Parsonstown spent heavily to try to quell the rebellion. It was fruitless and he, like an uncle in Dublin, Sir William Parsons, fled to England and there solicited aid from parliament. The nephew, haunted by the memory of what he too had lost, vowed to rebuild. Yet, the iron had entered his soul. He forbade any of his children to marry 'with any of the Irish papists' and counselled them to 'remember that horrid and bloody rebellion in Ireland'.³⁹

Death stopped either of the exiled Parsons enjoying the reconstructed Protestant Ireland for which each had pleaded. Their heirs discovered that this new world, for all its resemblances to pre-war Ireland, could disappoint. Sir William Parsons's eventual successor, his grandson, hitched himself to the Ormond caravan – despite the family enmity in the 1640s – and, in 1681, was

Ormonde Mss, new series, ii, p. 272; vi, p. 64; R. Armstrong, *Protestant war: the 'British' of Ireland and the wars of the three kingdoms* (Manchester, 2005), pp 82–4, 92, 170, 182, 186, 187, 195, 197, 207, 208; Canny, *Making Ireland British*, pp 249–50, 254–5, 259–61, 262, 379, 470, 558; H.F. Kearney, *Strafford in Ireland* (Manchester, 1959), pp 10, 39, 81–4, 174, 257. **35** Boate, *Irelands naturall history*, p 73; TCD, MS 834, ff 73, 92, TNA, PROB 11/215, 33; R. Gillespie, 'The trials of Bishop Spottiswood', *Clogher Record*, 12 (1987), p. 330. **36** TNA, PROB 11/215, 33. **37** Boate, *Irelands naturall history*, p. 162; T.L. Cooke, *The early history of the town of Birr, or Parsonstown* (Dublin, 1875), pp 35–51, 384–7. **38** BL, Add. MS 31,881, ff 152–4; Cooke, *Birr*, pp 42, 47, 384. **39** Birr Castle, Co. Offaly, MS A/1/92; TNA, PROB 11/231, 85; Bodleian, Rawlinson MS A 258, ff 39, 44; *CSP, Ireland, 1647–60*, p. 735; HMC, *Ormonde MSS*, new series, ii, pp 289, 290.

ennobled. By then, the inheritance was entangled and depleted, in part owing to lavish spending and loss of rents during the Confederate War. Viscount Rosse, as Parsons had become, could not live up to his elevated port and was reduced to borrowing from his wife and pawning a watch.[40] At Parsonstown itself after Charles II's restoration, although the landlord procured a new market-house, meetings of the assizes and quarter-sessions and the presence of a garrison, the townspeople, 'seemingly still beggars', showed scant gratitude and once more rose against the Parsons in 1689. Notwithstanding the improvements and an increased rent-roll, debts exiled Sir Laurence Parsons to England for much of the 1680s.[41]

Through their writing, the Boates aimed to attract, not to repel. Accordingly, they said little about the hazards of a landlord's life in Ireland. They did, however, expatiate on Catholic malevolence, but this was a universal theme which those from the Low Countries and Central Europe (like Hartlib) had reason to chant. By showing how the active, either singly or together, could amend Ireland, the Boates not only gratified their patrons within the exiled community but repeated a popular axiom: that landlords through their own example, prodding and spending, could animate an inert Ireland. The recent substitution of so many Protestants for the Catholic owners endorsed the pivotal role of these newcomers in improving the island. The belief in the centrality of individual exertions was accepted and then elaborated by the Boates, Hartlib and their acolytes. In the event only one of Hartlib's followers in Ireland, Dr Robert Child, was patronized by a local squire, who might apply the improved and improving techniques: Colonel Arthur Hill in County Down. (Hill was a connection of Sir William Parsons.)[42] In time, William Petty metamorphosed into a considerable Irish proprietor and would strive, quixotically, to make his remote holdings a showcase for the smart methods that he had picked up in the 1640s and 1650s.[43]

Most of the virtuosi who endorsed the approaches of Bacon and Hartlib had come to Ireland for gainful employment. The state, faced with the massive challenges of resettlement and recovery, had need of the talented. Worsley and Petty, as each in turn surveyed the forfeited property of the defeated, enjoyed the support of a militarized and virtually absolute governmental machine. Cohorts of soldiers were put at their disposal, to assist in measuring the terrain. In contrast, Child, relying on the patronage of an individual owner, quickly dis-

---

40 Birr Castle, MS A/1/144; HMC, *Ormonde Mss*, new series, vi, pp 56–7, 73, 83, 86, 130–1; vii, p. 20. **41** Birr Castle, MSS A/1/147–9; Cooke, *Birr*, pp 66–87, 391–5. **42** Letters of Robert Child, Sheffield UL, Hartlib Papers, 15/5; TNA, PROB 11/215, 33; W.A. Maguire, *The Downshire estates in Ireland, 1801–1845* (Oxford, 1972), pp 2–5. **43** See below, pp 41–72.

cerned the limitations of private enterprise. Child applauded Colonel Hill's dynamism as overseer and engineer of improvement in the tradition sketched by Boate. Moreover, in the north-east where Child worked, the craze for building, fencing, ditching, draining bogs and trying unfamiliar crops gripped farmers returning to, or newly arrived in, a region already undergoing agricultural and social change thanks to the plantations earlier in the century.[44] At the same time, Child had to concede that Hill was frequently absent from his estate: an inescapable consequence of the multiple interests of the rich, but one unnoticed in the Boates' account.[45] The absence of owners mattered less where tenants had already been won to industry, civility and Protestantism. Planters in Ulster and Munster were enjoined by the terms of their original grants to let lands only to such paragons. Tenants were to be kept to the mark through the example as well as the incentives of an improving proprietor. A resident owner was more likely than even the most dutiful agent to oversee such innovations.

The Boates and Hartlib repeated the adage that the individual owner was the vital instrument to change Ireland. The proposition was accepted and acted on by their followers, notably Petty. It would outlast the eighteenth century. At the same time, most acknowledged a role for government. Especially through legislation the state could either help or hinder landlords and entrepreneurs. Often it was felt that the Westminster parliament, increasingly intrusive into Irish affairs, thwarted fruitful developments. The situation improved from 1692, when the Dublin parliament met regularly and represented and responded to the interests of Irish Protestant landowners. The assembly helped ingenious squires and prosperous farmers with bounties and benevolences. Despite such incentives, not all proprietors exerted themselves. As the Boates had discovered earlier, the cult of improvement would be embraced only if it appealed simultaneously to the self-interest and altruism of the landed. Fashion as well as duty popularized active supervision and innovation. Following this belief, the Boates paraded the sensational successes of Coote and Cork. Later organizations, notably the Dublin Society, exploited print to publicize the meritorious.[46]

The Boates, although appreciative of the potential of publicity, bothered less about how the fads of the few were to be entrenched as a universal doctrine

---

44 R. Child to S. Hartlib, 13 Nov. 1651, 26 [Feb.] 1651[2], 11 March 1651[2], 23 June 1652, 8 April 1653, 7 July 1653, Sheffield UL, Hartlib Papers, 15/5; R. Gillespie, 'Landed society and the interregnum in Ireland and Scotland' in P. Roebuck and R. Mitchison (eds), *Scotland and Ireland, 1500–1939* (Edinburgh, 1988), pp 38–47; Gillespie, *Colonial Ulster*, pp 195–222; M. Perceval-Maxwell, *The Scottish migration to Ulster in the reign of James I* (London, 1973); Robinson, *The plantation of Ulster*, pp 172–94. **45** A.P.W. Malcomson, 'Absenteeism in eighteenth-century Ireland', *IESH*, i (1974), pp 15–35. **46** Royal Dublin Society, *A bibliography of the publications of the Royal Dublin Society from its foundation in the year 1731 ...*, 2nd edn (Dublin, 1953).

of improvement. In particular, they overlooked the value of the lease as an instrument for improving Ireland. Regulating tenurial relationships through the lease and other legal contracts supposedly marked off the new, anglicized Ireland from the old, in which economic and social relations were organized according to military contingencies and hereditary obligations.[47] By the mid-seventeenth century, leases, through their duration, charges, prohibitions and stipulations, encouraged, restricted and punished. Owners exerted considerable power through the grant of tenancies. However, it was far from absolute. Desirable tenants were often scarce, especially in the aftermath of the wars of the 1640s and 1689–91. Landlords were obliged to relax onerous terms: rent arrears were forgiven; reductions allowed; Catholics taken as tenants. Dues in kind, rendered in butter or labour, were accepted. In some districts, 'the custom of the country' moderated notional rigidities.[48] Furthermore, the owners' problems – shortage of capital, underdeveloped credit facilities, debts, family commitments and feuds or simple temperamental aversion from business – led many to barter close control over tenancies, and so over the character of their lands, for scarce cash.[49]

One familiar to the Hartlib circle who had not sacrificed control was the head of the Boyles, the second earl of Cork. In 1649, taking in hand his holdings after the disruptions of the war, he granted leases for only one or three years. The purpose was to bring in a little money, to arrest any further physical deterioration of his inheritance and yet to retain his freedom to profit when conditions improved.[50] In the more benign atmosphere of the 1660s, Cork reverted to his preferred policy of tenancies of eighteen or twenty-one years or for three lives. Detailed improvements were stipulated in the leases and sub-letting to others than Protestants or 'British' was banned.[51] Cork was favoured by a relatively dense concentration of Protestants within his territories. But even he had sometimes to waive the strict application of the terms in his leases.[52]

Lord Cork proved what the Boates and Hartlib group assumed. The second earl, like his father before him, cared for his purse and the wider Protestant

---

47 Dickson, *Old world colony*, pp 170–214; Gillespie, *Transformation of the Irish economy*. **48** H. Boyle to W. Conner, 3 April 1753, Chatsworth, Lismore MS 36/126. **49** PRONI, D 2707/A1/1/11; W.H. Crawford, 'The significance of the landed estates in Ulster, 1600–1820', *IESH*, 17 (1990), pp 44–56; Crawford, 'Landlord-tenant relations', pp 5–21; T.P. Power, *Land, politics and society in eighteenth-century Tipperary* (Oxford, 1993), pp 66–173; P. Roebuck, 'Landlord indebtedness in Ulster in the seventeenth and eighteenth centuries' in J.M. Goldstrom and L.A. Clarkson (eds), *Irish population, economy and society* (Oxford, 1981), pp 135–54; P. Roebuck, 'The making of an Ulster great estate: the Chichesters', *PRIA*, 79, sect C (1979), pp 12–25; P. Roebuck, 'Rent movement, proprietorial incomes and agricultural development, 1730–1830', in P. Roebuck (ed.), *Plantation to partition* (Belfast, 1981), pp 82–101. **50** NLI, MS 6143. **51** Abstracts of leases, Chatsworth, Londesborough Mss, box I (v); NLI, MS 6144. **52** Letter book of W. Hovell, s.d. 21 Dec. 1683, Farmar Mss, Dublin; Dickson, *Old world colony*, pp 176–81, 186–7.

interest.⁵³ Through meticulous, even obsessive oversight, Cork improved both. Rich, cosmopolitan and proud, he introduced novelties in diet, recreation, building and display which gradually percolated through the district. Locally, he revived the ironworks described by Boate. In his towns he fostered cloth-making. Thanks to his riches and status and to the deference of an intricate network of kinsmen, tenants and toadies, he abetted – but did little to originate – the culture of improvement. Books of husbandry and gardening were swapped and discussed; seeds, saplings, rare fruit and vegetables were exchanged; rams, stallions and bulls were lent in order to service the beasts of neighbours and subordinates. Experiments continued into reclamation and mineral extraction, while the meritorious were subsidized and advanced. Cork's apanage, vigilantly overseen for much of the century, was frequently praised as the *non-pareil* in an English Ireland.⁵⁴ In time, the estate succumbed to the genetic lottery as resident and attentive owners were succeeded by extravagant absentees. Before that decline, the first and second earls of Cork seemed to vindicate the thinking behind English plantations. Avarice and ruthlessness characterized the founder of the Boyle fortunes in Munster. What his heir contributed directly to the well-being of the property is harder to assess. Contemporaries applauded his assiduity and intimate understanding of the terrain and its inhabitants. He seized opportunities to enlarge his holdings during the confusion of the 1650s and 1660s. The larger acreage inevitably gave him an income bigger than his father's. As the largest proprietor in south Munster, he profited when the populous region recovered and prospered. Yet, innovations that added to those processes are harder to trace to the second earl.

VI

Hartlib's disciples in Cromwellian Ireland achieved less than they or their mentor had hoped. For some, such as Child and Worsley, Ireland formed a brief episode in careers mainly spent elsewhere. Landowners sympathetic to the objectives of the group, such as Richard and Roger Boyle, respectively earls of Cork and Orrery, busied themselves about basic reconstruction when they returned to their Irish estates. Initiatives deriving from the philosophies of

---

53 Barnard, 'Cork settlers', pp 309–65; Barnard, 'Land and the limits of loyalty: the second earl of Cork and first earl of Burlington, (1612–1698)' in T. Barnard and Jane Clark (eds), *Lord Burlington: architecture, art and life* (London, 1995), pp 167–99, both reprinted in Barnard, *Ascents and descents*, pp 35–83.
54 Smith, *Cork*, i, p. iv; pp 116–23, 151; C. Smith, *The antient and present state of the county and city of Waterford* (Dublin, 1746), pp 56–7.

Bacon and Hartlib are impossible to separate from routine operations. Restocking may have allowed unfamiliar strains of livestock, novel crops such as hops, woad, madder and clovers, and tenants with rare skills to be imported. However, such introductions, even if they started in the mid-1650s, shade imperceptibly into the dynamism of the 1660s, by which time the inspiration of Hartlib and his acolytes was seldom acknowledged. Educational institutions were targeted by the devotees of the 'new science'. In Dublin, it was hoped to add a second college to the existing Trinity College. This never happened. Instead it was left to individuals to use their positions to promote experiment and speculation. Miles Symner as professor of mathematics at Trinity and Robert Wood, master of a leading Dublin school, were best placed to do so, but had to push against the weight of orthodoxy and custom.[55]

Nevertheless, two legacies from the 1650s can be identified. The first was a stronger emphasis on collaboration, both among the enthusiasts in Ireland and between them and the like-minded elsewhere. Connected with the cooperative approach was the importance of communication, much of it still through personal correspondence, but also through the exchange and sponsorship of print. Hartlib presided over an intelligence network that reached from north America to eastern Europe and included Ireland and Britain. Soon his role would be taken over, though never entirely superseded, by the published transactions of learned societies, in London, Paris and Leipzig. These publications kept the curious in Ireland abreast of the wider developments and discoveries, although their own had still to be disseminated in manuscript.[56] Not until the 1730s was print exploited systematically to diffuse useful information in Ireland. Before that, though, formal societies committed to updated versions of Hartlib's agenda had been established.

A second function of Ireland in the Interregnum was to offer a unique outlet for the exponents of utility and empiricism. That so much of the island was surveyed, mapped and reallocated was thanks to what Worsley began and Petty then improved and completed. Moreover, the resulting data, seen by the government as the prelude to the better use of Irish resources, sparked further analysis and thought. Petty, in particular, having gathered so much of the material, based his radical prescriptions for Ireland's transformation on it. The mass of information also spurred him to devise better methods to make sense of it,

---

55 T.C. Barnard, *Cromwellian Ireland: English government and reform in Ireland, 1649–1660* (Oxford, 1975), pp 213–48. 56 T.C. Barnard, 'Marsh's Library and the reading public' in M. McCarthy and A. Simmons (eds), *The making of Marsh's Library: learning, politics and religion in Ireland, 1650–1750* (Dublin, 2004), pp 160–1.

reducing untidy data to the abstractions of 'number, weight and measure'. Petty pondered the implications and applications. Some findings he committed to print; others he discussed with intimates. He alone of the enquirers of the 1650s survived into the Ireland of the 1680s. As such he was a vital link between the earlier efforts and the more sustained and systematized work of the Dublin Philosophical Society, of which he was chosen president in 1684.

The accession of the Catholic James in 1685, no less than the advent of a republic in 1649, heralded a regime which would reconsider the premises on which English policy in Ireland was grounded. Petty was unusual not just in envisaging but thinking how best to utilize, the expected reduction, if not the total loss, of Protestant power in Ireland after 1685. His waywardness in contemplating and even encouraging the unthinkable diminished his influence during his own life, but made him the most intellectually powerful among the projectors from the 1650s. Many of his ideas circulated among a few intimates and possible patrons. However, by the end of the seventeenth century, his principal observations on Ireland, statistical and speculative, and his maps had been published. They offered more challenging prescriptions but did not altogether displace the orthodoxies of the Boates. Indeed, *Irelands Naturall History* was reissued in Dublin in 1726. There was even talk of reprinting Boate in 1787, as 'a good vehicle for new things, and the old trash there is not unpleasant as it shows the beginning and dawning of that science in this isle'.[57]

Petty, notwithstanding his ability to bring greater precision to the problems and possible solutions by expressing them through abstractions, fared badly as an innovator on his own estates.[58] Nor did the existence within Ireland of larger groups committed to the sorts of improvement beloved by the Hartlib circle bring dramatic transformations. In 1738, a Church of Ireland bishop, Robert Howard, reviewed the state of the nation. He found some comforting features. The defeated Irish Catholics were awakening 'from that pleasing dream in which they had long indulged themselves of recovering their imaginary possessions'. Reconciled to their losses, they had started 'to improve what was truly their own'. Moreover, Bishop Howard was cheered by the evidence that 'few countries have been more improved in the same compass of time than Ireland hath been since the happy revolution [of 1689–90], the era of labour and industry in this kingdom'. He believed that 'civil life has been refined, inventions perfected, manufactures improved and ornaments added to the plainness of nature'. Unfortunately, he concluded, that Ireland 'at this day [is] less cultivated

---

[57] E. Ledwich to J.C. Walker, 21 May 1787, TCD, MS 1461/2, f. 233v; G. Boate, *A natural history of Ireland in three parts* (Dublin, ?1726). [58] See below, pp 41–72.

and improved than any other country in Europe'. It still lagged behind the rest of Europe, maybe by as much as 100 years. The retardation might be corrected through the method favoured by Hartlib, a 'general inquisitiveness' about practices in other countries. Howard urged his listeners and readers to follow their God-given duty, for humans were 'designed for improvements and capable of further attainments'. The key attributes of 'will and choice' should be exercised so that 'industry and endeavour' resulted.[59]

Distinctive features in the Irish landscape, notably bogs, fascinated the inquisitive. The Boates, as befitted Dutchmen, revelled in describing how Irish bogs had been drained. They praised the work as conducing 'to the general good of the land'. From Ulster in the early 1650s, Child reported the renewed efforts in this direction.[60] The interest continued. In 1730, a pamphleteer celebrated the recent reclamation of a vast marsh outside Cork city. Its survival was attributed to the almost equally long reign of a Catholic potentate in the neighbourhood. The boggy waste, notorious in 1656 as a haven for wolves and tories, was now 'so drained and civilized that there is neither shelter for one or the other'. In terms that echoed the seventeenth-century praise of 'commonwealth work' of the first earl of Cork, the writer concluded, 'thus, in one age, the great fastnesses of Ireland might be destroyed and even the most barbarous parts, yet not amenable to the law and civil power, rendered habitable'.[61]

The landscape was scanned for its political and economic meanings. As the Protestant interest seemed more secure by the eighteenth century, so it was easier to enjoy the wild and unimproved aspects. Even so, this appreciation grew slowly. Uncultivated tracts rebuked their indifferent owners. One fervently evangelical improver saw surviving bogs not just as an indictment of slothful landowners but as a warning of deeper, collective ills.[62] Well-to-do clerics of the Church of Ireland attacked backwardness on both practical and ideological grounds. The clergymen, as substantial landowners themselves, were eager to increase the yield of estates; as apologists of and beneficiaries from Protestant privilege, they wished to end back-sliding among their co-religionists. Accordingly, bishops, such as Howard at Elphin, applied their funds, their pro-

---

59 R. Howard, *Sermon on Matthew 25, v. 29*, NLI, MS 7238; idem, *A sermon preached at St. Andrew's Dublin, before the honourable House of Commons. On Friday December the 8th 1721* (Dublin, 1721); idem, *A sermon preached in Christ-Church, Dublin; before their excellencies the lords justices, on Tuesday October the 23d, 1722* (Dublin, 1722); idem, *A sermon preach'd in the Parish Church of St. Mary, Dublin: March the 22d. 1729[30]* (Dublin, 1730); idem, *A sermon preach'd in Christ-Church, Dublin, before the Incorporated Society for promoting English Protestant Schools in Ireland* (Dublin, 1738). **60** R. Child to S. Hartlib, 23 June 1652, Sheffield UL, Hartlib papers, 15/5/12–13; Boate, *Irelands naturall history*, pp 114–17, 167–9. **61** [Rye], *Considerations on agriculture*, pp 74, 80–5. **62** W. Henry, *Love of our country. A sermon preached in the Cathedral Church of St. Patrick, March 17th 1756* (Dublin, 1756), p. 19.

ficiency in mathematics and 'hydrogasticks', and their quills to aquatic questions. Bogs must go; in their place, navigable rivers, canals, water-courses, fishponds, ornamental lakes, cascades and *jets d'eau* were to gush.[63]

The themes and activities of Bishop Howard reappeared among others in the established Church. Indeed, the clergy were in the vanguard of improvers, whether in the pulpit or on the lands from which they drew their livelihoods.[64] In chastising the backsliders and congratulating the pioneers, they deployed spiritual weapons. Fulfilment of the divine purpose required the attainment of the potential in individuals and the exploitation of all creation. Another bishop, Francis Hutchinson of Down and Connor, nagged the Irish parliament to assist. He begged the members to turn away from factious squabbles and instead to promote 'the undisputed ways of devising good for the improvement of our country and common happiness'. He itemized the projects deserving parliamentary support: 'learning, language, useful arts, and knowledge, employing and providing for the poor, educating youth, carrying on public works, and, in short, mending the state of everything that can be made better amongst us'.[65] Hutchinson's targets differed little from Hartlib's.

Even in the eighteenth century, optimism was regularly checked by natural disasters. Wars, although feared, did not disturb the island between the 1690s and 1790s. Famine, however, recurred. It offset self-congratulation among the more sensitive of the new Protestant proprietors. A lordly Englishman, elevated to the rich bishopric of Derry in 1734, was astonished that Ireland had to import grain despite 'a soil capable to become the granary of Europe'. The bishop connected the deficiency with the absence of a yeomanry and any widespread understanding of effective husbandry.[66] The same laments had been heard in the 1650s. Another observer, writing in 1729, reckoned that it was easier to ship grain into Dublin from Egypt than from Roscommon and Longford. By the eighteenth century, a favoured corrective was to improve transport – notably through public subsidies for building roads, canals and bridges. A supporter of better navigation along the River Shannon cited the example of the Vistula as the channel down which grain passed easily from Poland towards lucrative markets.[67] Also, parliament should reward those undertaking innovative agri-

63 Chatsworth, Lismore MS 32/82; H.F. Berry, *History of the Royal Dublin Society* (Dublin, 1915), p. 20; Sir John Browne, *The benefits which arise to a trading people from navigable rivers* (Dublin, 1729), pp v–vi; Hoppen, *The common scientist*, pp 195, 263. 64 T.C. Barnard, 'Improving clergymen, 1660–1760' in A. Ford, J.I. McGuire and K. Milne (eds), *As by law established: the Church of Ireland since the Reformation* (Dublin, 1995), pp 136–51, 257–65, reprinted in Barnard, *Ascents and descents*. 65 F. Hutchinson, *A sermon preached in Christ-Church Dublin, on Thursday, the 30th day of January 1723[4]* (Dublin, 1723[4]), p. 7. 66 T. Rundle, *A sermon preach'd in Christ-Church, Dublin, on the 25th Day of March 1736* (Dublin, 1736), pp 22–3. 67 Browne, *Navigable rivers*, pp 4–5, 7. Cf. A. Dobbs, *An essay on the trade and*

culture and industry.[68] Education was still valued. Founding and sustaining schools were essential; so too was the easier availability of information about superior methods. The greater use of print in Ireland and the existence of voluntary groups and formal associations willing to sponsor appropriate publications made the efforts of the Hartlib group look rudimentary. Yet, continuities in attitude between the 1650s and mid-eighteenth century persisted.

The divinely ordained duty to improve self, fellows and society expanded into, but was not lost in, an apparently secular obligation of every inhabitant to labour for the 'happiness of the nation wherein he lives'.[69] The good citizen and the true patriot were invariably portrayed as improvers. In 1756, another Church of Ireland incumbent, William Henry, argued that 'love of country' was best channelled into 'ameliorating and improving the soil', making good roads, navigable canals, comfortable houses and by sponsoring manufactures, industry and commerce.[70] Henry, true to his creed, undertook what he could on his own Sligo settlement of Ballymote. There, each male settler would be equipped with 'a bible and backsword to defend it, and to every woman a prayer book and a spinning wheel'.[71] The link between militant Protestantism and bracing industry was once again proclaimed. Even more explicit was a manifesto of 1758. This, while paying tribute to the efforts of the Dublin Society, felt that the resources of voluntary associations were too small and uncertain to sustain national improvement. Accordingly, it was proposed that the Irish parliament assume responsibility for the work. Central to the regeneration was the revival of religion and morality. Without them, material advances would never be achieved.[72]

Parliament awarded the Dublin Society annual grants. However, progress remained jerky, as the energetic jostled against the indifferent, indolent, indulgent and absent. Yet another bishop, James Traill, in 1777 felt that much still needed to be done. In his own diocese of Down and Connor, he decried 'the dreary and extensive waste which still remains a stranger to industry and to instruction'. Many locals preserved 'a ferocity in manners and a brutality in crimes not to be paralleled in any civilized nation in Europe'. Traill, like so many

---

improvement of Ireland (Dublin, 1727), p. 45. **68** These expedients are studied in D. Broderick, *The first toll-roads: Ireland's turnpike roads, 1729–1858* (Cork, 2002); B.M.S. Campbell, 'Economic progress in the canal age: a case study from Counties Armagh and Down' in D. Dickson and C. Ó Gráda (eds), *Refiguring Ireland: essays in honour of L.M. Cullen* (Dublin, 2003), pp 63–93; E. Magennis, 'Coal, corn and canals: parliament and the dispersal of public moneys, 1693–1772' in D.W. Hayton (ed.), *The Irish parliament in the eighteenth century: the long apprenticeship* (Edinburgh, 2001), pp 71–86. **69** Dobbs, *Essay on the trade and improvement*, p. 2. **70** Henry, *Love of our country*, p. 17. **71** Calendar of miscellaneous letters and papers prior to 1760, s.d. 15 March 1758, NA. **72** *Some thoughts on the general improvement of Ireland with a scheme of a society for carrying on all improvements* (Dublin, 1758), pp 19, 31–2, 34–41.

of his predecessors, trusted in education as a solution. He also looked to industry to soften brutality. Commerce, it was thought, 'necessarily enlightens the minds of men: it creates, indeed, artificial wants; but it excites a spirit of industry; it dispels that gloom and sourness of temper which is fostered by ignorance and idleness; it softens, polishes and refines the behaviour; and unites the hearts of men in loyal attachment to that state and government, under which our interests flourish'.[73] Unsettled conditions in Ulster, noticed by Bishop Traill, revealed problems that might arise from the modest prosperity accompanying industry. Luxury was a well-known danger.[74] Quickening but erratic economic and social change brought luxury and poverty to Protestants. Placebos were wanted. Protestant landlords, formerly idolized, were demonized as vicious, idle and vain, just as their Catholic predecessors had been. Similarly, education, if not strictly supervised, subverted. An improved Ireland might be more prosperous, though patchily so. It was not necessarily a placid island, as the last decades of the eighteenth century would show.

VII

It may be that attitudes towards land differed in Ireland from those in England. Land was easily lost or won in seventeenth-century Ireland. This feature deprived it of the *réclam* that it enjoyed in England. By the end of the seventeenth century, that which had been in the possession of the same family since the mid-sixteenth century or earlier was prized. The feeling was largely explained by practical calculation. Property that had been acquired then was less liable to be forfeited by the numerous threatened and actual redistributions. (The reversal of the Protestant reformation and the secularization of church lands would make some of the apparently secure holdings vulnerable.) With land easily available but with titles resting on insecure foundations, two tendencies resulted. Land in itself did not confer the kind of prestige carried by similar acreages in Britain. Nor indeed did it produce a comparable income. Owners, if they were to live in the style to which they aspired on the basis of their landed possessions, had to supplement their revenues. This need could spur them into improvements.

A less welcome consequence of the peculiarities of land-owning in Ireland was carelessness. Repeated and seemingly regular uprisings extruded incum-

---

[73] James Traill, *A sermon preached at Christ-Church, Dublin, on the 7th of February, 1779* (Dublin, 1779), pp 11, 14–15. [74] P.H. Kelly, '"Industry and virtue versus luxury and corruption": Berkeley, Walpole and the South Sea Bubble crisis', *ECI*, 7 (1992), pp 57–74.

bents from their properties. Uncertain when next they – or their heirs – would be ejected, the current occupants were tempted to make the most of what they held. Expedients adopted by Cork and advertised by the Boates, notably the felling of timber and its use as cheap fuel, remained popular. Few newcomers showed much compunction in selling parcels of land which had come into their possession so easily. As population gradually recovered from the mid-century catastrophe and then steadily grew, so the market for agricultural and manufactured goods expanded and with it the demand for tenancies. Individual profit rather than social calculus or *noblesse oblige* governed leasing policies. The ideological imperatives of the 1650s – always preferring Protestants and usually immigrants as tenants – faded. By the close of the seventeenth century, Irish politics were swinging into a patriotic mode. English malice was contrasted with the beneficial potential of Irish institutions. Of the latter, the Dublin parliament was the most important, and it was generous in awarding bounties to those who forwarded the crazes of the moment – corn- and flax-growing, spinning linen yarn, weaving linen cloth, cutting canals and turnpiking roads.[75] Voluntary groups, such as the Incorporated and Dublin Societies, equated civic duty with active improvement, and encouraged the latter.[76] In addition, Christian and humanist teaching emphasized the obligations of the propertied to devote a part of their resources to the education, employment and relief of the unlucky.

The private and public, mercenary and moral, threaded through schemes of improvement. Sometimes, seemingly, the larger benefits were invoked to salve uneasy consciences. In early-eighteenth-century Wicklow, a customarily absent owner converted much of the valuable timber into cash. He did order the replanting of the felled woodland. Moreover, anxious to popularize improvement among the tenantry, he donated packets of seed and catechisms. One of his tenants – a clergyman of the Church of Ireland – responded appropriately. The parson, 'reckoned as great an improver as any in the county', was reputed to love his coppices as much as his bible.[77] In the face of the prevailing enthusiasm, few openly dissented from the improving credo. The occasional sceptic suspected that it contained much hypocrisy and cant.[78] But it was hard to swim against the tide.

---

75 Magennis, 'Coal, corn and canals', pp 71–86. Fresh perspectives on the English situation are offered in S. Tarlow, *The archaeology of improvement in Britain, 1750–1850* (Cambridge, 2007).   76 J. Livesey, 'The Dublin Society in eighteenth-century Irish political thought', *Historical Journal*, 47 (2004), pp 615–40.   77 Sheffield City Library, WWM 14/14; WWMA 759, 383; 764, 12–17, 23–5; 766, 7; 769, 17.   78 R.J.S. Hoffman (ed.), *Edmund Burke, New York agent with his letters to the New York Assembly and intimate correspondence with Charles O'Hara*, Memoirs of the American Philosophical Society, 41 (Philadelphia, 1956), pp 281–2.

CHAPTER TWO

Sir William Petty, Irish landowner and improver

THE STOCK OF SIR WILLIAM PETTY continues to rise. Deviser and overseer of the massive land transfers of the 1650s, founder fellow of the Royal Society of London and inspirer (and first president in 1684) of the Dublin Philosophical Society, he has long been recognized as an intellectual and technological pioneer. His credo was to try to reduce all issues to number, weight and measure.[1] True to this philosophy – a personal amalgam of insights from Francis Bacon, Galileo, Descartes and Hobbes – he applied it to the tasks of surveying, evaluating, redistributing and improving the land and peoples of England and more especially of Ireland. Both his methods and deductions earn him accolades as pioneering demographer, cartographer, statistician and economic theorist.[2] He appreciated the importance of velocity in the circulation of money and of differences between price and value, and formulated a labour theory of value.

Easier access to his surviving papers, since 1993 in the British Library in London, have stimulated closer study of his activities and thinking, both in specific areas and in their totality.[3] The results have strengthened the view of him as an innovator. This is a conclusion that might have delighted Petty, in some vital ways deeply disappointed by his torpid public career after 1660. He himself wrote accounts of particular episodes, notably the Down Survey of the 1650s.[4] He did so to refute detractors and to advertise his own achievements.

---

1 Sir W. Petty to J. Rutter, 16 Jan. 1671[2], McGill UL, Osler MS 7612; same to P. Bunworth, 3 Nov. 1674, BL, Add. MS 72,858, p. 309; Sir R. Southwell, observations, ibid., Egerton MS 1633, ff 94–4v; H.W.E. Petty-Fitzmaurice, marquess of Lansdowne (ed.), *The Petty-Southwell correspondence* (London, 1928), pp 51, 96, 260.   2 T. Aspromourgos, 'Political economy and the social division of labour: the economics of Sir William Petty', *Scottish Journal of Poltical Economy*, xxxiii (1986); T. Aspromourgos, 'The life of Sir William Petty in relation to his economics: a tercentenary interpretation', *History of Political Economy*, xx (1988), pp 337–56; T. Aspromourgos, *On the origins of classical economics: distribution and value from William Petty to Adam Smith* (London, 1996); T. Aspromourgos, 'The mind of the oeconomist: an overview of the "Petty papers" archive', *History of Economic Ideas*, 9 (2001), pp 39–101; T. Aspromourgos, A.W. Coats, D.P. O'Brien, B. Schefold, *Sir William Petty und seine 'Political Arithmetick'* (Düsseldorf, 1992); A. Fox, 'Sir William Petty, Ireland, and the making of a political economist, 1653–1687', forthcoming; T.G. McCormick, 'Sir William Petty, political arithmetic and the transmutation of the Irish', unpublished Ph.D. thesis, Columbia University (2005); L.G. Sharp, ''Sir William Petty and some aspects of seventeenth-century natural philosophy', unpublished D.Phil. thesis, University of Oxford (1977); P. Slack, 'Government and information in seventeenth-century England', *Past and Present*, 184 (2004), pp 33–68.   3 *The British Library catalogue of additions to the manuscripts: the Petty Papers* (London, 2000).   4 W. Petty, *The history of the survey of*

Much within the archive has a similar purpose. It is weighted disproportionately to the schemes towards the end of his life, and tends towards self-justification if not self-glorification. In addition, numerous papers show how, with James VII and II's accession in 1685, Petty craved to influence official policy as strongly as he had during the Cromwellian interregnum.[5] Between 1655 and 1659, he served as secretary to the effective governor of the island, Henry Cromwell, and as a clerk to the Irish council. During the 1680s his pent-up energies poured into schemes that were startling, but frequently repetitive and impracticable. James II failed to give the ageing Petty the kind of eminence that he had enjoyed in Cromwellian Dublin.

Petty's vanity and how it affected what survives among his writings, published and unpublished, is fully appreciated by recent analysts. Yet, they conclude that he did indeed have much to be vain about. Moreover, if his hopes of shaping the Ireland that emerged from the fiery furnace of the Cromwellian reconquest were blighted, he had had a decisive effect on the nature and implementation of the new settlement. What he had not foreseen was how stubbornly Ireland might resist the detailed blueprint that he had drawn. At best it would be realized slowly and patchily. This failure resembled that of numerous less ingenious and industrious administrators who had wrestled earlier with the intractable Irish hinterlands. After 1660, Petty was powerless to prevent the restored Stuart monarchy from reversing some of the recent changes in property ownership. His attempts to salvage the principles underlying the land transfers of the 1650s, such as the substitution of newcomers who would supposedly implant industry and civility and thereby pacify and enrich Ireland, ran counter to the inclinations of Charles II and James II. The kings sympathized with loyal Catholics and helped some to be reinstated. Petty, arrogant by temperament, diminished in political stature the more he insisted on his view. Clever, entertaining, irreverent, his private talk diverted intimates, but his public stridency bored or angered the powerful. Petty, pushed towards the margins of power, had greater leisure in which to reflect, project and object.

The result is a voluminous archive. Several questions and arguments run simultaneously through the papers. Even when preoccupied with the topical and personal, he lifted his ruminations above petty antagonisms to formulate approaches and propositions that prefigure those of the nineteenth and twentieth centuries. He appreciated the power of the state, both to re-order popula-

---

Ireland commonly called The Down Survey, ed. T.A. Larcom, Irish Archaeological Society (Dublin, 1851); W. Petty, *Reflections on some persons and things in Ireland* (London, 1660). 5 F. Harris, 'Ireland as a laboratory: the archive of Sir William Petty' in M. Hunter (ed.), *Archives of the scientific revolution: the formation and exchange of ideas in seventeenth-century Europe* (Woodbridge, 1998), pp 73–90.

tions and to collect information (much of it connected with raising money and assessing fighting potential), and subjected the resulting data to endless interrogation. Political arithmetic – his digesting of detailed findings into the abstractions of number, weight and measure – was the substructure for the fiscal-military state that would arise in eighteenth-century Britain and (arguably) in Ireland too. Petty was not just a navvy labouring on the sprawling subterranean foundations, but the structural engineer who devised first in outline and then in detail how exactly it could be done.

During his own life, he knew what he had accomplished. Those who relaxed in his company realized it as well: not because he bored them with reciting his achievements, but because he was unsurpassed as a companion. Unfortunately too few in Restoration England and Ireland shared the unbuttoned intimacy for Petty to be appreciated fully. Something of this relaxed manner is caught in his wish to be painted *en dishabille* rather than with the conventional accoutrements of wig and finery.[6] His situation was in any case awkward. A prime example of a man of ability given full expression for his talents thanks to the revolution of 1649, this enthusiastic and profitable collaboration with the usurpers had to be glossed after 1660. Petty professed indifference to the form of a government so long as it wielded real power. Accordingly, he joined the talkers and thinkers who continued to toss about a republican ball in the Rota club of 1659. Others deeply implicated in the Cromwellian regime adjusted to the return to divine right monarchy after 1660. So, apparently, did Petty, elected to the Westminster and Dublin parliaments and knighted by Charles II. Yet Petty, less suave or oleaginous than many of the lapsed who regained their faith in kingship, never altogether obliterated his republican past.[7] These characteristics, combining with combativeness and intemperance, made later Stuart governments unwilling to allow him close to the heart of affairs. So, to his chagrin, he saw the mediocre overtake him.

Failure to be entrusted with work suitable to his talents mortified Petty. However, there were consolations. He was never wholly shunned by the makers of policy. In Ireland, for example, he served on the Council of Trade.[8] This position encouraged him to set out plans for commercial and political improvement. Also, he belonged to two groups – the Royal Society of London and, from 1683, the fledgling Dublin Philosophical Society – through which ideas of amelioration and betterment could be promoted.[9] These opportunities made Petty

---

6 Sir W. Petty to Lady Petty, 16 Feb. 1677[8], McGill UL, Osler MS 7612. **7** Sir W. Petty to J. Petty, 17 April 1660, BL, Add. MS 72,850. **8** Sir W. Petty to J. Rutter, Feb. 1672[3], BL, Add. MS 72,858; same to R. Wood, 10 April 1675, ibid., Add. MS 72,858; *CSP, Domestic, 1669–70*, p. 126; ibid., *1670*, pp 222–3. **9** For a succinct

indefatigable in analyzing the current condition of Ireland, and in suggesting exactly how it could be amended.

Alongside this activity, by turns severely practical and utopian, he pursued personal matters. Ireland throughout the seventeenth century was seen as a stock from which enterprising and ruthless Scots, English and Welsh could reward themselves. The career of the first earl of Cork, represented as that of a younger son and adventurer, was the most sensational example known by the mid-seventeenth century. Cork, who died in 1643, was reckoned to have an annual rental of about £20,000 on the eve of the devastating uprising of 1641.[10] In the next generation, Petty would personify a comparable ascent. Petty, like Cork before him, profited from rebellions, the subsequent redistributions of property and from government service. The indigent son of a Hampshire clothier, he was a conspicuous example of an autodidact and of self-help. After various adventures, including shipwreck and education by Jesuits in France, he gained a fellowship of an Oxford college and celebrity as a physician. Medical expertise brought him to Ireland as physician to the army that had been sent in 1649 to reduce the island to English rule. He arrived with £500 rather than the £5 that Cork was said (by himself) to have had in his purse when he landed in Ireland.[11] The difference showed how Petty had already hauled himself upwards in the propitious circumstances of the civil wars and their aftermath. Nevertheless, it was Ireland that opened the prospect of much more lucrative and challenging employments. Petty's success in supplanting the official appointed to survey and reallocate the forfeited property of the rebels (8,400,000 acres) was a feat of conception and organization that proved to contemporaries the utility of his theories.[12] He was handsomely recompensed. Furthermore, like others with precise knowledge of the Irish localities, he snapped up unwanted property at bargain prices. Through these methods he amassed estates scattered across five counties. By 1685 they yielded an annual £6,700. The total might look modest beside the rental of the earls of Cork,

---

account of the early Royal Society, M. Hunter, *Science and society in Restoration England* (Cambridge, 1981); on the Dublin Philosophical Society, see Hoppen, *The common scientist*. **10** N. Canny, *The upstart earl: a study in the social and mental world of Richard Boyle, first earl of Cork, 1566–1643* (Cambridge, 1982); T.O. Ranger, 'The career of Richard Boyle, first earl of Cork, in Ireland, 1588–1643', unpublished D.Phil. thesis (Oxford University, 1958); T.O. Ranger, 'Richard Boyle and the making of an Irish fortune', *IHS*, x (1957), pp 257–97. **11** Lord Edmond Fitzmaurice, *The life of Sir William Petty, 1623–1687* (London, 1895), p. 319; Lansdowne (ed.), *Petty–Southwell correspondence*, p. 211. **12** J.H. Andrews, *Shapes of Ireland: maps and their makers (1564–1839)* (Dublin, 1997), pp 118–52; W.J. Smyth, *Map-making, landscapes and memory: a geography of colonial and early-modern Ireland, c.1530–1750* (Cork, 2006); W.J. Smyth, 'Society and settlement in seventeenth-century Ireland: the evidence of the "1659 Census"' in W.J. Smyth and K. Whelan (eds), *Common ground: essays on the historical geography of Ireland* (Dublin, 1990), pp 125–58; W.J. Smyth, introduction to *A census of Ireland, circa 1659*, ed. S. Pender (Dublin, 2002), pp v–lxii.

which had grown to perhaps £25,000.[13] Even so, it made Petty the richest commoner in Restoration Ireland.

The ascent demonstrated anew the opportunities afforded by seventeenth-century Ireland. In contrast with England, Wales and Scotland, it witnessed a revolution in the identity of the propertied élite. Over the course of the century, more than 50 per cent of the profitable land in the island was transferred from Catholics to Protestants. The process was most dramatic during the 1650s, thanks in large measure to Petty's efficiency in directing the survey of confiscated lands. Petty's enrichment also suggested the unusual scope in Ireland for the energetic to thrive. The ambitious programme that England had set itself since the 1540s – to extend its authority throughout the entire island and to release its full potential as an appendage of England – required active executants. This need was especially urgent after 1649, owing to the magnitude of the resettlement and the exclusion of many potential helpers on political grounds. Petty benefited from a brief phase of meritocracy before the prevalent jobbery returned and washed nonentities back on the tide. Petty had to watch powerlessly while he was pushed aside by the mediocre. Galling too were the obstacles that impeded full enjoyment of his personal fortune. Petty frequently behaved as if he had been singled out to be thwarted. Personalizing his tribulations may be dismissed as an instance of his egocentricity. No matter how much he might fulminate against the official indifference and delays, he had become a rich man.

An examination of Petty's frustrations as an Irish landlord has two purposes. A gap opened between the theory and practice of plantation, which, if it was particularly wide on some of Petty's holdings, may have been an experience common to new proprietors. Many landlords faced intractable terrain inhabited still by obstinate indigenes. Yet, Petty argued that many of the problems resulted from the ambiguous and – by the 1680s – hostile attitude of government towards the newcomers' efforts to settle their holdings. Petty's litany of complaint raises a second question. The Cromwellian settlement, which he had done so much to devise, is traditionally treated not just as revolutionary but also as definitive in setting out the lineaments of landownership for more than a century and enabling a Protestant ascendancy over power as well as property to be constructed. Detailed studies have shown that the Cromwellian arrangements were modified but not dismantled under Charles II and James II.[14] When

---

13 T.C. Barnard, 'Land and the limits of loyalty: the second earl of Cork and first earl of Burlington, 1612–1698', in T. Barnard and J. Clark (eds), *Lord Burlington: architecture, art and life*, pp 167–99, reprinted in Barnard, *Ascents and descents*, pp 84–110. **14** For the settlement: L.J. Arnold, *The Restoration land settlement in County Dublin, 1660–1688: a history of the administration of the Acts of Settlement and Explanation* (Dublin, 1993), J.G. Simms, 'The Restoration, 1660–1685' in T.W. Moody, F.X. Martin and F.J.

James II used Ireland as the base from which to recover his other two kingdoms between 1689 and 1690, the dispossessed hoped soon to enjoy their own again. Catholic expectations were dashed by James's defeat. Instead the confiscations of the past century were confirmed and extended to encompass that small group of Catholics who hitherto had hung onto their lands. By the end of this final episode in the land settlement, the percentage of land owned by Catholics had dwindled to 22.[15]

These essentials are agreed. However, investigators of what was happening in particular places have revealed the unexpected: Catholic resilience as well as losses and sufferings. They are explained – in part – by the ingenuity of the losers in evading, or exploiting loopholes in, the discriminatory system. In part, too, Catholic survival, while reflecting simple superiority of numbers, reflected Protestant weakness. The state in Ireland, although increasingly intrusive and better manned, had difficulty in ensuring compliance with all its edicts. In addition, the new order in Ireland, Protestant and English (or British) remained numerically feeble. Fewer immigrants than expected arrived to settle the lands conferred on them in the 1650s. Only from Scotland did migration on a substantial scale continue until the close of the seventeenth century. This disparity strengthened the divergences between the north of Ireland – the destination of most Scots – and the rest of the island.[16] The paucity of settlers obliged compromise. For lands to be tenanted and tilled or for towns to offer specialized skills and services so that they would revive and thrive, Catholics had to remain. Recognition that this must be the case in the absence of a massive influx of newcomers had forced the government of the 1650s to abandon its plan of consigning much of the remaining indigenous population to the western province of Connacht and adjacent county of Clare. Petty had been privy to this modification of the original draconian utopianism. It did not prevent him, in his declining years, from advocating the wholesale transference of peoples between Ireland and Britain. In the interval between 1655 and 1685, he had grappled with the intransigence of the inhabitants long established on the lands that he had lately acquired. The ability with which those on the spot, notably in Kerry, blocked Petty's grand projects might have cautioned him.

An axiom underlying Petty's approach, as that of his contemporaries and collaborators influenced by Bacon, gathered into informal groups around

---

Byrne (eds), *A new history of Ireland*, iii (Oxford, 1976), pp 420–53; K.S. Bottigheimer, 'The restoration land settlement: a structural view', *IHS*, xviii (1972), pp 1–21. **15** J.G. Simms, *The Williamite confiscation, 1690–1703* (London, 1956). **16** T.C. Barnard, 'New opportunities for British settlement: Ireland, 1650–1700' in N. Canny (ed.), *Oxford history of the British Empire. I. The origins of empire* (Oxford, 1998), pp 309–27.

Samuel Hartlib and Robert Boyle during the Interregnum or later in the formal associations in London, Oxford and Dublin, was that theory could be applied.[17] The acquisition of extensive Irish estates gave him at once a laboratory in which techniques could be tested and refined and a showcase in which he would display the remarkable results. In this way, the speculations and experimentation of the learned would be verified and sceptics would be persuaded of the superiority of the innovations advocated by Petty and his ilk. Embarrassingly, Petty's projects failed to furnish sensational prototypes on which others might model their enterprises. But Petty was stubborn: he did not conclude that his presuppositions might be wrong. Rather he blamed the authorities for hindering him. Far from altering the approach, he redoubled his efforts.

This obstinacy encapsulates an aspect of Petty at variance with the fertile and original empiric whose stature has been heightened by recent studies. The disparity is a genuine contradiction within Petty's approach. It may do little more than confirm that Petty, so willing in much of his work to jettison tradition, never freed himself from conventional English views of Ireland and the Irish. Looking in detail at Petty's chastening experiences as an Irish propertyowner is not designed to topple him from his plinth within the pantheon of intellectual colossi. He contended that he was unique in the combination and severity of troubles that he faced. No doubt, the size of his holdings (and of his ego) magnified the problems. But Petty was not singled out: others who had recently been granted Irish property, such as the courtier, William Legge, had to battle against the uncertainties and alterations in policy, the feebleness of the Irish authorities, and the tenacity of those already on the spot.[18] Accordingly, Petty's record as an Irish landowner serves to warn of the gulf between intention and achievement: a gulf that many more than he struggled to bridge.

II

The Cromwellian confiscations reduced the Catholic share of land from 60 per cent to 22 per cent. Since the policy had been instituted by the English Long Parliament and implemented under the usurper Cromwell, it was reasonable to expect the restored Charles II to reverse it. However, confiscation followed by Protestant plantation belonged to a formula for anglicizing and stabilizing

---

17 For this atmosphere: T.C. Barnard, 'The Hartlib circle and the origins of the Dublin Philosophical Society', *IHS*, xix (1974), pp 56–71; Sharp, 'Petty and natural philosophy'; C. Webster, *The Great instauration: science, medicine and reform, 1626–1660* (London, 1975). **18** Something of Legge's troubles is sketched in T. Barnard, *The kingdom of Ireland, 1641–1760* (Basingstoke, 2004), p. 111.

Ireland too well-established to be abandoned lightly.[19] Policy for Ireland was decided invariably in London, and thither, between 1660 and 1663, rival groups repaired. Those bent on preserving the recent changes – mostly the Protestants established in Ireland before 1641 who had gained greatly from the forfeitures of the Interregnum, and the English soldiers and investors whose contributions were repaid with land – resisted a lobby of Irish Catholics.[20] Some Catholics argued that they had not participated in the uprising of 1641, with the attendant atrocities, and had indeed sought to restrain the headstrong. Many contended that they had fought loyally for Charles I and Charles II, even sharing exile with the latter. They were, therefore, being penalized for their loyalty to the Stuarts. The king sympathized with this proposition. He hoped to please all. Favoured Catholics were restored immediately to their hereditary estates. At the same time, prominent Irish Protestants, usually those with direct access to the court or helpful in the restoration, were pardoned and had their new land grants confirmed. Charles II wanted a similar generosity to inform the general settlement of Ireland. The very idea enraged the Protestants, who had no wish to lose so quickly their monopoly over office, power and the lushest lands. They argued that Ireland would never be secure so long as the Catholic Irish owned sizeable estates; they also pointed out that Ireland lacked enough acres to satisfy all claimants.

The revised settlement of the 1660s allowed those Catholics who could prove their innocence of any role in the 1641 risings or their subsequent good conduct to regain lost possessions. Where these older claims conflicted with those of the recently established proprietors, the newcomers would be compensated with lands elsewhere. Also, in order to provide a sufficient stock of property, the soldiers and adventurers (investors in the reconquest during the 1640s) had to disgorge one-third of their awards. The stages through which these arrangements had evolved – discussions at the royal court and in the English privy council, more talks and drafting in the Irish council, debate and passage in the Dublin parliament – were attended by political manoeuvres and intrigue in which the Protestants showed themselves to be superior. Controversy did not cease with the passing of the statutes by the Irish parliament in 1662 and 1665. A Court of Claims, staffed by English commissioners, sat in Dublin to adjudicate the claims of innocence and to re-instatement. Rumours of the commissioners' friendliness towards powerful Catholics provoked Protestant protest, including a sinister conspiracy against the govern-

---

19 N. Canny, *Making Ireland British, 1580–1650* (Oxford, 2001).   **20** Sir W. Petty to J. Petty, 9 Jan. 1660[1], 5 and 23 March 1660[1], BL, Add. MS 72,850.

ment. To stop further contentions, the sittings of the Court of Claims were terminated. What was left to accomplish was to apportion lands, decide compensation for displaced Protestants and for the legal owner to take possession of the allotted properties.[21]

The compromise pleased neither Protestants nor Catholics. The latter, embittered by their modest compensation, schemed to re-open the question. Protestants, doubting that they were entirely secure, remained vigilant against what they saw as Catholic wiles and the pusillanimity of English rulers. In consequence, the settlement, formally completed in 1669, was not treated as definitive. While the disappointed and nervous awaited an opportunity to improve the legal situation, individuals exploited the uncertainties. Loss of records, unclear boundaries, ill-defined land law and partial judges, jurors and witnesses meant that wrangles over ownership and physical possession proliferated. Particularly in remoter regions, Protestants were kept from occupying what they had been granted. Elsewhere, Catholics were denied repossession of their lands by partisan Protestant officials. Violence sometimes erupted between the competitors. More generally, many Catholics felt that they had been accorded scant justice from a Court of Claims that was short-lived and staffed by Englishmen, and from a settlement, the authors of which were Protestants. The Catholics' agents, headed by Richard Talbot (later earl of Tyrconnell), schemed at court to re-open the matter. Charles II's readiness to listen to the complaints, to appoint fresh commissioners to review the earlier process and, by virtue of his prerogative, to override statutes and restore some Irish Catholics further unsettled Irish Protestants. The unease of the latter made them link themselves to English critics of the later Stuarts.

Irish Catholics had long realised that no English parliament would improve their lot. Instead they looked to the monarch to use his prerogative on their behalf. Not only did they lobby assiduously, they fluently defended royal powers. One Irish Catholic assured James II that Ireland, 'by the king's prerogative is at his disposal independently of the Parliament of England', and insisted that if only Catholics were returned to power in Ireland 'they could make you [James II] as absolute in Ireland as your heart could wish'.[22] Protestants naturally seized on such utterances to show the danger of leniency towards the papists and questioned both the Catholics' constitutional reasoning and Charles

---

21 Geraldine Tallon (ed.), *Court of Claims: submissions and evidence, 1663* (Dublin, 2006). 22 'A series of eight anonymous and confidential letters to James II about the state of Ireland', *Notes and Queries*, cxxiv (1882), pp 361, 401; A.C. Creighton, 'The Catholic interest in Irish politics in the reign of Charles II', unpublished Ph.D. thesis, Queen's University, Belfast (2000).

II's and James II's actions in undermining the acts of 1662 and 1665. Protestants asserted that the king could not dispose of confiscated Irish lands without parliamentary consent, that those lands had merely been vested in the king as parliament's trustee and that consequently any letters patent or grants made by royal commissioners were invalid until confirmed by the Irish parliament.

After 1660 there was much Protestant nervousness about the monarch's intentions towards the settlement. What so far had been achieved had resulted from and must henceforward be maintained by intense lobbying. Yet fears for the future could not be allowed to let Protestants neglect what they currently but maybe precariously held. In the future, the lands might be overrun and seized by insurgent Catholics. For the time being, however, the proprietors dedicated themselves to exploiting what they possessed. Despite uncertainty over royal attitudes, the times were propitious: years of peace, a growing population and buoyant trade increased demand for Irish produce. Propertied Protestants displayed their wealth in modish houses and gardens, furnished with artefacts and plants shipped from England and continental Europe.[23] Petty grew rich with his fellow landowners. Yet he was less fortunate than the stereotype suggests. Indeed, if his strictures are accurate, they may modify that stereotype.

III

Most who obtained land in Cromwellian Ireland did so through fighting there or through advancing money towards the costs of reconquest. Petty, in contrast, owed his estates to his service as a civilian administrator. Such state servants formed a group which in the past had done well when confiscated property was parcelled out. It was, after all, the route to riches taken by the first earl of Cork. As the English state expanded westwards, Ireland was turned into an arena for advancement. Those unable to find promising openings in England, whether in the administration, the law or the church, turned – often reluctantly – to Ireland. They accepted posts there in the hope of stepping from them into better ones back in England. Plans seldom worked quite as hoped. These functionaries, reluctant and (they fondly supposed) temporary settlers in Ireland, found themselves marooned there. Since lands were cheap and abundant, the expatriates consoled themselves by founding dynasties and amassing the wealth that would enable their heirs to buy their passages back into the upper reaches

---

23 For examples, see: T.C. Barnard, 'The political, material and mental culture of the Cork settlers, c.1650–1700' in P. O'Flanagan and N.G. Buttimer (eds), *Cork: history and society* (Dublin, 1993), pp 309–65, reprinted in Barnard, *Ascents and descents*, pp 35–83.

of English society. This, within a generation, was what the successors of the first earl of Cork did.[24] It would be what Petty's own heirs later contrived.

The upheavals of the 1640s and 1650s, like the aftermath of earlier Irish wars, presented the active and unscrupulous with exciting possibilities. There was much to be done, and few with the right talents. Petty, as has been seen, exchanged the relative calm of Oxford, admittedly remodelled to reflect the new political and religious orders of the English Commonwealth, for the clamour and dolour of a subjugated country awaiting reconstruction. The immensity of the undertaking, together with the belief that a fresh template could be imposed on Ireland, promised to stretch Petty's abilities even more than the resuscitation of a hanged criminal had in Oxford. So it proved. Intellectual gratification was matched by the pecuniary. His nest-egg of £500 swelled to £9,000. In addition, he had gained an unrivalled knowledge of the terrain and resources of Ireland: capital with which he would continue to trade for the rest of his life. Petty invested a little of his profits in London property. But the bulk was either received in or converted into Irish lands. By 1660 Petty was a substantial Irish landowner. His holdings earned him election as knight of the shire to the Irish parliament in 1661. Although it was fortuitous that he had secured this stake in Ireland and by no means clear that his subsequent interests would remain there, he was necessarily concerned with the fate of the forthcoming settlement. He was both a principal architect of the present redistribution and a prime beneficiary. The first role, speaking as it did of his closeness to the powerful of the Interregnum, might make him apprehensive about how he would fare in the next stage.

The Cromwellian regime in Ireland, no less than in England, was divided by ideologies and personalities. Petty aligned with what most viewed as the more conservative: with Henry Cromwell, the actual governor in Dublin from 1655, rather than with the titular lord deputy, Charles Fleetwood, and against the incumbent surveyor-general, Benjamin Worsley, whose scheme Petty belittled in order to substitute his own for the Down Survey.[25] Petty was also condemned publicly by Hierome Sankey, a heresiarch of the Baptists in Ireland.[26] Fleetwood, Worsley and Sankey were radicals in religion; Petty, soon suspected of an indifference that bordered on atheism, eschewed sectarian enthusiasm.[27]

---

24 Barnard, 'Land and the limits of loyalty', pp 167–99. **25** On these divisions, T.C. Barnard, 'Planters and policies in Cromwellian Ireland', *Past and Present*, 61 (1973), pp 31–69, reprinted in Barnard, *Ascents and descents*, pp 1–34. **26** Sir W. Petty to Tomkins, 7 Dec. 1672, BL, Add. MS 72,858; same to Mrs Cromwell, 10 June 1679, ibid., Add. MS 72,850; W. Petty, *A brief of proceedings between Sr Hierom Sankey and Dr William Petty* (London, 1659); Petty, *Reflections*. **27** Sir W. Petty, 'A sermon preached upon ye 23 October', BL, Add. MS 72,884, ff 127–40v; Sir R. Southwell, observations, BL, Egerton MS 1633, f. 68; Sir

In 1659, Petty returned to London. A seat in the parliament there was one reason; others were the crisis that impended following the death of the Protector, Oliver Cromwell, in the previous September. Soon Petty's main patron in Ireland, Henry Cromwell, would be recalled to England, and confusion threatened to envelop Irish affairs. In London, Petty could more effectively protect himself against those who were aggrieved by the allocations under the new settlement or attacked him as a surrogate for his patrons. Petty steered through the turbulence that followed the fall of the Cromwellian protectorate and culminated in the return of Charles II. The king, diverted by Petty's talk, pardoned and knighted him. More materially, his Irish land holdings were first confirmed by letters patent and then enlarged.[28] Petty had surmounted dangerous hurdles, but others remained. Like most interested in the Irish settlement, Petty moved back to Dublin in 1663, as the scene shifted there. He was fortunate in being able to call on the backing of the two principal controllers of Irish affairs, the duke of Ormond and earl of Orrery. He had helped both in the 1650s to save or extend their estates. He paid the Irish lord chancellor £100 in order to have inserted into the bills clauses to confirm his lands.[29]

Petty's behaviour between 1660 and 1666 was not all defensive. He knew there were pickings to be had while men were uncertain what belonged to whom. He tried to buy up cheaply and secretly dilapidated property in Dublin. He negotiated to develop housing and to introduce building with brick into the city of Limerick. Knowing from his observations of the 1650s that the soldiers who had obtained or awaited payment in land would grow restless and impecunious as their acquisition of secure titles was further delayed, he bought up their entitlements contained in paper debentures. Through grants and by purchasing, he secured lands in five counties. Acumen was also demonstrated when, in 1667, he married the widow of an Irish baronet. The marriage brought him estates, concentrated in County Cork, worth a further £1,000 p.a.[30] It also gave him a formidable assistant in his varied ventures.

None of this property was free from trouble. The rival claims of those adjudged innocent by the Court of Claims jeopardized some portions; royal

---

R. Southwell, 'Preparations for an answer to Sir W. Petty's paper of religion', RIA, MS 12 F 42. On his attitude to Christianity, R. Lewis, 'William Petty, God and the order of nature: an unpublished manuscript treatise', forthcoming, is illuminating. **28** Letter of Charles II, 1 Feb. 1661[2], Bodleian, Carte MS 42, f. 492. **29** Sir W. Petty to J. Petty, 8 Aug. 1660, BL, Add. MS 72,850; T. Dance to Lady Petty, 4 Aug. 1688, ibid., Add. MS 72,864; *The statutes at large, passed in the parliaments held in Ireland*, 8 vols (Dublin, 1765–86), ii, pp 281, 298; iii, pp 40–1, 63–4. **30** Sir W. Petty to J. Petty, 13 Nov. 1660, 4 and 15 Dec. 1660, 9 Jan. 1660[1], 26 March 1661, BL, Add. MS 72,850; same to J. Rutter, 18 April 1668, 2 June 1668; same to J. Graunt, 18 April 1668; same to Capt. Phillips, 13 May 1668; same to J. Hall, 23 June 1668, McGill UL, Osler MS 7612.

grants, others. Even those lands for which his title looked unassailable had still to be possessed physically and the previous owners displaced. Furthermore, after those preliminaries had been completed, the influence of the ejected proprietor might persist, especially if still living nearby. Suitable agents, tenants and labourers had then to be introduced. These anxieties were worsened by the vagaries of royal policy. One part of his acquisitions excited the highest hopes and caused Petty the greatest worry. The largest acreage lay in the distant southwestern county of Kerry, still thought a redoubt of old ways and resistant to change. Contemporaries presumed that the vast holding in Kerry was the chief source of Petty's wealth; his own obsession with it seemed to prove the belief. The assumption is not borne out by the estimates in his papers. Petty, towards the end of his life, reckoned that £4,800 of his annual income of £6,700 derived from Ireland. Of that £4,800, no more than £1,100 was expected from Kerry. Usually, it yielded less.[31]

In 1657, Petty had accepted lands in Kerry, at the mouth of the Kenmare River, because no one else wanted them. The region was remote, English influence was slight and resident Protestants few. Much of the land was bog or mountain. A range of mountains separated the district from the rest of the country, and even the sea voyage around Mizen Head was perilous. It was the contrast between what the region appeared to be and what Petty believed that it might be made which beguiled him into accepting it and then adding to the initial grant. Here was a locality overdue for assimilation to English ways. It cried out to Petty for planting with industrious and skilled Protestants, and for intensive economic exploitation. Petty, having presided over the survey of so much of Ireland (twenty-nine of its thirty-two counties), detected or suspected rich natural resources. The pasture was fertile, the seas teemed with fish and rivers glistened with pearls. Trees clad the hill-sides and could be shipped away profitably as timber. What was not fit for export could fuel local manufactures. Iron-ore, copper, lead and even silver were thought to be buried in the hills. There was marble to be quarried. Even the inhabitants were reported to be industrious if only they could be freed from the oppressive rule by heads of their septs and the debilitating routines of their religion. In Kerry, Petty aimed to enrich himself, assist the government by quieting and improving a wild area, and set an example to others in 'the terrible work' of planting Kerry. The further attraction was the chance to advertise the utility of his science by applying it to the unimproved place.[32]

---

[31] Sir W. Petty to Lady Petty, 24 Sep. 1683, 14 Oct. 1683, BL, Add. MS 72,856; Fitzmaurice, *Petty*, pp 320–3; J. Aubrey, *Brief lives*, ed. A. Clark, 2 vols (Oxford, 1898), ii, p. 142.   [32] Sir W. Petty to J. Rutter, May 1668,

From 1660, Petty devoted disproportionate efforts to defend and develop his original grants, and to add to what he held in Kerry. Any enlargement of the holdings depended on what the Court of Claims decreed. Two of the leading Catholic landowners displaced from the area and now seeking restoration – Donough McGillicuddy and Donough McFinin – commanded the support of the king and Ormond, the lord lieutenant, having soldiered with them.[33] The situation was also complicated by a claim to estates in Kerry from Ormond that dated back to the 1580s. Ormond wanted the restitution of the Kerry estate so that he could endow a younger son. Although massively wealthy, with a rental of approximately £25,000 matched only by the earls of Cork, Ormond was already beset by accumulated and worsening debts.[34]

Petty waited apprehensively for the decision of the Court of Claims, and intrigued to try to influence the verdict. Kerry gave Petty an interest opposed to that of Ormond. Given Ormond's power, not just as the lord lieutenant in Ireland but as a courtier and counsellor at the English court, the rivalry was unfortunate. It began a process of estrangement which would damage Petty. His political affiliations, his religious outlook and his temperament distanced him from the duke. The distance was increased dangerously owing to the zeal with which Petty pursued his claims over Kerry. Petty broadened his campaign. He represented the matter as indicative of Ormond's avarice and incompetence. He joined the claque of discontented who criticized the duke's lax administration. He also impugned his honesty, elaborating on how much Ormond personally had gained from the revised land settlement. At first, Petty's partisanship was rewarded. Ormond withdrew his claims in Kerry; then, in 1669, he was dismissed as lord lieutenant.[35] But these victories did little to improve Petty's

McGill UL, Osler MS 7612.   **33** Charles II to lords justice of Ireland, 18 April 1661, Bodleian, Carte MS 42, f. 190; Sir L. Dyve to Ormond, Sep. 1662, Bodleian, Carte MS 32, f. 17; D. McGillicuddy to Ormond, 17 Nov. 1668, Carte Ms, 36, f. 565; D. McFinin to Ormond, 24 Nov. 1674, ibid., Carte MS 38, f. 181; 44, ff. 72, list of those restored by Court of Claims, undated, c.1667, ibid., Carte MS 44, f. 479; Orrery to Ormond, 23 July 1667, ibid., Carte MS 48, f. 116; Ormond to Orrery, 27 July 1667, ibid., Carte MS 48, ff. 120–1; Ormond to Sir W. Petty, 25 July 1674, ibid., Carte MS 219, f. 135; privy council [England] to Essex, 28 June 1676, BL, Stowe MS 209, f. 382; letters patent for Lt.-Col. Donough McGillicuddy, 16 Nov. 1678, NLI, D 10,000; Sir W. Petty to J. Rutter, 29 Oct. 1672, BL, Add. MS 72,858; *CSP Ireland, 1669–70*, pp 678–9; HMC, *Ormonde Mss*, new series, i, p. 252.   **34** Bodleian, Carte MSS 35, f. 80; instructions for R. Southwell, 18 May 1664; R. Southwell to Ormond, 10 June 1664, Carte MS 40, ff 645, 647; Ormond to R. Southwell et al, 25 May 1664, Carte MS 144, f. 50; same to same, 1 March 1664[5], Carte MS 145, f. 146; same to T. Crosby et al., 24 Sep. 1663, Carte MS 159, f. 78; Sir W. Petty to Major Goodwin, 16 Oct. 1666; same to ?Sir G. Carteret, 26 Oct. 1666, same to J. Graunt, 21 July 1668; Lady Petty to Sir R. Southwell, 9 Aug. 1670, BL, Add. MS 72,852; J. Petty to sheriff of Co. Kerry, 25 July 1671, BL, Add. MS 72,859; T. Barnard, 'Introduction' in T. Barnard and Jane Fenlon (eds), *The dukes of Ormonde, 1610–1745* (Woodbridge, 2000), pp 21–6.   **35** Papers relating to Ormond, BL, Add. MS 72,884, ff 96–105v; Sir W. Petty to J. Petty, 30 March 1661[2], BL, Add. MS 72,850; J. Walsh to Ormond, 18 Sep. 1666, Bodleian, Carte MS 35, f. 80; Lady Petty to Sir R. Southwell, 9 Aug. 1670, BL, Add. MS 72,852; Ormond to Ossory, 5 Oct. 1667, 16 Dec. [1667], Bodleian, Carte MS 220, ff. 290, 431; Ormond to Ossory, 15

prospects in Kerry or elsewhere. Worse, he had incurred Ormond's displeasure. The duke recovered from the setback and would return to the Irish viceroyalty in 1677, in which capacity he resisted Petty's renewed quest for official favours. Ormond politely acknowledged Petty's remarkable abilities, but made sure he had narrow outlets for them in Ireland.[36]

The Court of Claims, in dismissing Ormond's pretensions, upheld the grant of much of south Kerry to three regiments in satisfaction for their arrears of pay. The judgment was the cue for Petty to act. Dealings with soldiers during the 1650s had convinced him that they could not tell 'what to do with this body nor have they stock or brains to manage it'. Petty believed that they would be easily prevailed upon to sell. An asking price of £35,000 was mentioned. Prosperous as he had become, Petty alone could not command sums of this magnitude. Tantalized by a prospect just beyond his grasp, he wailed, 'Lord, what might one do now with ready money in Ireland'.[37] For Petty it was an awkward time. He faced the loss of rents and the costs of rebuilding his London houses destroyed in the Fire. His recent marriage burdened him with the debts and complicated legal proceedings inherited by Lady Petty from her first husband.[38] Credit facilities in Ireland were primitive, and those in London seem to have been closed to Petty. In these circumstances, he had to find a partner. He hit on Sir George Carteret, recently connected with Ireland through appointment as its vice-treasurer. Carteret was interested in colonizing projects, both in America and Ireland.[39] These interests, together with the possibility that he might entice settlers from the Channel Islands (where he had been governor) to Kerry, recommended Carteret to Petty. But Carteret's chief attraction was the cash he would put into the joint venture. He was expected to invest £8,000 and lend a further £2000 or £3000 to Petty at 10 per cent interest.[40] Later, Carteret alleged that he had advanced £12,000.[41]

Oct. 1667, Bodleian, Carte MSS 48, f. 221; W.M. Brady (ed.), *The McGillicuddy papers* (London, 1867), p. 84; J.I. McGuire, 'Why was Ormond dismissed in 1669?' *IHS*, xviii (1973), pp 295–312. **36** Sir W. Petty to J. Rutter, 3 March 1667[8], 18 April 1668, McGill UL, Osler MS 7612; list of Ormond's alleged profits, Bodleian, Carte MS 70, f. 368; Arlington to Lord Lieutenant and Irish council, 12 Nov. 1669, ibid., Carte MS 40, ff 727–8; Charles II on behalf of Ormond, 20 Dec. 1673, ibid., Carte MS 40, f. 770; Ormond to Sir R. Southwell, 27 May 1676, BL, Add. MS 72,851; Ormond to Sir R. Southwell, 20 Oct. 1678, Carte MS 70, f. 456. **37** Sir W. Petty to Major Goodwin, 16 Oct. 1666; same to ?Sir G. Carteret, 26 Oct. 1666, McGill UL, Osler MS 7612. **38** Sir W. Petty to ?Sir G. Carteret, 22 June [1667]; same to J. Rutter, 14 March 1667[8], 23 June 1668; same to Bp. E. Worth, 14 March 1667[8]; same to J. Graunt, 13 May 1668, 28 Feb. 1670[1]; same to W. Chealy, 13 May 1668; same to Lady Petty, after 3 June 1668, McGill UL, Osler MS 7612; P.E. Jones, *The Fire Court*, 2 vols (London, 1970), ii, pp 154–5. **39** Bodleian, Carte MSS 33, f. 237; 49, f. 163; K.G. Davies, *The Royal African Company* (London, 1957), pp 62, 65; K.H.D. Haley, *The first earl of Shaftesbury* (Oxford, 1968), pp 186, 231, 233; D.T. Witcombe, *Charles II and the cavalier House of Commons* (Manchester, 1966), pp 92–3, 94, 98, 198. **40** Sir W. Petty to unknown, 16 Oct. 1666, 30 March 1667; same to ?Sir G. Carteret, 26 Oct. 1666, 9 and 22 June 1667, 26 Jan. 1668[9], 12 March 1668[9], 12 Dec. 1668, McGill UL, Osler MS 7612. **41** Brady,

To entrap Carteret, Petty drew up an alluring prospectus. The size of their Kerry colony would be such that 'no man in Ireland has so much lands in one spot, nor do I believe many of the sovereign princes in Italy and Germany have so much, perhaps not much more for their dominion, much less for their prosperity'. He emphasized the region's hidden assets, and predicted that the investment would soon return £10,000 annually. Carteret was not convinced. If he ever entered into a formal partnership with Petty, it was short-lived. Petty was forced to scale down his original, grandiose plans. In the end, he spent £3,700 on 164,000 acres. In addition, he received scattered scraps to compensate for lands elsewhere that had to be returned to Catholics.[42]

Petty's stake in Kerry, although smaller than he had hoped, was vast. Its availability told of the unparalleled opportunities of the 1640s and 1650s. Yet this great estate never matched Petty's imaginings. At first, he had planned to reside there for part of the year. Residence and personal oversight had been crucial factors in the success of the first earl of Cork's stewardship. The very remoteness of Kerry militated against frequent and prolonged stays. Geography and earlier settlement ensured that the centres of Cork's apanage at Lismore and Youghal allowed relatively quick and easy access to Dublin, south-west England and ultimately London. Petty in Kerry enjoyed no such advantages. His visits, as a result, remained occasional and fleeting. Instead, he was obliged to rely on subordinates. Again, in contrast to the situation in Lord Cork's empire, Petty had only a meagre human stock on which to draw, whereas Cork had identified and nurtured potential among his numerous tenants. Cork's more mature system did not prevent the appointment of the dishonest and incompetent, but, at least until Cork's successors ceased to reside in Ireland, such mistakes were far fewer than those made by Petty.[43]

Petty approached the planting of Ireland conventionally. The essential was to attract suitable tenants. Not only should they be English and Protestant, but 'honest, willing to take pains, skilled in their employments, have some stock and ... [such as] do delight in improvement and good husbandry'.[44] To attract

---

McGillicuddy Papers, p. xxv. **42** Sir W. Petty to ?Sir G. Carteret, 26 Oct. 1666, 12 Dec. 1668; same to Sir P. Pett, 26 Aug. 1676; same to L. Kingdon, April 1683, McGill UL, Osler MS 7612; Petty Papers, box D, items 79 and 98, now BL, Add MS 72,900; Sir W. Petty to Lady Petty, 14 and 24 Sep. 1681, BL, Add. MS 72,856; Lansdowne (ed.), *Petty–Southwell correspondence*, p. 75. **43** Barnard, 'Land and the limits of loyalty', pp 167–99, reprinted in Barnard, *Ascents and descents*, pp 84–110; M. MacCarthy-Morrogh, *The Munster plantation: English migration to southern Ireland, 1583–1641* (Oxford, 1986), pp 168–74, 218–20, 245–53, 274–83; L.J. Proudfoot, *Urban patronage and social authority: the management of the duke of Devonshire's towns in Ireland, 1764–1891* (Washington, DC, 1995), pp 66–296; T.O. Ranger, 'The career of Richard Boyle, first earl of Cork, in Ireland, 1588–1643', unpublished D.Phil. thesis, Oxford University (1959). **44** Sir W. Petty to Davy, 18 Feb. 1667[8], 9 March 1667[8], 13 May 1668, 17 Nov. 1668; same to Lt. Taylor, 3

such paragons he offered preferential terms. But lures could not entice enough of the right sort into his pool. The appeal of Ireland to those with the desired attributes had diminished sharply over the seventeenth century. Moreover, those who might still seek a life in Ireland, such as refugees from persecution in Catholic Europe, gravitated to more accessible and longer established settlements. In the end, Petty had little to tempt immigrants to prefer him as their landlord. Initial obduracy gave way gradually to accommodations, accepting as tenants the existing inhabitants, regardless of confession or habits.[45]

IV

Petty's belief in the great potential of his Kerry estate and in the superiority of his methods for tapping it, shaken by repeated setbacks, did not vanish. In his opinion, neither his assessment nor his technique was at fault. The government was to blame. His persistence with approaches that were at once traditional and wrong-headed sat strangely with a philosophy that elevated the observed and concrete above inherited learning. In focussing on official unhelpfulness, Petty deflected attention away from structural inconveniences in his project. If official policy hampered his efforts, so to did the collapse of his partnership with Carteret and the reluctance of tenants from outside Kerry to hazard themselves there. Other planned developments disappointed, as his investments in iron-making and fishing will demonstrate.

For Petty to blame the authorities for his misadventures in Kerry was not unusual. Moreover, in castigating official policies, Petty was sticking to his belief that only the state could provide the framework in which the anglicizing of Ireland would proceed. He also shared with numerous contemporaries disquiet over the later Stuarts' inadequate support for the Protestant interest in Ireland after 1660.[46] However, he differed from many of his co-religionists in welcoming the accession of James VII and II in 1685. For Petty, it revived dreams of returning to influence and presaged the resolution of a grievance to which he attributed his misfortunes in Kerry. The grievance was the requirement to pay quit rents to the crown.

Quit-rents were a standard yearly charge on Irish lands granted in the monarch's name. Otherwise landowners in Ireland were lightly taxed and resented any attempt to alter this agreeable situation. Numerous landowners

---

March 1667[8]; same to J. Rutter, 18 April 1668, [May 1668], 16 June 1668, McGill UL, Osler MS 7612; same to T. Crookshanks, 13 March 1674[5], BL, Add. MS 72,858. **45** Sir W. Petty to J. Rutter, May 1668, 16 Jan. 1671[2]; same to Hutchinson, 17 Oct. 1677, McGill UL, Osler MS 7612; cf. Ormond to ?Sir C. Wyche, 7 March 1678[9], Bodleian, MS Eng. Hist. C 266, f. 16. **46** T.C. Barnard, 'The Protestant interest, 1641–1660' in J.H. Ohlmeyer (ed.), *Ireland from independence to occupation* (Cambridge, 1995), pp 218–40.

complained that the level of quit-rents set on grants in the 1660s was unrealistically high. In some cases, the amounts exceeded the annual value of the property. Twice commissioners were empowered to reduce the quit-rents. Also, the king, the English and Irish councils and the law courts authorized reductions for Protestant and Catholic proprietors. In Petty's case, the quit-rents to be paid on the Kerry lands had not only been set too high – at over £1,600 annually – but were also based on a clerical error. Petty's liability had been calculated on the total acreage that he held, not, as was customary, solely on the profitable lands: 'the reduced column'. This mistake occurred simply because the columns in the official records relating to Kerry had been wrongly labelled.[47]

Petty, the unrivalled master of Irish surveying, was incensed at falling victim to the carelessness of a clerk recording the results of the survey that he himself had supervised. He sought redress through the obvious channels – the commissioners appointed specially for the purpose, the Irish viceroy and his council, the law courts, the privy council and the king in London – and yet was given no satisfaction. More than once the Irish lord lieutenant and the Irish law officers recommended a dramatic reduction.[48] But Petty was not allowed the benefit of these favourable rulings. In 1683, with feigned resignation, he commented to one official that the latest remission 'is another vibration of the swing swang of my Kerry business, which for this 15 years hath keeled from side to side like a drunken man'.[49] So far from having the debt to the state cancelled, he was presented with an alarming bill for arrears of unpaid quit-rents. For the period between 1660 and 1668, even before he was legally possessed of the Kerry estate, £20,000 was demanded.

The authorities accepted the contention of Petty and other objectors that, until the mistake was corrected, English plantation would be hindered. The case looked clear-cut, mechanisms for settling it existed, and others exposed to the same injustice had been relieved. However, Petty failed to secure effective redress. This failure requires explanation.

Petty suffered, like many of his contemporaries, from the haphazard and ill-defined procedures for considering and deciding Irish cases. The jurisdiction

---

[47] Material relating to the issue is scattered through Petty's own papers (particularly in BL, Add. MSS 72,900–72,902, those of Ormond and Essex and the State Papers. A comprehensive account is in Petty's anonymous and previously unattributed tract, *The case of the Kerry quit-rent, 1681* (n.p., [1681]); Sir W. Petty to Lady Petty, 16 and 28 Aug. 1681, BL, Add. MS 72,856; Fitzmaurice, *Life*, p. 263. [48] For example: letter of Charles II, 28 April 1676, BL, Add. MS 72,852; Bodleian, Carte MS 40, ff 621–32; reports of Sir J. Temple, 3 May 1678, 2 May 1679, 21 March 1683[4], BL, Add. MSS 72,900–1; Bodleian, Rawinson MS C. 439, ff 301v–3; *CSP, Domestic, 1679–80*, p. 415; Sir W. Petty to Sir W. Domville, 21 April 1683; same to Lady Petty, 23 and 30 June 1683, McGill UL, Osler MS 7612; Petty papers, box D, item 79. [49] Sir W. Petty to J. Ellis, 21 April 1683, McGill UL, Osler MS 7612.

of the Irish courts over estate and legal matters was blurred. Suits might be interrupted by executive action or transferred without warning. Decisions of the Irish government were routinely overturned in London. Even there, the Privy Council and Treasury could be circumvented by the king. These informalities meant that access to the court and royal favour mattered more than a just cause. Petty, then, fell victim to the structural defects of the administration and law in both kingdoms. In addition, and more important in explaining his predicament, was political weakness. The finances of Ireland were enmeshed in the factionalism of English politics throughout Charles II's reign. The political sensitivity of questions affecting Irish revenues became particularly acute in the 1670s. Charles II hoped that Ireland, after decades of being subsidized by England, would not only pay its way but supplement his English income. The king was encouraged in this hope by a powerful syndicate of English and Irish politicians and merchants who competed for the farm of the Irish finances. The group that secured the contract to run much of the tax system in Ireland formed a powerful interest, and one to which the king felt indebted, both literally and politically. Unhappily for Petty, he incurred the animosity of the syndicate. In 1675, it had seemed that he was to be one of the group of revenue farmers, but he was dropped mysteriously.[50] In 1682, he made a fresh but unsuccessful bid for the farm. Through his attempts to participate in the lucrative work of revenue farming, Petty demonstrated his fiscal expertise and unrivalled understanding of Ireland. On this basis and, no doubt, from chagrin at being beaten in the race for the contract, he attacked the detail of the successful farmers' estimates and also impugned their honesty. His assaults hardly endeared Petty to the incumbent syndicate. Furthermore, the farmers wanted to maintain taxes in Ireland at as high a rate as was practicable in order to maximise their profits. Accordingly, they could be expected to oppose any reduction of liabilities or cancellation of arrears. When coupled with the personal animosity between Petty and the farmers, the former had little likelihood of triumphing over such a well-organized gang.[51]

[50] Sir W. Petty to E. Roberts, 15 June 1674; same to R. Wood, 4 July 1674, 27 July 1675; same to Sir H. Ford, 13 Oct. 1674, BL, Add. MS 72,858; Sir W. Petty to the Lord Treasurer, 10 March 1675[6], Bodleian, Carte MS 52, ff 566–7; *Letters written to his excellency Arthur Capel, earl of Essex* (Dublin, 1770), p. 343. [51] Sir W. Petty to Lady Petty, 8 May 1680, BL, Add. MS 72,856; R. Wood to Sir W. Petty, 29 June 1674, 8 Oct. 1674, 24 June 1675, 11 March 1681[2], BL, Add. MS 72,850; Sir W. Petty to R. Wood, 23 Oct. 1675, ibid., Add. MS 72,858; BL, Stowe MS 206, f. 153; Bodleian, Carte MSS 39, f. 547; 54, ff 197, 242; Ormond to Arran, 18 July 1682, Bodleian, Carte MS 70, f. 556; Arran to Rochester, ibid., Carte MS 168, f. 131; 218, f. 503; 232, f. 63; HMC, *Ormonde Mss*, new series, vi, pp 367, 411–12; vii, pp 150, 162, 174; Lansdowne (ed.), *Petty–Southwell correspondence*, p. 100; Aubrey, *Brief lives*, ii, p. 144; *CSP. Domestic, 1675–6*, p. 442; *CSP, Domestic, Addenda, 1660–85*, p. 454; *Calendar of Treasury books*, v, p. 27. Different views are taken in G.E. Aylmer, 'The first

Neither diplomacy nor courtliness came naturally to Petty. They were needed to navigate between the reefs and rocks of Charles II's court. The repulse over rectifying the simple but expensive mistake relating to the quit-rents fitted into a larger pattern in which Petty was stranded on the fringes of influence. This apparent powerlessness at court contrasted with the high standing that he had enjoyed between 1654 and 1659 and again immediately after Charles II's restoration. The days when he basked in the king's favour did not last.[52] Politics quickly reverted to an adversarial mode. In the polarization, Petty, though he was happy to see power concentrated in a strong ruler, tended towards the critics of divine right and absolutism. The king ceased to seek Petty's amusing conversation. Others high in power found him more irritating than entertaining. Petty failed to ingratiate himself with the successive lords lieutenant in Dublin. The viceroys, wrestling with the Irish hydra, wearied of the inventive projects – a statistical survey of resources, the establishment of banks and the rebuilding of Dublin Castle. Ormond, so foxed by experimental science 'that it is all the most clear demonstration can do to make me comprehend the necessary consequences and effects of a windmill', was bored by Petty's loquacity. In 1679, Ormond vetoed the suggestion that Petty be added to the Irish council, because 'he will make so many objections and propose so many motions that much of our time will be lost in them'. In public, Ormond praised Petty's outstanding talents, but privately regarded him as a tedious projector, unsound in religion, suspect in politics and a personal irritant, since he had competed against Ormond for the Kerry lands and disparaged the duke's government in London.[53] Civilities were observed, but the two men eyed each other warily. Ducal gifts of venison did not stop Petty from detailing how Ormond and his family had profited since the restoration. After dancing attendance at Kilkenny Castle – the duke's seat – in the futile hope of favours, Petty reported, 'I can't say that I believe the Ormond family to be our friends beyond fair and civil words, nor do we think they have done for us what we deserved from them.'[54]

Essex, lord lieutenant between 1672 and 1677, presented a more promising prospect as an ally of Petty. The latter bombarded the new viceroy with advice.[55]

---

duke of Ormond as patron and administrator' in Barnard and Fenlon (eds), *The dukes of Ormonde*, pp 115–35; S. Egan, 'Finance and the government of Ireland, 1660–1685', unpublished Ph.D. thesis, 2 vols, TCD (1983). **52** Sir W. Petty to J. Petty, 5 and 19 Feb. 1660[1], BL, Add. MS 72,850. **53** Bodleian, Carte MS 143, f. 154; HMC, *Ormonde Mss*, ii, p. 286; new series, iv, pp 377, 506, 527; v, pp 332, 336; Barnard, 'Introduction: the dukes of Ormonde', pp 2–3. **54** Sir W. Petty to Lady Petty, 10 Sep. 1681, 25 March 1682, 11 and 21 April 1682; same to Mrs M.W., 12 March 1681[2], BL, Add. MS 72,856; Sir W. Petty to Sir R. Southwell, 23 May 1676, ibid., Add. MS 72,851; same to same, 14 Sep. 1681, ibid., Add. MS 72,852; BL, Add MS 21,484, f. 64v; Lansdowne (ed.), *Petty–Southwell correspondence*, pp 73, 77, 317, 327; HMC, *Ormonde Mss*, ii, pp 265, 306. **55** Sir W. Petty to W. Herbert, 21 July 1674, BL, Add. MS 72,858.

Drafts of what would become *The political anatomy of Ireland* were read with apparent enjoyment by Essex. Yet, the lord lieutenant, although closer in political outlook than his predecessors to Petty, declared roundly, 'that in all His Majesty's three kingdoms there lives not a more grating man than Sir William Petty'. Essex was at least disposed to end the saga of the quit-rents in Petty's favour, but discovered that he lacked the power to do so definitively.[56] Petty might be admired in high places, but possessed no powerful patron to further his interests. Those whose company he found most congenial, and to whom in return he showed his most engaging qualities, tended to be administrators like himself occupying the middling ranks (Samuel Pepys, Peter Pett, Sir Joseph Williamson and Sir Robert Southwell) and the virtuosi of the learned societies in London and Dublin. Companions of this sort diverted him from his obsessions and disappointments. Furthermore, they – particularly Southwell – encouraged him to apply his inquisitive mind and immense knowledge to analysis. Notwithstanding the consolations, Petty repined at the decline in his influence over public affairs since the Interregnum. Everything thereafter was anti-climatic. He became obsessed with the injustice of the Kerry quit-rents, even publishing a tract on the topic. It embodied his resentment at being blocked from exercising his superlative abilities. He acknowledged, 'if my wrongs were but of middle and common nature I should be ashamed to complain, but they have been as mountains set on mountains'.[57] Briefly, after 1685, it looked as if his internal exile from power would be ended. In a frenzy of creativity, Petty composed and amended papers, including several to resolve the problems of Ireland. James II, for whom most were written, had advisers and an agenda of his own. The new king failed even to decide the disputed quit-rents in Petty's favour.[58]

Petty's chances of ingratiating himself with James could have been increased by his open outlook on religion. Petty knew its value to the stability

[56] Petty Papers, box D, item 79; Sir W. Petty to Lady Petty, 5 June 1675, BL, Add. MS 72,856; same to R.Wood, 3 Nov. 1674, BL, Add. MS 72,858; R. Wood to Sir W. Petty, 25 Oct. 1673, 28 April 1674, 10 Oct. 1674, ibid., BL, Add. MS 72,850; T. Waller to Sir W. Petty, 12 June 1675, Add. MS 72,860; Sir W. Petty to Lady Petty, 28 Aug. 1677, 20 Nov. 1677; same to R. Aldworth, 18 Sep. 1677; same to T. Crookshank, 6 Oct. 1677, McGill UL, Osler MS 7612; Bodleian, Carte MS 38, f. 579; *CSP, Dom, 1677–8*, pp 404–6, 499–500; Lansdowne (ed.), *Petty–Southwell correspondence*, pp 33–4; O. Airy (ed.), *Essex Papers, I, 1672–79*, Camden Society, new series, xlvii (1890), p. 83; J.C. Beckett, 'The Irish viceroyalty in the restoration period', reprinted in Beckett, *Confrontations: studies in Irish history* (London, 1972), pp 75–80. [57] Sir W. Petty to Mrs Cadogan, 24 April 1683, McGill UL, Osler MS 7612. [58] Report of Ranelagh, 20 April 1687; Sir W. Petty, notes on Tyrconnell's letter of 21 June 1687, BL, Add. MS 72,902; Petty Papers, box D, item 72, p. 14; Sir W. Petty to S. Pepys, 4 and 8 Sep. 1687, Bodleian, Rawlinson MS A. 189, Lansdowne (ed.), *Petty–Southwell correspondence*, pp 213, 215, 233, 283. His widow continued the unavailing struggle for remission: Dowager Lady Shelburne to Sir R. Southwell, 13 March 1695[6], BL, Add. MS 72,902.

of the state and the well-being of society. For this reason, he was prepared to accord an official role to the Catholic clergy, since in Ireland their reach went much further than their Protestant counterparts. In addition, Petty had been schooled by Jesuits, lived for a time in a country in which the state cult was Catholicism and for longer in one in which the majority of inhabitants were Catholic. Among intimates, Petty indulged not just in anti-clericalism which may have been permissible in such educated quarters, but displayed a gift for satire that bordered on blasphemy, even heresy. It was said that he could 'preach extempore incomparably either Presbyterian way, Independent, Capuchin friar or Jesuit'. A mock sermon by Petty – in the mode of a Church of Ireland divine – survives.[59] Petty himself observed sardonically that he was accused sometimes of being 'of no religion and sometimes of all successively, viz. of that which *pro tempore* is esteemed worst'.[60]

After 1685, Petty's natural inclinations and deference to James II might have combined in an approach to Ireland which discarded atavistic anti-Catholicism and anti-Irishness. Petty sensed that James and his advisers wanted to assist Catholics throughout the three kingdoms.[61] Despite this intellectual mischievousness and lumbering efforts at courtliness, Petty never conquered the common prejudice against the Irish. The last term was still treated by most in England, even if Catholic, as a synonym for barbarism and backwardness. Petty's thinking coincided with the prejudice. Long service in Ireland, although it had sometimes aroused a humane pity for the unlucky indigenes, had left him with a crude Anglo-centric outlook.[62] Moreover, it was Irish Catholics who stood between him and full enjoyment of the spoils of office. The continuing local leverage of Donough McFinin, who 'pretendeth to be chief and head of West Munster, vilifying the power of any other there', dismayed Petty.[63] Disturbing too was the appointment of another rival, McGillicuddy, as a justice of the peace for County Kerry in 1672. Not only did it give the potentate formal powers to inconvenience newcomers like Petty and his subordinates; it also told of the royal favour enjoyed by McGillicuddy.[64]

---

59 Aubrey, *Brief lives*, ii, p. 142, from Bodleian, Aubrey MS 6, f.13v; Sir W. Petty, 'A sermon preached upon ye 23 October', BL, Add. MS 72,884, ff 127–40v. **60** Sir W. Petty to J. Petty, 27 March 1661, BL, Add. MS 72,850; Lansdowne (ed.), *Petty–Southwell correspondence*, p. 186. **61** Sir W. Petty to Lord Tyrconnell, 19 May 1687, BL, Add. MS 72,850. **62** Sir W. Petty to J. Rutter, 15 March 1672[3], BL, Add. MS 72,858. **63** Sir W. Petty to Lord Orrery, 17 July 1672; same to J. Rutter, 24 Sep. 1672; same to T. Waller, 20 Dec. 1673, BL, Add. MS 72,858; J. Rutter to Sir W. Petty, 26 July 1672, 6 and 16 Aug. 1672, 7, 20 and 23 Oct. 1672, 28 Nov. 1672, 17 March 1672[3], 29 June 1673, ibid., Add. MS 72,861; same to Lt.-Col. Donough McFinin, 11 Oct. 1672, ibid., Add. MS 72,861; same to M. Connell, 23 Feb. 1672[3], ibid., Add. MS 72,861; Lady Petty to D. McFinin, 7 Jan. 1672[3], BL, Add. MS 72,858; T. Waller to P. Bunworth, 17 Oct. 1674, ibid., Add. MS 72,858; Sir W. Petty to Lady Petty, 23 Feb. 1683[4], ibid., Add. MS 72,856. **64** J. Petty to J. Rutter, 24 June 1671, BL,

V

The inequitable treatment over the quit-rents overshadowed Petty's appraisal of what was happening in Kerry. If his heavy investment was slow to yield profits, he could reasonably object that any proceeds were ear-marked for the exigent revenue officers. Occasional trips into Kerry, the reports from his wife and subordinates, and scrutiny of the accounts warned of problems.[65] He attended to the sickly settlement and amended his approach. Some whom he employed had proved wanting; they were replaced. Defects in management and accounting were dealt with. Especially in the two ventures that he promoted – iron-making and the fisheries – patience and persistence were required.

The experience of others who started to make iron in rural locations – earlier, Lord Cork; in Petty's own time, a partnership at Enniscorthy in County Wexford – met the same difficulties.[66] The industry appealed because it was an obvious way to make money from the thick woodlands. Also, it provided employment for tenants. Specialists, to be sure, had to be imported, but in time it was hoped that their skills would percolate through to the locals. The venture was intended to stimulate and diversify the economy in and around his estate. It was not an innovation, but part of the standard battery of any enterprising landlord.

Petty was tempted because of the abundance of timber in the valleys draining into the Kenmare River. Water-power, the existence of local demand, the leavening effect of introducing artificers with specialized skills and the likely profits were further incentives. It was a rural industry that had existed in the locality in the remembered past. Also it had been adopted with apparent success by other settlers blessed with a good stock of trees. In the event, the cheap fuel – charcoal from the timber – was the sole asset. Local iron ore was of poor quality and had to be supplemented with costly imports from the Forest of Dean. Skilled specialists, able to build and run furnace and forge, were rare. The few in Ireland were hard to induce into Kerry and even harder to retain. Contrary to propaganda about the desirability of rural industries – stimulants to the local economy, sedatives to the workers and their dependants – the reverse was nearer the truth. The settlements were unruly; the benefits to the

Add. MS 72,859; Sir W. Petty to D. McGillicuddy, 29 Oct. 1672, BL, Add. MS 72,858; T. Waller to Sir W. Petty, 2 Dec. 1673, ibid., Add. MS 72,860; Sir W. Petty to Lord Chief Baron, 17 April 1675; same to T. Waller, 17 April 1675, ibid., Add. MS 72,858; P. Bunworth to Sir W. Petty, 8 April 1675, ibid., Add. MS 72,860. **65** H. Wood, 'Sir William Petty and his Kerry estate', *JRSAI*, lxiv (1934), pp 22–40. **66** J.H. Andrews, 'Notes on the historical geography of the Irish iron industry', *Irish Geography*, iii (1954–58), pp 139–49; T.C. Barnard, 'An Anglo-Irish industrial venture: iron-making at Enniscorthy', *PRIA*, lxxxv, sect C (1985), pp 101–44; H.F. Kearney, 'Richard Boyle, ironmaster', *JRSAI*, lxxxiii (1953), pp 156–62; Ranger, 'The career of Richard Boyle, first earl of Cork', pp 135–66.

economy minimal. The iron made in Kerry was of low grade. Neither in price nor quality did it find many buyers. Petty summed up the sorry history when he wrote, 'our iron, it seems, is ill-made and but little of that, and what is made is squandered away. It's made at excessive charge and sold at less rates.'[67]

The remoteness of Kerry meant that cash rents collected there had then to be conveyed across wild terrain to Cork, Limerick or Dublin.[68] The dangers could be avoided if his Kerry estate produced commodities that would be bought by substantial traders who could then arrange to pay him in London. This arrangement had persuaded Lord Cork to continue with an otherwise unprofitable iron manufacture. Petty may have been similarly motivated to go on with what seemed troublesome and unprofitable.[69]

Fishing was an obvious activity to encourage. As a supplement to what could be earned from farming, it would help those along the coasts and estuaries to pay their rents.[70] Just as mature woods were seen as mines above ground, so the shoals were gold beneath the waves. But for fisheries to add more than marginally to the livelihoods of tenants or to Petty's rentals, considerable outlay was needed. So long as timber survived, boats could be built locally. Nets, ropes, tar and other necessities had to be bought further afield and at high prices. Salt was essential to preserve the catches, and that too had to be purchased from others. Commercial fishing, no less than forge and furnace, required the knowledgeable and experienced. Even when all the prerequisites were in place, success depended on the unpredictable movements of the shoals and on supplying regular, accessible markets. As a seasonal occupation that added modestly but vitally to the income and diet of some on the Kerry estates, the encouragement of the fisheries was sensible. However, as a device for habituating the inhabitants to regular work, to a cash economy and to appreciation of the benevolence of their new landlord, fishing did not succeed.[71]

Successive generations of improvers, confronted by the untapped potential of their own lands or by endemic poverty and regular famines, repeated Petty's appeal for more to be done to harvest what swam in the sea. These advocates encountered similar problems and discovered it was beyond the power of any

---

67 T.C. Barnard, 'Sir William Petty as Kerry ironmaster', *PRIA*, lxxxii, sect C (1982), pp 1–32. Petty's efforts might be compared fruitfully with those of the Brownes of Westport in the 1680s and 1690s. **68** Sir W. Petty to T. Beecher, 16 April 1672, BL, Add. MS 72,858; T. Waller to T. Heald, 21 Nov. 1674, BL, Add. MS 72,860; same to Sir W. Petty, 31 Nov. 1674, BL, Add. MS 72,860. **69** Sir W. Petty to Sir G. Rawdon, 13 April 1672, BL, Add. MS 72,858; M. MacCarthy-Morrogh, 'Credit and remittance: monetary problems in early seventeenth-century Munster', *IESH*, xiv (1987), pp 5–19; Ranger, 'The career of Richard Boyle, first earl of Cork', pp 135–66. **70** Sir W. Petty to T. Heald, 23 May 1674, BL, Add. MS 72,858. **71** T.C. Barnard, 'Fishing in seventeenth-century Kerry: the experience of Sir William Petty', *Kerry Archaeological and Historical Journal*, xiv (1981), pp 14–25.

single proprietor to achieve significant structural improvements in the fishing industry. Similarly, iron-making and other extractive and metallurgical processes bewitched owners and improvers alike. With only rare exceptions, the gleam which dazzled the credulous proved that of fool's gold. There were moments when Petty was on the verge of following the logic of the heavy investment and meagre returns by abandoning his experiments in rural industry. Yet, there was merit in perseverance. He was confident that his basic premises were correct. Moreover, his division of labour and analyses of costs, continuing the system that he had employed so triumphantly in the surveys of the Interregnum, had a value beyond the running of his own affairs. He appreciated the desirability of assigning separate tasks to specialists. He realised that some preferred leisure to labour. His reflections led into the formulation of general theories about labour and its costs.[72]

When Petty reviewed his affairs in 1685, he was disheartened, notably by the intractability of Kerry. Yet, he vowed 'to attend to the improvements of my lands in Ireland', especially by promoting 'the trade of iron, lead, marble, fish and timber, whereof my estate is capable'.[73] This unquenchable optimism and his determination to persist with the ventures look at odds with the rational approach to which Petty subscribed. Kerry, seemingly inimical to his well-conceived schemes, stood as a tangible confutation of his ideas and methods. Already he had been publicly humiliated when the prototype of a catamaran had capsized and sank in Dublin Bay. There were too many detractors who rejoiced in his discomfiture. In practice, many of the methods and results differed little from the traditional expedients of hopeful settlers. Orthodox means of making money and employing tenants displaced the innovative. Trees were felled and made into staves for barrels and pipes: an easy expedient to turn timber to profit and one that in others he had condemned as destructive.[74] And, if a few arrows pierced him alone, much of what he endured was common among planters in Ireland. All suffered from the political twists and turns, the inefficiency and bias of the law and administration in the Irish provinces and the obstructions, both natural and man-made, in the way of farming and trading.

---

[72] Barnard, 'Petty as Kerry ironmaster', pp 1–32. [73] Fitzmaurice, *Petty*, p. 324. [74] Sir W. Petty to Capt. Dawly, 18 Feb. 1667[8], 2 June 1668; same to J. Rutter, May 1668, 14 July 1668; same to J. Graunt, 10 Oct. 1668; same to Capt. Phillips, 10 Oct. 1668, McGill UL, Osler MS 7612; same to J. Rutter, 2 April 1672, BL, Add. MS 72,858; same to T. Waller, 23 Aug. 1673, BL, Add. MS 72,858; T. Waller to Sir W. Petty, 21 March 1673[4], 23 May 1674, ibid., Add. MS 72,860; L. Sharp, 'Timber, science and economic reform in the seventeenth century', *Forestry*, xlviii (1975), pp 69–71.

VI

Petty was hampered by the fragmentation of his Irish estates, divided between five counties. Non-residence and consequent dependence on underlings were inevitable. Absenteeism, whether internal within Ireland or away from Ireland, also told of Petty's indecision as to where he wanted to make his and his family's future. Extended stays in London could be justified on the grounds that it was there that the fate of Ireland, and with it of Petty's stake, would be settled. However, the absences went beyond those necessary to pursue personal business. Petty was unusual if not unique among those of his wealth in Ireland in lacking a base on any of his holdings outside Dublin. Again, the failure to reside in the provinces reveals something about the way in which he regarded his rural estates: principally they were to support his and his family's lives in Dublin and London. A second function of the properties might to be to test notions. The lack of any urge to set up as an Irish squire was matched by the same disinclination to do so in England. He contemplated the purchase of an English estate, but in the end decided against it. This was represented as a rational avoidance of the extra spending that inevitably would follow. It connected, too, with Petty's refusal of a peerage. Again, any accretion of influence through a seat in the House of Lords was outweighed by the likely costs of living as a peer should. Petty did not prize what many contemporaries and his successors craved; sometimes indeed he dismissed such ambitions contemptuously.[75]

If he scorned one badge of worldly honour, he did not disdain others. He amassed enviable wealth, and continued to explore ways to increase it. Riches of this order purchased pleasures and security, as well as being envied. Petty had other ambitions, as his will revealed. He instructed his elder son to buy an English estate and to invest in an English office. He wanted the younger son to live in Ireland and manage the estates there. For his daughter he proposed an Irish match. Comparable choices had to be made by the increasing number of landowners much of whose income came from property in Ireland, but whose activities were concentrated in England. Examples include the Boyles, earls of Cork and Burlington and of Orrery, the Percevals, later earls of Egmont, the Temples, Viscounts Palmerston, and the Southwells.[76] Petty knew that Ireland was the fundamental financial base, and therefore should not be neglected: the mis-

---

[75] Sir W. Petty to Lady Petty, 20 Nov. 1677, 27 April 1680, Osler MS 7612; Sir W. Petty to Lady Petty, 11 Aug. 1679, 16 Aug. 1681, 14 and 27 Sep. 1681, 4 Oct. 1681, 24 Dec. 1681, 18 and 28 Feb. 1681[2], 25 March 1682, 7 May 1682, 5 June 1682, BL, Add. MS 72,856; Sir R. Southwell to Sir W. Petty, 28 Sep. 1687, BL, Add. MS 72,851; same to Lady Petty, 17 Sep. 1688, ibid., Add. MS 78,251; Lansdowne (ed.), *Petty–Southwell correspondence*, pp 289, 296–7. [76] Barnard, *New anatomy*, pp 30–7.

take of many absentees. Accordingly, he advised his successors to go on sailing in 'a double bottom' (a not very auspicious reference to his double-hulled boat that had turned turtle).[77] This they did: with startling success. His only daughter married into the dynasty of Fitzmaurice, long settled in Kerry. Indeed, the prominence of the family in the area had led to their ennoblement as earls of Kerry. It was this daughter's son who eventually reunited the Petty's Irish and English properties.

Petty, although apparently fixated on his lands (especially in Kerry), also appreciated the value of office. He advised his heir to buy a patentee office as well as English property. It may reflect Petty's own career. Offices – the Oxford professorship, physician to the army in Ireland, the clerkship of the Irish council and secretary to Henry Cromwell during the 1650s – had given him status, an assured income from fees and allowances, and power. Later, in the 1670s, he was appointed judge of the admiralty court in Ireland (by the lord high admiral, the duke of York, soon to be James II). Petty used the position to try to free mariners from irksome restrictions and thereby to help trade. His interventions made him unpopular among prominent Dublin merchants.[78] Also, Petty observed closely the place of office in the successful public life of his friend, Sir Robert Southwell. The Southwell tribe split into two branches after they settled in Ireland. One established itself in the port of Kinsale. Judicious accumulation of offices in the customs administration and in the admiralty brought the elder Robert Southwell modest prosperity and local, but hardly national eminence. The father used some of his wealth to launch his heir into the service of the Caroline state. The younger Robert Southwell regularly consulted Petty about possible changes of direction. In 1663, freshly returned from continental travels, Southwell weighed the rival attractions of England and Ireland. In Ireland, he and his father had cultivated the main patron, the lord lieutenant, Ormond. However, on investigation, Southwell concluded that there was nothing in the viceroy's gift 'agreeing with the method of my education'. His lengthy exposure to continental culture looked irrelevant to an Irish career, but might assist him in England. Southwell, conscious of his abilities, craved fame. Once won in England, he believed it would follow automatically in Ireland, but not the reverse. Petty cited Southwell's example when he argued that buying an office was the best way to provide for a son. The elder Southwell spent £2000 on an office for his heir, which then paid the holder an annual £1000. In addition, an office could be traded. Despite efforts to stamp out the practice, it was possible for the owner and occupant to sell it, as indeed the younger Southwell did with his clerkship of the English council. It was a moot point whether freehold

---

77 Sir W. Petty to Lady Petty, 4 Oct. 1681, BL, Add. MS 72,856; Fitzmaurice, *Petty*, p. 324. 78 Sir W. Petty to T. Crookshank, 29 July 1676; same to Sir A. Apsley, 9 Sep. 1676, 31 July 1677, Aug. 1683, McGill UL, Osler MS 7612.

land or a patentee office kept and increased its value better. It was a calculation that Petty might have been expected to make. Perhaps he did, because, when quizzed by Southwell as to why he had not acquired an English estate, he answered that office was the sounder investment.[79] Petty's son, Charles, shared the opinion, seeking the clerkship of the Irish council in the 1690s.

It was thought an oddity in Petty that he did not buy an English estate; an oddity, too, that he declined a peerage. So far as the acquisition of Irish lands was concerned, the nucleus had come in part payment for his official work. More were grabbed at what he considered knock-down prices. Longer engagement disillusioned him, but never caused him to contemplate disembarrassing himself of them. After 1660 Petty shifted backwards and forwards between the two kingdoms. Hopes of a prestigious appointment in England never materialized. He had to console himself with the judgeship of the admiralty, which, given his activism, obliged personal attendance in Dublin. At the same time, he was realising that his absence retarded the improvement of his estates. As early as 1668, he had concluded that 'our estates here [in Ireland] are mere visions and delusions and require more attendance than a retail shop'. He was soon convinced that an Irish estate 'cannot subsist without the owner's daily presence and inspection'.[80] He did not altogether obey his own commands. Sorties into Kerry remained occasional. Sometimes Lady Petty went as his deputy. Usually he relied on resident agents, some of them kindred, others recruited from the Protestant tenantry shallowly rooted in the vicinity. There was no denying that the Irish holdings, so far from being the concealed support to an elevated station in England, demanded constant care.

For all the entanglements, Petty believed that eventually he would be able to apply his blue-print in Kerry and make it the model of enterprise and industry for others to imitate. This had not happened before he died in 1687. In this sense, he went to his grave a disappointed man, for Ireland had not answered his, perhaps extravagant, expectations. Yet in the programme that he outlined for the closing phase of his life, it was not just the improvement of his Irish lands that concerned him. He would still study and experiment, chiefly in relation to 'the anatomy of the people and political arithmetic'. The materials that

---

[79] R. Southwell to R. Southwell the elder, undated, BL, Add. MS 72,852; Sir W. Petty to Sir J. Brooke, 19 Jan. 1674[5], ibid., Add. MS 72,858; Lansdowne (ed.), *Petty–Southwell correspondence*, pp 296–7; G.E. Aylmer, *The crown's servants: government and civil service under Charles II, 1660–1685* (Oxford, 2002); Barnard, *New anatomy*, pp 146–8; A.P.W. Malcomson, *Nathaniel Clements: government and the governing élite in Ireland, 1725–75* (Dublin, 2005), pp 206–88. [80] Sir W. Petty to J. Graunt, 30 June 1668, 21 July 1668; same to Mrs Hutchinson, 15 Jan. 1669[70], McGill UL, Osler MS 7612; Sir W. Petty to Lady Petty, 18 June 1672, 30 July 1672, 26 July 1679, 22 May 1680, 23 Feb. 1683[4], 27 March 1684, 16 May 1685, BL, Add. MS 72,856; same to J. Graunt, 24 Dec. 1672; same to J. Waller, 1 Aug. 1674, BL, Add. MS 72,858.

he planned to subject to his statistical approach included much that had arisen from the maps, surveys and censuses that he had earlier oversaw.[81] At the same time, more recent returns from his own estates supplemented and sometimes modified the national picture. The estates might yet repay some of the effort that he had expended by furnishing him with valuable information and insights: for example, into household size.[82] The supposition that the lands mattered to Petty only as the source of the income that bought him the leisure to speculate and write ignores their less obvious value to him. Puzzling over details in the accounts from the iron-works and fisheries could set him thinking about abstract issues relating to labour, leisure and value.[83]

Deductions based on the working papers for his plantations do more for Petty's posthumous fame than his thinking about plantations. The wholesale transfer of peoples between Britain and Ireland proposed repeatedly throughout the 1670s and 1680s was no more practicable than the permanent corralling of the residue of Catholic Irish away from the coast in Connacht and Clare.[84] In 1655 Petty was associated with the party gaining control of the Irish government which realized the transplantation to Connacht could not be implemented and, furthermore, would be deleterious to agriculture, manufacturing and trade. In the 1680s, his scheme, so far from proposing the separation of the distinct confessional and ethnic communities, put faith in the acculturation that would result from the mingling of populations. The steady assimilation of the longer settled in Ireland to English habits and to Protestantism was the aim of plantations. Reports from Petty's own lands, as from those of many others in later seventeenth-century Ireland, indicated that progress was pitiably slow. In some places, beleaguered Protestant settlers adopted local habits and went native. If the establishment of settlements were left only to private initiatives, then Ireland was likely to remain under-developed, restive and Catholic. In order to quicken change, Petty wanted the state to intervene. It had done so in the 1650s. Then the authorities had backed his programme for the Down Survey and had re-deployed the forces – a complement of 1000 soldiers – to achieve it. Even the enfeebled Irish state of 1660 and 1661 had been able to order cadastral surveys that had assessed some part of national wealth through local enquiries. After 1685, Petty revived ideas of swapping populations between Ireland and England. The project presumed a powerful state. The effective absolutism of military rule in the immediate aftermath of war during the 1650s helped him to complete what remained his

---

81 Fitzmaurice, *Petty*, pp 318–24. 82 T.C. Barnard, 'Sir William Petty and Irish population', *IESH*, vi (1979), pp 64–9. 83 Sir W. Petty to Lady Petty, 8 June 1675, 6 July 1675, with enclosed computation, BL, Add. MS 72,856. 84 BL, Add. MSS 72,865, ff 140–4; 72,879, f. 71; 72,886; Hull, *Economic writings*, ii, pp 545–621; T.G. McCormick, 'The idea of alchemy in the Political Arithmetic of Sir William Petty (1623–1687)', *Studies in*

most startling achievement, the Down Survey. But even as the work was in hand, authority was passing from the army to civilians, and being devolved to the lackadaisical in the localities. Charles II and James II in the 1680s, badgered by admirers of centralization, militarism and absolutism, were keen to preside over a system capable of the same degree of ruthlessness and control as that of the Cromwellians. Petty was hopeful that in this harsh climate, his grandiose scheme of transplantation and transmutation would become royal policy. Had it done so, Petty could have written eloquently and sycophantically on behalf of unfettered Stuart power. Instead, Petty was brushed off once more by impatient politicians as an elderly crank with a republican past.[85] He retired to his intimates and his papers. Staccato memoranda and admonitions were dashed off. Concurrently, he gave lasting meaning to a welter of confusing figures and comments by sorting them according to number, weight and measure.[86]

Thanks to durable achievements, Petty towers above the pigmies who opposed, oppressed and defrauded him. However, the Lilliputians did tie him down. And their ability to pinion him owed a good deal to his own failings. Also, Petty's ideas about plantations were stale. By the 1650s, they could hardly be otherwise. Both the idea and practice had been current in Ireland for more than a century. At most, fresh permutations not new conceptions might be devised. Other Irish landowners, content to use the materials to hand, rather than dreaming of importing the different, fared better than Petty. Gradually, Petty and his agents compromised. They discovered painfully that there was no profitable alternative to traditional occupations and the existing tenants. Petty's successors settled into any easy-going regime of intermittent absenteeism and compromise. Opportunities for future improvements were sacrificed for immediate ease in the 1690s.[87] Simply through massive acreages rather than through innovative management, the dynasty prospered. Great wealth was recognized first by an Irish and then (in 1760) by a British peerage (the earldom of Shelburne).[88]

The inappropriateness and lack of success of Petty's adventurous schemes for Kerry are demonstrated finally though comparison with neighbours and

history and philosophy of science, 37 (2006), pp 290–307. **85** T. Dance to Lady Petty, 4 June 1687, BL, Add. MS 72,864. **86** Sir W. Petty to T. Heald, 16 Jan. 1671[2], McGill UL, Osler MS 7612; calculation relating to the iron works, BL, Add. MS 72,860, p. 264. **87** Observations of R. Orpen, *c.*1693, RIA, MS 12 I 2, pp 49–77; J. Waller to H. Petty, 9 March 1696[7] and 25 March 1697; BL, Add. MS 72,864; same to Dowager Lady Shelburne, 20 March 1696[7], ibid., Add. MS 72,864; H. Petty to J. Waller, 8 May 1697, 9 Jan. 1697[8], ibid., Add. MS 72,902. The later history of the estate can be traced through H.W.E. Petty-Fitzmaurice, *Lansdowne, Glanerought and the Petty-Fitzmaurices* (Oxford, 1937); G.J. Lyne, 'Land tenure in Kenmare and Tuoist, 1696–*c.*1716', *Journal of the Kerry Archaeological and Historical Society*, x (1977), pp 19–54; Lyne, 'Land tenure in Kenmare and Tuoist, 1720–70', ibid., xi (1978), pp 25–55; G.J. Lyne, *The Lansdowne estates in Kerry under W.S. Trench, 1849–72* (Dublin, 2001). **88** J. Hort to Lady Caldwell, 15 Dec. 1755, JRL, B 3/30/112; Sir J. Caldwell to Lady Caldwell, 12 Nov 1772, ibid, B 3/29/37.

with the observations of the second Lord Shelburne. The Herberts had been settled in Kerry for nearly a century before Petty irrupted into the area. Less ambitious to storm smart English society than the later Pettys, the Herberts contented themselves with an existence reminiscent of that which their forbears had enjoyed a couple of centuries earlier on the borderlands between England and Wales. They tolerated many archaic features of the local society and culture, and – to a degree – were acculturated to them. Belatedly, the Pettys and their agents realised that this was the readiest way to enjoy what they owned in Kerry.[89] However, the accommodations offended the second earl of Shelburne. After inheriting in 1761, he inspected his Irish inheritances and was dismayed by what he found. Like his illustrious forbear, Petty, Shelburne adored novel theories and wished to show their utility.

Shelburne, briefly prime minister in 1782–3 and subsequently marquess of Lansdowne, may consciously have seen himself as an intellectual as well as legal heir.[90] Some of Petty's works were republished in Glasgow in 1751 as appropriate forerunners of the gathering enlightenment there.[91] A new edition was then printed in Dublin in 1769 at a time when Shelburne was involving himself actively in Irish affairs. Included in this volume was Petty's will.[92] Shelburne took a crash course on Irish history before touring the patrimony.[93] He bewailed familiar shortcomings, such as the peccadilloes of agents and the obsessive litigiousness of the locals. He further regretted the generous terms granted to tenants following Petty's death. Having viewed Kerry, he concluded that 'the country is wild and unimproved either by tillage, manufactures or arts'. He linked the lawlessness and political disaffection with the prevalent Catholicism. Britain's enemies recruited soldiers for their armies in the remote region. An invincible optimism, akin to Petty's, nevertheless re-surfaced. 'The country, though wild is very capable of improvement'. Many favoured expedients – fishing, iron-making, textiles – were suggested. Although roads, canals and coastal traffic had improved greatly since the seventeenth century, the very remoteness of the Kerry holdings militated against any transformation. The

---

89 Glimpses into the Herberts' practices come from NLI, MS 7861; Barnard, *New anatomy*, pp 227–30, 233, 237; D. Dickson, *Old world colony: Cork and south Munster, 1630–1830* (Cork, 2005), pp 77–8, 512–13; P. O'Connor, 'The seignory of Castleisland in the seventeenth century', *Journal of the Kerry Archaeological and Historical Society*, iii (1970), pp 43–7; W.J. Smith (ed.), *Herbert correspondence* (Cardiff and Dublin, 1963). The voluminous papers of the Herberts of Powis Castle in National Library of Wales await full exploitation. **90** Petty's manuscripts were listed by the earl's librarian in the 1780s, though apparently not in a manner to facilitate their study, see *The Petty papers*, pp xx–xxi. **91** W. Petty, *Political arithmetic* (Glasgow, 1751). It was prefaced with a dedicatory epistle from Lord Shelburne to the king. Also in the same volume was Xenophon's *Discourse upon improving the revenue of the state of Athens*. **92** W. Petty, *Tracts chiefly relating to Ireland* (Dublin, 1769). These had evidently been prepared for publication by Petty's son during William III's reign. **93** Bill of W. Wilson, 1770, Bowood House, MS 131, now in BL.

Pettys' estates in more accessible counties offered brighter prospects. Instead Kerry began to be appreciated because it was not improved. The taste for the sublime, picturesque and romantic meant that traits once reviled were now revered. Yet the unceasing need for larger remittances obliged Shelburne still to endorse and to try to practise improvements.[94]

A further comparison with the fate of Petty's estates and descendants is offered by the history of an associate. Thomas Taylor acted as an adjutant in the Down Survey in the 1650s. Rewarded like Petty with lands, Taylor did not return to England or make a career that spanned the Irish Sea. One reason may have been that, as a subordinate, his acquisitions were considerably smaller than Petty's. Nevertheless they served to raise his family. The Taylors' advance can be detected when, in the 1680s, they purchased one of the plots in the Dublin development at Smithfield, on the north bank of the River Liffey, and had a 'great house' constructed there. It was furnished in a manner appropriate to its scale. The Taylors' rentals steadily increased throughout the 1690s. By 1713, they were reckoned at an annual £1,200 (possibly an under-estimate). This income was modest when set against that of the Pettys: at best 20 per cent of what Petty's heirs commanded. Nevertheless, Sir Thomas Taylor was hailed as an active improver.[95] Improvements enhanced formal standing as well as reputation. So, in 1704, the Taylors received a baronetcy; then a peerage in 1760.[96] Also, the plebeian Taylors became Taylours. The focus of the family's activities remained Ireland. In 1766, Thomas Taylour, created earl of Bective, invited Robert Adam to design him new quarters on his Meath estate of Headfort.[97] In the previous decade, Shelburne had chosen Adam to reconstruct his house at Bowood in Wiltshire. Further convergence occurred when each was advanced to a marquisate: of Lansdowne for Petty's descendant in 1784 and Headfort for Taylor's in 1800.

Lansdowne resembled Sir William Petty in the variety of his interests and in his liking for speculation and experiment. Other hereditary traits may have been arrogance, volatility and virtuosity. Moreover, Lansdowne suffered a long eclipse after a brief time in power. The other continuity, it can be contended, was an obsession with the untapped potential of the Kerry estates. The need still to improve the district after a century of ownership, together with the revival of projects dear to Petty, warned of how little had been changed.

---

[94] Lansdowne, *Glanerought and the Petty-Fitzmaurices*, pp 61–88, 106–15. [95] List of MPs, 1713, BL, Add. MS 61,637A; rent receipts, NLI, MS 25,300; *Letters written by his excellency Hugh Boulter*, 2 vols (London, 1769–70), i, p. 189. [96] A.P.W. Malcomson, 'Report on the Headfort MSS', NLI, list 238; Barnard, *Making the Grand Figure*, pp 133, 146, 201, 230–1; GEC, *Complete peerage*, vi, pp 426–9; *HIP*, vi, pp 379–82. [97] C. Casey and A. Rowan, *North Leinster* (London, 1993), pp 313–17; John Harris, *Headfort House and Robert Adam* (London, 1973).

CHAPTER THREE

Interests in Ireland: Richard Lawrence as improver

RICHARD LAWRENCE IS CHIEFLY REMEMBERED as the pamphleteer who entered the lists against Vincent Gookin in 1655. Lawrence defended the scheme to transplant many of the defeated Irish west of the River Shannon.[1] That controversial episode was merely one in Lawrence's long career in Ireland. Having arrived with the Cromwellian army in 1649, he stayed until his death in 1684. This in itself is unusual among the high-ranking officers, especially those, like Lawrence, radical alike in politics and religion. Unusual, too, is the evidence – from his publications – of how his outlook shifted. Initially he championed the English interest in Ireland; latterly, he upheld the interests of locals in Ireland. So much is proclaimed by the titles of the books. The brace from the Interregnum were *The interest of England*[2] and *England's great interest in the well-planting of Ireland*.[3] By contrast, the compendium published in 1682 was entitled *The interest of Ireland in its trade and wealth stated*.[4] Lawrence's journey can be likened to that taken by others from England, Scotland and Wales in the sixteenth and seventeenth centuries. Lawrence's altered perspectives have an intrinsic interest. Through his reactions something of the rapid physical and cultural transformations can be discerned. Moreover, his approach to the improvement of Ireland – both theoretical and practical – can be compared with that of his contemporary, Petty.

Lawrence is valuable less for his originality than as a conductor of what was in the air. Anxieties that he voiced often had long histories. In several cases – dislike of luxury and absenteeism – they would concern commentators throughout the eighteenth century. A few later reformers, such as Francis Hutchinson, the indefatigable bishop of Down and Connor, in the 1720s and 1730s referred explicitly to what Lawrence had written.[5] In 1772, the prominent

---

1 S.R. Gardiner, 'The transplantation to Connaught', *EHR*, 14 (1899), pp 700–34; T. C. Barnard, 'Crises of identity among Irish Protestants, 1641–1685', *Past and Present*, 127 (1990), pp 58–68; D. Rankin, *Between Spenser and Swift: English writing in seventeenth-century Ireland* (Cambridge, 2005), pp 61–74. 2 R. Lawrence, *The interest of England in the Irish transplantation, stated* (London, 1655). 3 [R. Lawrence], *England's great interest in the well-planting of Ireland with English people discussed* (Dublin, 1656). 4 2 parts (Dublin, 1682). 5 [F. Hutchinson], *A second letter to a member of parliament recommending the improvement of the Irish fishery* (Dublin, 1729), pp 4–5. A copy of Lawrence's *Interest of Ireland* was included in the books from Hutchinson's library and sold for 1s. 2d. with another volume: *A catalogue*

73

Dublin publisher dismissed Lawrence as 'very partial and creduluous'. At the same time, Faulkner conceded that in the ninety years since Lawrence wrote, 'I do not think our country much improved.'[6] More generally, organizations such as the Dublin Society and the Physico-Historical Society continued to press a programme which, both in ideological underpinning and detailed agenda, recalled Lawrence's.[7]

Recently it has been argued that approaches to social reforms of the kind wanted by Lawrence changed in the mid-seventeenth century. These shifts were associated especially with the Hartlib group and its leading adherent in Cromwellian Ireland, William Petty. A new methodology which reduced hitherto intractable problems to 'number, weight and measure' gave the pioneering political arithmeticians the confidence to address poverty and under-development more constructively. Pessimism over an unbreakable cycle of degeneration and renewal gave way to a linear conception of improvement. At much the same time, during the 1650s, the notion that improvements could be achieved through collective action led to the foundation of voluntary bodies dedicated to such ends.[8]

These developments touched the Ireland of Lawrence's time. As has been seen already, several of Hartlib's disciples laboured there. Petty, most notably, directed his talents into analysing and alleviating Irish problems. Lawrence knew Petty, sat with him on the Council of Trade in Dublin after 1664 and later debated with him how best to reform Ireland's coinage.[9] Lawrence, therefore, might have been expected to fall under the spell of the novel approach. Indeed, superficially it looked as if Lawrence was bewitched. He used quantification to back his contentions: for example, as to how much specie was drained annually from the island by absentee landowners and office-holders.[10] However, he did not repudiate an essentially religious conception of what was wrong with Ireland and how it could be rectified. This outlook might make him seem old-fashioned by some standards. Yet, it persisted among many active in the work of the Dublin Society and the Physico-Historical Society after 1731. Lawrence borrowed heavily from

of books being the library of the Right Rev Dr Francis Hutchinson, late bishop of Down and Connor (Dublin, 1756), lot 327. **6** [F. Hutchinson], *A second letter to a member of parliament recommending the improvement of the Irish fishery* (Dublin, 1729), pp 4–5; R.E. Ward (ed.), *Prince of Dublin printers: the letters of George Faulkner* (Lexington, 1972), p. 114. **7** *The Dublin Society's weekly observations* (Dublin, 1739), pp 18–19, 27–8, 41, 146–7, 342; Richard Barton, *Lectures in natural philosophy* (Dublin, 1751), pp v–vi, 111–13; Richard Barton, *A dialogue, concerning some things of importance to Ireland* (Dublin, 1751), pp 21–2; W. Henry, *An appeal to the people of Ireland* (Dublin, 1747); W. Henry, *Religion and virtue. The foundation of courage and victory* (Dublin, 1744). **8** P. Slack, *From reformation to improvement* (Oxford, 1999), pp 81–3; P. Clark, *British clubs and societies, 1580–1800* (Oxford, 2000), pp 49–50, 85. **9** W. Petty, *The history of the survey of Ireland commonly called the Down Survey*, ed. T.A. Larcom (Dublin, 1851), pp 12, 30, 269, 277, 279; HMC, *Ormonde Mss*, new series, vii, p. 14. **10** Lawrence, *Interest of Ireland*, i, pp 80–9.

contemporaries, including those whose vision appeared more secular and rational – Petty, William Temple and Francis Brewster – but still used explanatory and expository frameworks which invoked hidden and supernatural powers.[11]

In so far as Lawrence set his account of Ireland in a providential cosmography, his mentality can be linked with what is known of his biography.[12] He arrived in Ireland as an officer of the Cromwellian army. He was soon identified with the party of radical republicans favoured by the lord deputy, Charles Fleetwood. This alignment was strengthened when Lawrence emerged as a public proponent of the enforced removal of much of the indigenous population to Connacht and Clare.[13] He subscribed wholeheartedly to the anti-Catholic and anti-Irish sentiments prevalent in England and in Ireland among English soldiers and administrators around Fleetwood. After Charles II's return in 1660, Lawrence may briefly have contemplated exile in the Low Countries. However, he had no need to skip overseas. He had not been a regicide, and soon agilely accommodated himself to the restored monarchy. When James Butler, duke of Ormond, arrived in Dublin as lord lieutenant in 1662, Lawrence placed himself under the duke's protection. By 1668, Lawrence gallantly declared his intention henceforward to 'trust God's providence and my Lord's [Ormond's] nobleness for a livelihood'.[14] Before this, Ormond had appointed him to the Council of Trade, made him manager of the prestigious textile works at Chapelizod outside Dublin, and even restored him to an army command during the invasion alert of 1666. Later Ormond read *The interest of Ireland* in manuscript and encouraged Lawrence to publish it.[15] Deferentially Lawrence would dedicate the volume to Ormond's grandson and heir, Lord Ossory.

Against this political flexibility has to be set Lawrence's steadfastness as a Baptist. Unusually among survivors from the Interregnum in Restoration Ireland, he continued in the Dublin congregation. As such he was the city's most prominent Baptist. This affiliation brought him under suspicion: first, in 1663 during the alarm lest Dublin Castle be seized and then in 1683 at the time of the Rye House Plot in England.[16] In the event, he did nothing seriously to

---

11 F. Brewster, *Essays on trade and navigation* (London, 1695); W. Petty, *The political anatomy of Ireland* (London, 1691); W. Temple, 'An essay on the advancement of trade in Ireland (written to Lord Essex), 22 July 1673' in W. Temple, *Miscellanea* (London, 1680), pp 97–145. Cf. D. Armitage, 'The political economy of Britain and Ireland after the Glorious Revolution' in J. Ohlmeyer (ed.), *Political thought in seventeenth-century Ireland* (Cambridge, 2000), pp 227–8. 12 The fullest accounts are in C.H. Firth and G. Davies, *A regimental history of Cromwell's army*, 2 vols (Oxford, 1940), i, pp 356–9 and *Oxford DNB*. 13 T.C. Barnard, 'Planters and policies in Cromwellian Ireland', reprinted in Barnard, *Ascents and descents, 1641–1770* (Dublin, 2004), pp 1–34. 14 R. Lawrence to Sir G. Lane, received 20 May 1668, Bodleian, Carte MS 36, f. 330. 15 HMC, *Ormonde Mss*, new series, vii, p. 27. Cf. ibid., iv, pp 38–40. 16 Bodleian, Carte MS 45, f. 437; HMC, *Ormonde Mss*, new series, vii, pp 54, 63, 65, 70–1.

disturb the authorities. Indeed, rather the reverse: he kept the Dublin government informed of thinking in the dissenting communities.[17] Little in his public stance after 1660 could be traced to the specific doctrines of the Baptists. Yet his experiences as a non-conformist, subject to legal disabilities, help to explain two emphases in his writings. Lawrence insisted on the fundamental loyalty of the Irish Protestant dissenters both to the crown and to English rule over Ireland. He contrasted this outlook with the subversiveness of Irish Catholics. Lawrence stressed the good affection of his non-conformist colleagues in the hope that their condition would be eased. The government was unmoved by his pleas. In the absence of any official relaxation of statutory penalties, Lawrence urged a second strategy. Convinced of the vitality of the Catholic menace, he reiterated the importance of Protestant unity. The ideal way to achieve it would be for the state to comprehend all the more theologically orthodox Protestant sects. Hopes that this might happen rose and fell between the early 1660s and 1680s, but came to nothing. In default, Lawrence, residing in an Ireland where the protestant minority seemed beleaguered by aggressive Catholics, was prepared to rally to the established episcopalian Church of Ireland. A 'national religion', he believed, would guard against atheism, 'popery and confusion', and promote godliness.[18] In an increasingly nervous atmosphere, as the accession of a Catholic king impended, Lawrence may have obeyed his own published advice. His last-born son was baptized according to Church of Ireland rites in 1682.[19]

II

Reformation and improvement exercised Lawrence. In 1655, Ireland was thought to be 'a white paper' or 'clay on the potter's wheel', awaiting a distinctive impress.[20] Lawrence, like many before him, designed a blueprint for the pacification, Anglicization and enrichment of the island. By 1682, Lawrence admitted that the materials had proved more stubborn than he had predicted. His disappointment, it can be argued, was as much personal as at the collective failures of the Irish Protestants. Lawrence, having stayed on in Restoration Ireland, struggled for a living and a status commensurate with what he had enjoyed under the Cromwellian regime. After 1660, he was styled variously as 'merchant', 'esquire' and 'colonel'.[21] Movement between the different designa-

[17] R. Lawrence to Sir G. Lane, received 20 May 1668, Bodleian, Carte MS 36, f. 330.   [18] Lawrence, *Interest of Ireland*, ii, pp 269–70.   [19] J. Mills (ed.), *The register of the parish of S. Peter and S. Kevin, Dublin, 1669–1761* (Dublin, 1911), p. 234; K. Herlihy, 'The Irish Baptists, 1650–1780', unpublished Ph.D. thesis, TCD (1992), p. 98.   [20] T.C. Barnard, *Cromwellian Ireland: English government and reform in Ireland, 1649–1660* (Oxford, 1975), p. 14.   [21] Petition of 20 Oct. 1663, Bodleian, Carte MS 154, f. 40; HMC, *Ormonde Mss*, new

tions accurately reflected his assorted stratagems and somewhat precarious situation. He dabbled in commercial and proto-industrial ventures, of which the textile factory at Chapelizod was merely the most celebrated. Lawrence had gained large estates in the 1650s, partly in payment of his arrears of salary and also in the busy speculative market. Part of the spoils had to be disgorged in the 1660s. More were lost thanks, apparently, to those who purported to help, notably Roger Boyle, earl of Orrery, a fly operator, who was later accused of cheating Lawrence of £1000 per annum in lands.[22]

Lawrence compensated for the loss of the recently acquired holdings in Counties Dublin and Limerick through a marriage which brought him more property in County Down. Concern with the distant lands gave him greater insight – as it did Petty – into the predicament of the internal absentees: those who lived in Ireland but remote from portions of their property.[23] Rents alone could not keep Lawrence in the manner to which he had grown accustomed. He may have sunk as much as £2,000 of his own into the cloth factory, which, in the event, brought a sorry return.[24] To supplement his income, he traded. His business – in wool, hides, tallow and butter – emboldened Lawrence to lecture his contemporaries.[25] The commodities were the hardy perennials of Irish commerce. Even so, by 1679, all had gone awry. At a low ebb, he confided, 'my whole dependence is on my rents and if I must wait three or four months after they are due, I must run upon ticket [credit] for my family and supply, which goeth against the grain'.[26]

The fragility of Lawrence's finances was remembered by his descendants. The family preserved a tradition in which he had apportioned blame for his setbacks between tricksters and impersonal forces. Despite these rubs, Lawrence contrived to live in a style which befitted his standing in Protestant Dublin. Towards the end of his life he was able to move into the up-market housing development in Smithfield, just north of the River Liffey. Other residents included Petty's associate, Thomas Taylor and Robert Wood, the schoolmaster follower of Hartlib. Setbacks in his money-making enterprises led Lawrence to generalize about the causes. He identified institutional and structural deficiencies. Ireland, he concluded, suffered from retarded economic development

series, vii, p. 97. **22** Surrey CRO, 84/49/1–4; paper why R. Lawrence should not lose his lands, Petworth House, West Sussex, Orrery Mss, general series, 13; J. Hall to Orrery, 14 Nov. 1671, 18 May 1672, ibid., 28; E. MacLysaght (ed.), *Calendar of the Orrery papers* (Dublin, 1941), pp 59–60, 77, 84–5; *A memoir of Mistress Ann Fowkes (Née Geale) ... with some recollections of her family* (Dublin, 1892), pp 25–6. **23** Indenture between R. and Agnes Lawrence and F. Hall, 3 May 1674; A. Lawrence to W. Waring, 30 Dec. 1698, private collection, Co. Down; cf. A.P.W. Malcomson, 'Absenteeism in eighteenth-century Ireland', *IESH*, i (1974), pp 15–35. **24** Bodleian, Carte MS 160, f. 36v; *CSP, Ireland, 1669–70*, p. 635; HMC, *Ormonde Mss*, new series, v, pp 450–1. **25** Account book of D. Johnson, Birr Castle, MSS of earl of Rosse, MS A/16; HMC, *Ormonde Mss*, new series, iii, pp 332–7, 346–51; Lawrence, *Interest of Ireland*, ii, pp 31–2. **26** R. Lawrence to R. Trueman, 30 Dec. 1679, private collection, Co. Down.

because the state failed adequately to back promising initiatives like his at Chapelizod, and because most in government and the propertied elite were openly contemptuous of trade. Furthermore, inadequate credit facilities and unsound coinage hampered commerce. All cried out for reform.[27]

The way in which Lawrence widened his criticism of government indifference into critiques of English policy towards Ireland and of absenteeism was undiplomatic. Lawrence contended that the Council of State, on which he sat, made excellent recommendations. They were then ignored by the Irish council. The latter was turned into a sepulchre in which hopeful plans were interred.[28] He traced much of the fault to the ignorance of and prejudice against trade among the councillors. More blame attached to the lord lieutenant. Lawrence contrasted the zest with which Ormond had sponsored improving ventures with the sorry performance of his successors. The duke had persuaded the government to assist the works at Chapelizod. Meanwhile, on his own estates at Carrick-on-Suir and Callan, he introduced foreign textile workers. Those who followed Ormond – Robartes, Berkeley and Essex – seemingly lacked his enthusiasm. It suited Lawrence to shift responsibility for his own losses at Chapelizod onto others. Accordingly, he berated the administration in Dublin for its meagre backing after 1669. Although the works had diversified to cater for the growing market in furnishing fabrics, making tapestry and turkey-work, their staple was to clothe the Irish army.[29] However, promised contracts never materialized. Lawrence explained the lack of backing by the fact that Robartes, Berkeley and Essex were all English. With no stake in Ireland, they peddled the English line obediently. By the 1670s, this was to subordinate the Irish economy to that of England and to stifle any enterprises that might compete against English industries.[30]

An analysis which emphasized personal and institutional opposition allowed Lawrence to suggest why most of the fourteen manufactures started in the 1660s had collapsed by 1682.[31] In stressing such factors, he overlooked structural problems which later analysts have invoked.[32] His criticism developed into an indictment of others who apparently harmed Irish interests. Chief among the culprits were England and the English government. Not only were unsympathetic strangers sent to rule the kingdom, the English, Welsh and (more rarely) Scots gained much of the property and many of the profitable offices in

---

27 Lawrence, *Interest of Ireland*. **28** Ibid., sig. †7. **29** R. Lawrence to Ormond, received 30 Oct. 1668, Bodleian, Carte MS 36, f. 521; HMC, *Ormonde Mss*, new series, iv, pp 38–40; vii, p. 27; *Memoir of Ann Fowkes*, pp 26–7; W. Penn, *My Irish journal, 1669–1670*, ed. I. Grubb (London, 1952), p. 22. **30** Lawrence, *Interest of Ireland*, ii, pp 102–5. **31** Ibid., i, sig. *4; ii, pp 104, 189. **32** L.M. Cullen, *An economic history of Ireland since 1660* (London, 1972), pp 26–49; D. Dickson, *New foundations: Ireland 1660–1800* (Dublin, 2000), pp 109–41.

Ireland. The majority of these beneficiaries were absentees, so that money flowed away from Ireland and the country was denied potential leaders.[33] To reverse the trend, Lawrence pleaded that Ireland should always be governed by one of its own. This was a surprising *volte face* from his attitude in the 1650s, when even Protestants of Irish birth were not to be trusted with the government. Sycophancy towards Lawrence's new patrons, the Butlers, may be suspected as a factor in his changed opinion. In addition, longer residence familiarized Lawrence with the needs of the island. The damage from absenteeism was beginning to trouble other of his contemporaries, notably Petty and the elder Sir Richard Cox.[34] Along with several matters that worried Lawrence – the adulterated coinage and uncertain credit – the curse of absentees featured conspicuously in the patriots' agenda of the 1720s and 1750s.[35] In identifying these problems, Lawrence stood near – if not at – the start of a tradition of 'patriotism' among Irish Protestants.[36] It was a surprising change of role for the upholder of English interests in the 1650s.

Lawrence's premonitory diagnosis of the causes of Irish economic weakness coexisted alongside traditional explanations, more in keeping with what was to be expected from a Cromwellian sectary. In this interpretation, certain attitudes hampered Ireland's improvement. The obvious leaders of local society were not only uninterested in commerce but set bad examples. Lawrence's religion did not make him argue that an elite based on spiritual merit should be substituted for the existing carnal one. Rather, he was dismayed that those who had inherited high responsibilities with their properties seldom fulfilled them. He stated baldly that 'nobles' titles void of nobles' estates and noble qualities renders nobility contemptible, and not the reproach but the pest of the country'.[37] Lawrence pilloried those peers who engaged in less obviously useful pastimes. He may have had Orrery, a villain since the debacle over Lawrence's lands, in his sights when he lampooned playwrights 'as no more useful in a commonwealth than fiddlers in a country parish, to incite to idleness and debauchery'.[38]

---

33 For the trend, T.C. Barnard, 'Scotland and Ireland in the later Stewart monarchy' in S.G. Ellis and S. Barber (eds), *Conquest and union: fashioning a British state, 1485–1715* (London, 1995), pp 252–8, 265–70. 34 *The economic writings of Sir William Petty*, ed. C.H. Hull, 2 vols (Cambridge, 1899), i, pp 46, 185, 193; R. Cox, 'Regnum Corcagiense; or a description of the kingdom of Cork', ed. R. Day, *Journal of the Cork Historical and Archaeological Society*, 2nd series, viii (1902), pp 70–1. 35 T. Prior, *A list of the absentees of Ireland* (Dublin, 1729); Malcomson, 'Absenteeism in eighteenth-century Ireland'. 36 P.H. Kelly, 'The politics of political economy in mid-eighteenth-century Ireland' in S.J. Connolly (ed.), *Political ideas in eighteenth-century Ireland* (Dublin, 2000), pp 105–29; J. Livesey, 'The Dublin Society in eighteenth-century Irish political thought', *Historical Journal*, 47 (2004), pp 615–640; S. Rashid, 'The Irish school of economic development, 1720–1750', *The Manchester School of Social and Economic Studies*, 54 (1988), pp 345–69; J.G. McCoy, 'Local political culture in the Hanoverian empire: the case of Ireland, 1714–1760', unpublished D.Phil. thesis, University of Oxford (1994), pp 131–58. 37 Lawrence, *Interest of Ireland*, i, p. 12. 38 Ibid.,

Lawrence was particularly severe towards those who, by virtue of possessions and status, should have guided Protestant Ireland. Individuals were adjudged wanting. But fiercer fire was directed on collectives. He followed convention by expecting leadership from the peerage. Indeed, in his writings, he devoted considerable space to this order. The peers had so far done too little to support entrepreneurial schemes. In another sphere, they had been more forward. With a flurry of statistics, Lawrence demonstrated how, between the 1630s and 1680s, the Irish parliamentary peerage had shifted decisively towards Protestantism.[39] This change encouraged Lawrence to hope that other influential groups in Irish society would move in the same direction. He recognized, however, that the government had to assist the process. In an entirely traditional fashion, he advocated a mixture of coercion and cajolery.

As he scrutinized in turn Catholic and Protestant communities, he observed much that was amiss. His anti-catholicism was profoundly conventional. Often it was interwoven with antipathy towards the Irish. Yet this prejudice diminished as he dealt more regularly with the indigenes. Even so, there survived until the close of his life traces of a determinism which assumed that the native Irish were by nature incapable of living amicably alongside the English.[40] Lawrence was never entirely consistent in his arguments. In the same book, as well as in the interval between 1655 and 1682, he veered between optimism and pessimism. In the 1650s, he endorsed the complaints of Spenser and Davies, that the intermingling of ethnic and confessional populations had led to a dangerous acculturation of English Protestant settlers. To avoid such 'degeneration' in the future, he supported the project to corral the Irish west of the River Shannon. Elsewhere, he approved the likely gains if the separate peoples lived together. Strict prohibitions against distinctive Irish language, dress, housing and husbandry, when coupled with the examples of English industry and prosperity and a stronger Protestant presence, would induce the majority to adopt 'civil deportments'.[41] By 1682, Lawrence detected numerous signs that Ireland was undergoing social and cultural transformations to become 'West England'.[42] He had still to concede that progress towards that goal was slow. Both in the 1650s and 1680s he looked to the state to speed change: an expectation that he shared with Petty. By 1682, the failure of government to do so became one of his strictures.

Also to blame were the failings of both Protestants and Catholics. Tactfully he distinguished between the respectable and restless. He nodded approvingly at the 'more serious and better principled papists', who had stood aloof from

i, sig. *6v–*7v. **39** Ibid., i, p. 69; Barnard, *New anatomy*, pp 21–40. **40** Lawrence, *The interest of England*, pp 13–16, 24–6; Lawrence, *England's Great Interest*, pp 6–9, 12–13. **41** Lawrence, *England's Great Interest*, pp 37–9. **42** Lawrence, *Interest of Ireland*, i, p. 51.

the alleged massacres of the 1640s and who lived as dutiful subjects of their English king. In contrast, adherents of 'bloody, savage Tridentine principles' and of the Jesuits were attacked relentlessly.[43] Lawrence repeated the commonplace that the priesthood had become addicted to incendiary notions and had spread them among the laity. An axiom of those in power in Ireland was that the Catholic clergy, together with their lay adjutants, had infected a vulnerable population and so brought war and devastation to Ireland.[44]

Lawrence, returning to the theme in 1682, suspected continuities in the power over the Irish of Catholicism and the attendant dangers. Whereas the 1650s had been a time when the English could freely express their antipathy towards Catholicism, especially that professed by the Irish, 1682 was a less auspicious moment to do so. Charles II had ridden out a storm whipped up in part by an unscrupulous exploitation of fear of Catholicism in England and Ireland. Both the king and his younger brother, soon to succeed as James II, were inclined to sympathy with Catholics. Accordingly, Lawrence tempered his anticatholic invective. He adopted a popular distinction: 'it is not the religion of the Church of Rome ... but the policies of the state of Rome that render them so incompatible with civil order and society'. He prefigured Protestant denials throughout the eighteenth century when he insisted that he had no wish to constrain the Catholics in their worship.[45] But the generosity was not consistently applied. Erroneous doctrines did more than delude the Catholics alone. The tenacity with which they stuck to and defended misguided opinions, he believed, increased their propensity to sin. Through this reasoning he traced much of the behaviour which stunted the economy of Ireland back to the prevalence of Catholicism there.[46] Catholicism in the end was unfitted to be a civic religion, because inimical to 'civil order and society'. Lawrence's view uncannily foreshadowed a declaration from Dublin in 1725, to the effect that popery constituted 'the grand enemy to our religious and civil liberties'. The tenets of 'popery' – according to Lawrence – undermined society.[47] His observations suggested that Catholics sabotaged 'neighbourly society and civil converse betwixt private persons'. The harmonious functioning of society and the conduct of trade required trust. Lawrence argued that this was impossible so long as the Catholics practised mental reservation when swearing oaths. The practice, for which Catholics were taxed routinely, rendered nugatory the oaths and contracts on which a prospering trading nation depended. It also engen-

---

43 Ibid., i, sig. ††2v–††3v; ii, pp 222, 239; T.C. Barnard, '"Parlour entertainment in an evening": histories of the 1640s' in M. Ó Siochrú (ed.), *Kingdoms in crisis: Ireland in the 1640s* (Dublin, 2001), pp 20–43. 44 Lawrence, *Interest of England*, p. 11; Lawrence, *England's Great Interest*, p. 16. 45 Lawrence, *Interest of Ireland*, ii, p. 93. 46 Ibid., i, p. 70. 47 Ibid., ii, pp 194–5

dered suspicion, so that there 'can be no true friendship nor comfortable neighbourhood'. Lawrence accused ardent Catholics of reducing social life to something akin to a Hobbesian state of nature. Their principles were worse than 'little peccadilloes only inconvenient to neighbourly society and civil converse between private persons' and threatened to return humanity to 'a condition worse than brutish'.[48] What he feared from the loose, unstable (and largely unknown) world of Irish Catholicism contrasted with his knowledge of the compact congregation of Dublin Baptists. Fellowship, based on the keeping of a scriptural and sacral covenant, provided an ideal of trust and neighbourliness.

The charges, familiar long before Lawrence made them, remained in the Irish Protestants' armoury. In 1698, Bishop Foy of Waterford believed that the unsocial or anti-social habits of the Irish Catholics were worsened by their living in scattered and makeshift settlements. The bishop wanted to herd them into nucleated villages centred on church and manor, copying the model of lowland England.[49] By the mid-eighteenth century, sociability was regarded as a vital badge of civility and civic responsibility. It led Irish Catholics, who persisted in the views attributed to them by Lawrence, to be impugned for 'dissociability'.[50] As such they unsettled society and, resistant to its norms, could legitimately be debarred from full citizenship.[51]

A sense of imminent danger from the assertive Irish Catholics pulsed through *The interest of Ireland*. When, in 1682, Lawrence wrote, 'while God blesses us with an English Protestant king and parliament, Ireland can never degenerate from an Irish Protestant interest', it hardly amounted to a resounding affirmation of confidence in a Protestant future for Ireland.[52] Within three years, the Catholic James had ascended the throne, but by then Lawrence had died. Lawrence ingeniously linked the nature of Catholicism to the principal topic of his treatise: the economic condition and betterment of Ireland. The space that he allowed to his rants not only unbalanced the survey but drowned what might otherwise have been timely and dispassionate advice as to how to improve the kingdom.[53] Lawrence had picked up some of the vocabulary and method of the innovative political arithmeticians, but those novelties had not

---

48 Ibid., ii, pp 194–5, 199, 225, 271. **49** N. Foy, *A sermon preached in Christ's-Church, Dublin; on the 23d of October, 1698* (Dublin, 1698), pp 27–8; H. Maule, *A sermon preached in Christ-Church, Dublin ... on Tuesday the 23d day of October 1733* (Dublin, 1733), p. 21. **50** John Brett, *A friendly call to the people of the Roman Catholick religion in Ireland* (Dublin, 1757), p. 12. **51** T.C. Barnard, 'The languages of politeness and sociability in eighteenth-century Ireland' in D.G. Boyce, R. Eccleshall and V. Geoghegan (eds), *Political discourse in seventeenth- and eighteenth-century Ireland* (Basingstoke, 2001), pp 193–221; Barnard, *Making the Grand Figure*, pp 345–72. **52** Lawrence, *Interest of Ireland*, ii, p. 58. **53** Bibliographical evidence, with the pagination from pp 96–113 in the second part of *Interest of Ireland* duplicated, suggests that this section – on the imperative for Protestant unity – was inserted while it was in the press. Also, the final section, a partisan Protestant history of Catholic conspiracies, has the appearance of having been tacked on.

supplanted older and sometimes chiliastic thinking. Powerful traditions sustained Lawrence's diatribes against Protestant neglects. He endorsed a widely held interpretation that Irish Protestants had provoked divine wrath in 1641 through their sin, and might do so again unless they amended their behaviour.[54] He saw material improvement and moral reformation as causally connected. Sins stopped economic advances, characteristically by wasting money.

In *The interest of Ireland*, Lawrence attacked four pernicious 'wealth-wasting' and 'God-provoking' sins: swearing, gambling, adultery and drunkenness. He argued that 'these evils not only hazard the eternal safety of immortal souls, but also are superlatively destructive to the trade and wealth of this nation'.[55] This outlook, treating material and immaterial worlds as conjoined, had long prevailed among Protestant zealots in England. It inspired campaigns to reform conduct, stimulate industry and relieve the poor. Practical measures taken in Colchester, Coventry, Dorchester, Gloucester, Leicester and Salisbury were belatedly to be imported into Ireland.[56] A similar philosophy underlay the drive to reform manners in England, Wales and Ireland during the 1690s.[57] In Ireland, it persisted in the eighteenth century and expressed itself in the hospitals opened in Dublin, the charter schools and in some of the schemes advanced by the Dublin Society, the Physico-Historical Society and (near the end of the century) in the Society for Discountenancing Vice.[58] Lawrence's direct influence on the later undertakings can occasionally be detected, as in Bishop Hutchinson's published reference to *The interest of Ireland* when he urged the Irish parliament and Dublin Society to help the Irish fisheries.[59]

The godly milieu in which Lawrence moved in Dublin was one source of his preoccupations. Essentially a colony transplanted from England, the Baptist community in the Irish capital acquired its own local colouration, including an acute sense of the Catholics by whom they were surrounded. At the same time, it shared concerns that survived in England. Neither the poor themselves nor their relief were problems unique to the Baptists. Every denomination struggled with the theoretical and practical challenges of poverty. In Lawrence's case, his grand-daughter recalled that he boasted that 'he was fond of employing the poor

---

[54] Lawrence, *Interest of Ireland*, i, sig. ††v; T.C. Barnard, 'The uses of 23 October 1641 and Irish Protestant celebrations', *EHR*, 106 (1991), pp 889–920, reprinted in Barnard, *Ascents and descents*, pp 111–42. [55] Lawrence, *Interest of Ireland*, i, pp 37, 51, 57. [56] Slack, *From reformation to improvement*, pp 29–32. [57] T.C. Barnard, 'Reforming Irish manners: the religious societies in Dublin during the 1690s', *Historical Journal*, 35 (1992), pp 805–38, reprinted in Barnard, *Ascents and descents*, pp 143–78. [58] Barnard, 'Hartlib circle'; J. Liechty, 'Irish evangelicalism, Trinity College Dublin and the mission of the Church of Ireland at the end of the eighteenth century', unpublished Ph.D. thesis, St Patrick's College, Maynooth (1987); K. Milne, *The Charter Schools* (Dublin, 1997). [59] Hutchinson, *A second letter*, pp 4–5. Lawrence's *Interest of Ireland* is found in the libraries of Charles Willoughby and Claudius Gilbert, both of which later passed to Trinity College, Dublin. TCD, MSS 10, f. 104; 11, f. 19.

and giving them bread'. In *The interest of Ireland*, he detailed the plight of the destitute in Dublin; in his will, he arranged doles.[60] The two executors named by Lawrence had a wider concern with helping the poor. One, the Revd Daniel Williams, ministered to a dissenting congregation in Dublin until the Catholic *revanche* of 1688 drove him back to England. Throughout the 1690s, albeit from a distance, he put his weight (and purse) behind the Irish efforts to reform manners.[61] The second executor of Lawrence's will, James Knight, belonged to similar pious groups. He endowed charities and schools in Dublin.[62]

Lawrence was among the first among the Protestants in Ireland to address the alarming incidence of poverty. Like earlier and contemporary observers, he explained it as a choice made by the superstitious and backward. He also treated it as a condition arising from a variety of tyrannies – English as well as Catholic and Irish. In the longer term, he agreed with other reformers that the remedy lay in providing more employment. Living in Dublin and seeing for himself the plight of his fellows, he stressed two matters that bothered his cleverer contemporary, Petty, rather less. The luxury enjoyed by a few accentuated the straits of the majority. Lawrence lived in comfort and seems not to have disdained the accessories of smart city life. But it is improbable that his annual income was even a tenth of Petty's. One result was that Lawrence confined his activities to Ireland after 1660, rather than voyaging between the two islands. Enforced residence in one place may have made Lawrence more sensitive to the situation of the less fortunate around him. At all events, his critique of excess, speaking of a religious morality, differed from Petty's dispassionate appraisal of human needs and spending. In addition, Lawrence bequeathed money to the poor in Dublin. Petty schemed and projected to cure the endemic poverty of Ireland, but limited his charity to the deserving of the parish from which he hailed – Romsey in Hampshire. Cynically, Petty remarked that Englishmen needed to ingratiate themselves with the parish in which they were born.[63] Petty's may have been the more constructive approach, but it lacked Lawrence's humanity.

---

60 Proposal for Chapelizod, *c.*1668, Bodleian, Carte MS 36, f. 523; will of R. Lawrence, 26 June 1684, private collection, Co. Down; *Memoir of Ann Fowkes*, p. 26; Lawrence, *Interest of Ireland*, i, pp 45–6. **61** J. Richardson to Society for the Promotion of Christian Knowledge, 18 July 1718, Abstract Letter Book [ALB], 8, no 5289, Society for the Promotion of Christian Knowledge [SPCK]; D. Williams, *Sermon preach'd before the societies for reformation of manners, in Dublin: July the 18th, 1700* (Dublin, 1700), R.L. Greaves, *God's other children: Protestant nonconformists and the emergence of denominational churches in Ireland, 1660–1700* (Stanford, 1997), p. 260. **62** St. J.D. Seymour, *The Puritans in Ireland, 1647–1661* (Oxford, 1921), pp 155, 215 indenture of 12 April 1698, NAI, 6252; J. Bulkeley to J. Bonnell, undated [1720s], NLI, PC; H. Maule to R. Stearne, 10 Jan. 1717[8], ALB, no 5502; H. Newman to J. Knight, 14 April 1718, ibid., CS 2/7, ff 17v–18; *Faulkner's Dublin Journal*, 15 Nov. 1726; Monck Mason, collections relating to Dublin, Gilbert MS 67, p. 726, Dublin City Library; J. Knight, will, 21 Feb. 1725[6], PRONI, D 3168/2/7. **63** Sir W. Petty to T. Waller, 10 Dec. 1671, McGill UL, Osler MS 7612; Lord Edmond Fitzmaurice, *The life of*

The interest of Ireland appeared at a time when the seriousness of poverty in Dublin was starting to prompt individual and collective responses. Church of Ireland parishes, dissenting congregations, the municipality and philanthropists helped the deserving.[64] Mostly the schemes copied what had already evolved in England. In addition, Lawrence shared with observers of the English scene, a sense that the poor constituted an unrealised resource. He conceded that some, owing to their stage in the cycle of life, had been reduced to indigence and were fitting objects for Christian charity. The able-bodied, in contrast, needed employment. Increasingly the cultivation of flax and hemp and the making of linen were best at providing it. Not the least of Ormond's merits, in Lawrence's account, was his support of such ventures. Lawrence himself, in his work for the Council of Trade, prepared instructions for the planting of hemp and flax.[65] The Irish council ordered that they be printed, but no copy is known to have survived. Such manuals again prefigure what was done in the first half of the eighteenth century under the auspices of the Linen Board and the Dublin Society.[66] Chapelizod itself disappointed Lawrence's perhaps exaggerated hopes. Incidentally, his failure to turn it into a profitable enterprise blasted his reputation with censorious contemporaries.[67] The experiment, always conceived as a showpiece akin to the Mortlake tapestry factory or the Gobelins works, was revived. As Lawrence had dreamt, it became the focus of patriotic endeavour, though not in his own lifetime.[68] One unwelcome result of the proto-industry had been to crowd unruly workers onto a single site. Other pioneering entrepreneurs discovered that labour did not always conduce to discipline, instead proving a source of unrest.[69]

Lawrence was also linked with the embryonic linen industry of Ulster. Through his wife he gained lands in County Down, which were managed by a local resident, William Waring. The latter keenly promoted the cultivation and spinning of flax. The extent to which the experience at Chapelizod informed schemes elsewhere in Ireland remains elusive. Notable among Lawrence's

Sir William Petty, 1623–1687 (London, 1895), pp 323–4. **64** T. Barnard, 'The eighteenth-century parish' in E. Fitzpatrick and R. Gillespie (eds), *The parish in medieval and early modern Ireland* (Dublin, 2006), pp 297–324; R. Dudley, 'The Dublin parish, 1660–1730', op. cit., pp 277–96; R. Gillespie, 'Urban parishes in early seventeenth-century Ireland: the case of Dublin', op. cit., pp 228–41; B.F. Gurrin, 'Land and people in Wicklow, 1660–1840', unpublished Ph.D. thesis, NUI, Maynooth (2006). **65** Lawrence, *Interest of Ireland*, sig. †7. **66** Royal Dublin Society, *A bibliography of the publications of the Royal Dublin Society from its foundation in the year 1731 ...*, 2nd edn (Dublin, 1953), items 3, 8, 18; H.D. Gribbon, 'The Irish Linen Board, 1711–1828' in L.M. Cullen and T.C. Smout (eds), *Comparative aspects of Scottish and Irish economic and social history, 1600–1900* (Edinburgh, 1977), p. 81. **67** HMC, *Ormonde Mss*, new series, iv, p. 156. **68** *CSP, Domestic, 1691–2*, pp 321–2; A. Longfield, 'History of tapestry-making in Ireland in the seventeenth and eighteenth centuries', *JRSAI*, 68 (1938), pp 92–9; A. Longfield, 'Some tapestry makers in Ireland', *Burlington Magazine*, 85 (1944), p. 250. **69** T.C. Barnard, 'An Anglo-Irish industrial venture: iron-making at Enniscorthy', *PRIA*, lxxxv, sect C (1985), p. 141; T.C. Barnard, 'Sir William Petty as Kerry ironmaster', *PRIA*, lxxxii, sect C (1982), p. 26.

achievements was the despatch of a specialist, Alexander van Fornenbergh, probably a Protestant refugee, to observe and evaluate techniques in England and the Low Countries. Fornenbergh's reports, together with the arrival in Ireland of foreign artificers, may gradually have disseminated better methods.[70] The Warings intermarried with the Lawrences.[71] The Warings, innovators in the Ulster industry, had sources other than Lawrence and Chapelizod from which to learn of continental processes. In the 1680s, the heir to the Waring estate toured the Low Countries, the Rhineland and Italy.[72] Accordingly innovations in the northern industry may have been independent of any contribution from Lawrence.

Improvers insisted that their exertions bettered not only themselves but also the commonwealth. This was a view to which Lawrence subscribed. Later analysts have tended to be sceptical about what could be done by particular proprietors, no matter how energetic and civic-minded. Notwithstanding the favourable publicity that at first surrounded Chapelizod or the value of printed manuals such as Lawrence's, structural and ecological factors did most to implant linen-making in late seventeenth- and early eighteenth-century Ireland.[73]

Other barriers to the economic development of Ireland, notably the lack of a bank and the shortage and adulteration of the circulating coin, continued to trouble pamphleteers. High interest rates (often over 10 per cent) deterred investors and improvers. Lawrence proposed that a joint-stock company be formed. This solution was recommended by others, and would be tried in the 1690s as a means to nourish the puny linen industry.[74] Soon enough it was replaced by a state subsidy. Fresh efforts in the 1720s were directed into founding an Irish equivalent of the Bank of England, but they failed.[75] Similarly, successive administrations wrestled with the defects in the coinage. The problems of bimetallism and the habit of consistently over-valuing the main medium of Irish exchange – silver – inhibited trade. Not enough low value coins circulated. The shortage was to some extent overcome by urban traders issuing tokens. But

---

[70] R. Lawrence to Sir G. Lane, received 20 May 1668, received 30 Oct. 1668, 16 Dec. 1668, Bodleian, Carte MS 36, ff 330, 521, 609; instructions from Lawrence to A. van Fornenbergh, recd. 20 May 1668, ibid., ff. 332–3; A. van Fornenbergh's reports, recd. 26 May 1668 and Sep. 1668, ibid., ff 347–8, 497–8. [71] A. Lawrence to W. Waring, 30 Dec. 1698, private collection, Co. Down; *Memoir of Ann Fowkes*, p. 26. [72] T.C. Barnard, 'What became of Waring? The making of an Ulster squire' in V. Carey and U. Lotz-Heumann (eds), *Taking sides? Colonial and confessional mentalities in early modern Ireland* (Dublin, 2003), reprinted in Barnard, *Ascents and descents*, pp 235–65. [73] W.H. Crawford, 'The origins of the linen industry in North Armagh and the Lagan valley', *Ulster Folklife*, 17 (1971), pp 42–51; W.H. Crawford, 'The evolution of the linen trade in Ulster before industrialization', *IESH*, 15 (1988), pp 32–53, both reprinted in W.H. Crawford, *The impact of the domestic linen industry in Ulster* (Belfast, 2005). [74] W.R. Scott, 'The king's and queen's corporations for the linen manufacture in Ireland', *JRSAI*, 31 (1901), pp 371–7. [75] L.M. Cullen, 'Landlords, bankers and merchants: the early Irish banking world, 1700–1820', *Hermathena*, 135 (1983), pp 25–41; M. Ryder, 'The Bank of Ireland, 1721: land, credit and dependency', *Historical Journal*, 25 (1982), pp 557–80.

the confused situation was thought to discourage trade and to slow modernization by necessitating barter. Matters were further muddled by large quantities of foreign specie, particularly from Spain and Portugal. Lawrence, like others, pressed the Council of Trade to tackle these questions, but his suggestions were too contentious to be adopted. In 1683 Lawrence and Petty wrangled before the Irish Council of Trade over revaluing the coinage, 'but with little edification to the hearers'.[76] Lawrence hoped to turn his knowledge of monetary matters to personal advantage. In 1676 he offered unsuccessfully to manage the inland revenues of Ireland. With equal lack of success he sought the post of accountant-general.[77]

Projectors had long inundated the makers of policy for Ireland with ideas: some utopian, others severely practical. Many resembled what had been tried in Tudor and Stuart England.[78] Governments, although eager for a placid and prosperous Ireland, seldom looked beyond instant gains. This was notoriously the case under Charles II. Not just Lawrence with his rag-bag of prejudices and pretensions, but also the seemingly more rational Petty, failed to persuade the administration to apply their nostrums to Ireland.[79] Instead, Charles II and his ministers listened to the well-connected and unashamedly venal, like Lord Ranelagh.

Much that the hopeful Lawrence suggested was ignored. Yet he expressed thoughts important to future policies in Ireland. There was no novelty in pondering lessons from the economic miracle which had so enriched the Low Countries. Sir William Temple, Dr Benjamin Worsley, Sir Francis Brewster and Petty applied Dutch practices to Ireland. Furthermore, within Ireland itself, several grandees – Ormond, Orrery and Lane – knew the Low Countries at first hand either through exile or travel. After 1660, they exploited their earlier contacts to pick up ideas and personnel. Possibly Lawrence was directly in touch with the fertile overseas source thanks either to his exiled Baptist kinsman, Henry Lawrence, or the sectarian diaspora.[80]

Another craze of the moment besotted Lawrence. Whether as novice political mathematician or failed businessman he constantly totted up costs. Sometimes his efforts at quantification were more ingenious than persuasive. He berated notables in Restoration Ireland for importing mistresses along with other non-Irish goods. Lawrence reckoned that between £300 and £400 were annually spent on each.[81] Fiscal losses were compounded by other harmful consequences. Effeminacy set in, turning the once 'courageous lion' into 'the las-

---

[76] HMC, *Ormonde Mss*, new series, vii, p. 14. [77] HMC, *Ormonde Mss*, new series, v, pp 434, 451; vi, p. 39. [78] J. Thirsk, *Economic policy and projects* (Oxford, 1978). [79] See above, pp 41–72. [80] I am grateful to Professor John Morrill for telling me of Henry Lawrence's connections with Arnhem. [81] Lawrence, *Interest of Ireland*, i, pp 45–6.

civious goat'. From the era of Sardanapalus and the fall of the Assyrian empire, such indulgences enfeebled states.[82]

Lawrence was not the first analyst of social and economic malaise in Ireland to posit sin – collective and individual – as the principal cause. More innovative was his attack on the evils which arose from prosperity: the damage from poverty was a hackneyed topic. In print, he expatiated on the consumerism which was gripping Dublin and which others were starting to satirize.[83] It endangered alike the physical well-being and immortal souls of Dubliners. Ironies can be detected in his invective. The success of the Chapelizod works depended on the fashion for more sumptuous furnishings. The enterprise sought both to stimulate and satisfy the demand. Moreover, in his own house, Lawrence adopted these same comforts.[84] As yet only isolated voices – the bishop and archdeacon of Cork and ascetic Quakers – joined Lawrence's.[85] By the eighteenth century, the volume of complaint against luxury had risen to a crescendo. Later pamphleteers combined anger at the financial waste with anxiety over the spiritual damage. As with other aspects of the manifesto of the eighteenth-century 'patriots', a strong moral dimension survived behind the statistics and more impersonal language.[86] Many of the matters that obsessed Lawrence during the 1680s – Catholic vitality, malevolence and error, Protestant sin and insouciance, English misgovernment and incomprehension of, if not malice towards, Ireland – continued to perplex public-spirited commentators. Into the 1750s and beyond, those interested in the well-being of Ireland clamoured still for the official and private measures which Lawrence had urged. More precarious in his circumstances than Petty, Lawrence's experiences remained nearer those of the generality of Protestants in Ireland. For those reasons, his responses and solutions, although frequently confused and contradictory, had more in common with his contemporaries' than did those of the more original Petty.

---

[82] Ibid., i, pp 48–9. [83] R. Gillespie, 'Richard Head's *The Miss Display'd* and Irish restoration society', *Irish University Review*, xxxiv (2004), pp 213–28. [84] Proposal for Chapelizod, c.1668, Bodleian, Carte MS 36, f. 523; R. Lawrence, will, 26 June 1684, private collection, Co. Down; *Memoir of Ann Fowkes*, p. 26; Lawrence, *Interest of Ireland*, i, pp 45–6. [85] R. Synge, sermon, 30 March 1684, private collection, London; *A narrative of the Christian experience of George Bewley* (Dublin, 1750), pp 11, 15, 33, 43; *Some account of the life of Joseph Pike of Cork* (London, 1837), pp 59–61, 64–6; R.L. Greaves, *Dublin's merchant-quaker: Anthony Sharp and the community of Friends, 1643–1707* (Stanford, 1998), pp 201–10; E. Wetenhall, *A sermon preached Octob. 23. 1692* (Dublin, 1692), p. 18. [86] T.C. Barnard, 'Integration or separation? Hospitality and display in Protestant Ireland, c.1660–1800' in L. Brockliss and D. Eastwood (eds), *A union of multiple identities: the British Isles, c.1750–1850* (Manchester, 1997), pp 127–46; T.C. Barnard, 'Public and private uses of wealth in Ireland, c.1660–1760' in J.R. Hill and C. Lennon (eds), *Luxury and austerity: Historical Studies XXI* (Dublin, 1999), pp 66–83; P.H. Kelly, '"Industry and virtue versus luxury and corruption": Berkeley, Walpole and the South Sea Bubble crisis', *ECI*, 7 (1992), pp 57–74.

CHAPTER FOUR

Improving Ireland's past

IN 1741 SIR RICHARD COX, a landowner and member of parliament from west Cork, discussed the possibility of his writing a history of Ireland. This 'drudgery' (as he termed it) would continue a family tradition. In 1689, his grandfather, the elder Sir Richard Cox, lord chancellor of Ireland between 1703 and 1707, published *Hibernia Anglicana*: a learned defence of the English and Protestant interest in Ireland. The younger Cox's intention was to bring the story closer to the present. In particular, he hoped to handle 'the great revolutions of property' under Elizabeth I and James VI and I, and those that followed the wars of the 1640s and 1689–91. 'I am much deceived if any revolutions of the world afford a more copious subject for history,' he pronounced. However, Cox intended to end with the death of Queen Anne, 'because the late times are too modern ... and too delicate to be treated of candidly for one hundred years to come'.[1]

For the work, Cox planned to utilize manuscripts and scarce pamphlets owned by his family. He would also advertise in the Dublin press for other materials. In addition, he recruited a collaborator, Walter Harris. To the latter Cox promised 'your share of the credit and the profit of the work'. Harris was already known to Cox through his publication of a greatly enlarged edition of the writings of the seventeenth-century antiquarian, Sir James Ware. Cox had supplied Harris with a lengthy account of his grandfather, the former lord chancellor, for the supplemented *Ware*.[2] In the event, Cox, although he published several slight and topical works, never produced the history.[3] In contrast, Harris completed his version of Ware and issued other historical, as well as controversial, books.

The proposed literary partnership of Cox and Harris introduces several themes that merit closer scrutiny. Cox wished to avoid contemporary events

---

[1] Sir R. Cox to W. Harris, 6 March 1740[1], Armagh Public Library, papers of the Physico-Historical Society, K.I.II.14. [2] Sir R. Cox to W. Harris, 3 and 17 Feb. 1740[1], 6 March 1740[1], ibid. [3] R. Cox, *A charge delivered to the grand jury, at a general quarter sessions of the peace held for the County of Cork at Bandon-Bridge, on the 13th of January 1740[1]* (Dublin, 1741); *A letter from Sir Richard Cox, Bart. to Thomas Prior, Esq;* (Dublin, 1749); also the unpublished 'Letters between the Sp[eake]r, B[isho]p of C[or]k and Sir Richard C[o]x', of which there are manuscript copies in RIA, MS 12 W 25 and RCB, MS D7/12/1/3.

because too controversial. Others were not so reticent. Nor, it could be contended, did Cox avoid powerful prejudices in his allegedly objective publications. He wrote both as a fervent improver and a stalwart of the dominant Protestant order. Moreover, he was keen to appear in a wider world, through print, as the very model of an improving landlord. Cox's motives in venturing into a comprehensive history of Ireland are not entirely clear. He had reacted angrily to recent compilations, such as Carte's and Plunkett's, which he berated as too generous to the Irish Catholics.[4] Cox intended to correct the bias. The financial inducement to Harris, well-known for his cupidity, is blatant. So, too, is the appeal to vanity, with the lure of fame.

What can be reconstructed of Cox's motives prompts an examination of the longer tradition into which his efforts fitted. Three themes in particular are worth pursuing. There were more projects comparable with Cox's than is usually suspected, the majority of them, like his, never completed or published. Second, mercenary calculations entered into most of the schemes. Indeed, most failed because enough money to publish them was not subscribed. Nevertheless, profit was not the sole motor. Defence of past Catholic or Protestant, English or Irish, conduct inspired many compositions. Rehearsing distant events could either justify or undermine the existing regime. Less blatantly partisan was a belief that a detailed knowledge of the past would assist towards a better Ireland. Through careful reconstruction of earlier times Ireland might be freed from the monotonous aspersions about its barbarism and backwardness.

Attempts to write more sympathetic chronicles necessarily involved the location and study of scarce materials. Their very scarcity gradually induced greater care to collect and preserve them. Chroniclers turned first to the written remains, but because they were so sparse and so difficult of interpretation, the potential of other kinds of sources, including artefacts and buildings, was realised. In time, the appreciation brought a similar concern to locate, save and understand what survived. This interest in the past was a paradoxical result of the desire to improve Ireland materially and morally.

II

By 1741, when Cox contemplated his project, some of the events that he singled out for attention had received seemingly authoritative treatment. Sir John

---

4 For Nicholas Plunkett's work, see: P.H. Kelly, '"A light to the blind": the voyce of the dispossessed élite in the generation after the defeat at Limerick', *IHS*, xxiv (1985), pp 431–62.

Temple in *The Irish rebellion* supplied the canonical text for the tempestuous 1640s; Archbishop William King's *State of the Protestants of Ireland* did the same for 1688–91. Those with different perspectives, notably the Irish and Catholic, struggled against the dominance of the Protestant propagandists.[5] The latter, as the victors, had command of the surviving evidence, especially in official repositories, and readier access to the printing presses in Britain and Ireland. Even so, by the 1720s and 1730s, entrepreneurial booksellers, sensing that controversy helped sales, published a series of histories and memoirs that traversed the stormy seventeenth century. The sequence seemed to be inaugurated with the Dublin publication in 1720 of Clarendon's history of Ireland during the 1640s.[6] By 1743, one publisher wrote how 'of late years, a series of literary anecdotes have appeared, greatly contributing towards an insight and digestion of that rude chaos wherein the history of Ireland and particularly the rebellion of 1641 lay involved'.[7] As these accounts diverged from Temple, Cox and Harris were angered. They planned – both in tandem and separately – to re-impose an interpretation friendly to the Protestants and unflattering to the Catholics. The seventeenth century might be the most hotly contested terrain, but in the linked campaigns to vindicate or vilify the present order, to rebut the libels on Ireland and to quicken change, earlier periods could also serve.

One axiom that was to be tested was whether or not the English (or Anglo-Norman or Cambro-Norman or Scots) settlers were indeed the introducers of all that was good into the island. Sometimes in parallel, sometimes fused with it, was an insistence on the Protestantism of the Church of Ireland as the heir of patrician Christianity. In pushing back into those distant times, the curious hoped to prove that Ireland had once been a bastion of civility, the island of saints and scholars. Unsubtle champions of Protestant dominance employed these evidences so that 'the Irish themselves [can be] taught how much they have changed for the better'. Yet others derived less strident lessons: of primitive virtues, long-lost liberties and skills, even uncorrupted Christianity. 'All the darkness of ancient times' was hard to penetrate, yet the dedicated might dis-

---

5 Much of the material is surveyed expertly in B. Cunningham, 'Historical writing, 1660–1750' in R. Gillespie and A. Hadfield (eds), *The Oxford history of the Irish book. III. The Irish book in English, 1550–1800* (Oxford, 2006), pp 264–81; J. Leerssen, *Mere Irish and Fíor-Ghael studies in the idea of Irish nationality, its development and literary expression prior to the nineteenth century* (new ed., Cork, 1996), pp 254–376; C. O'Halloran, *Golden ages and barbarous nations: antiquarian debate and cultural politics in Ireland, c.1750–1800* (Cork, 2004). J. Waddell, *Foundation myths: the beginnings of Irish archaeology* (Bray, 2005) performs a similar function for archaeological enquiries. Also helpful for many of the issues is A. de Valera, 'Antiquarian and historical investigation in Ireland in the eighteenth century', unpublished MA thesis, UCD (1978). 6 Edward Hyde, earl of Clarendon, *The history of the rebellion and civil wars in Ireland* (Dublin, 1719/20). 7 *A collection of the state letters of the Right Honourable Roger Boyle, the first earl of Orrery*, 2 vols (Dublin, 1743), i, p. iii.

cern 'at least the form of their government, their laws, &c'.[8] Study of the few remains, abstruse and taxing, was of itself so challenging as to attract only occasional dogged or eccentric investigators. Theories were propounded. If many reflected the original presuppositions – about indigenous Irish ignorance or precocity – some moved away from stereotyping to more nuanced and better informed evocations of the Irish past.

Surveys of historical materials lurking in Ireland generally followed English models. Indeed, they were frequently conceived as elements within English surveys, notably for William Camden's *Britannia* and its updated editions. As English authority was extended further into Ireland, so incentives grew to chart convergences and continuing divergences between the two kingdoms. By the mid-seventeenth century, English imperialism and disinterested antiquarianism were given fresh twists as Baconian ideas took hold. Knowledge of historical structures and systems, as well as of natural resources, was the prerequisite for their more effective exploitation.

The recovery of ancient knowledge was widely regarded as a route to a better future. If the Egyptians, Babylonians and Greeks were the favoured ancients, interest in the earlier inhabitants of Britain and Ireland was growing. Written records relating to ancient Ireland were rare and difficult of interpretation. Moreover, they carried the risk that they might have been forged, as the exposure of tricks elsewhere warned. Therefore, alongside efforts to preserve, collect, decipher and interpret old Irish documents, curiosity about artefacts, above and below ground, arose. In England and Wales, antiquarian tastes, while sometimes nostalgic and conservative, were shared by improvers. The remains spoke of wisdom and skills that had been lost but might be recovered. Also, the relics could reassure the hopeful that the backwardness and errors, once understood, could be avoided or corrected. A gradual increase in curiosity about the antiquities of Ireland had sources and characteristics common to the parallel movements in Britain and continental Europe.[9] However, the Irish manifestation possessed distinctive features. The history of Ireland was contested not just by 'Ancients' and 'Moderns', by exponents of the rival philosophical and *érudit* approaches, but by apologists of the Old Irish, Old English and New English, and by Catholics and Protestants. More obviously than in the parts of Britain, history justified – or indicted – the recent revolutions in the distribution of property and power.

8 Sir R. Cox to W. Harris, 6 March 1741[2], k.I.II.14, Armagh. **9** S. Piggott, *Ancient Britons and the antiquarian imagination* (London, 1989), pp 13–35; R. Sweet, *Antiquaries: the discovery of the past in eighteenth-century Britain* (London, 2004).

Imported ideas merged with imperatives peculiar to Ireland. Wars, devastation and re-settlement recurred. Each episode necessitated an appraisal of the country, which the ingenious schemed to make the pretext for the compilation of its civil and natural histories. Accordingly, during the Cromwellian interregnum, the correspondents of Samuel Hartlib began to answer his 'interrogatories', alongside the mundane but urgent work of mapping and reallocating confiscated properties. Two noteworthy accounts came from this group, which prided itself on its intellectual innovativeness. In each – the Boates' *Natural History* and Petty's *Political anatomy* – analysis was subordinated to ideology and topicality. Each elaborated on the latent riches of the island, and argued that only under secure English rule could they be exploited fully.

Although the works of the Boates and Petty entered the public domain, they did not supplant older accounts such as that of Sir John Davies, which had appeared originally in 1612.[10] Indeed, the continuing grip of Davies's description and prescription – the full implementation across Ireland of English laws – was revealed in a 1673 publication.[11] The anonymous *The present state of Ireland* silently reproduced chunks from Davies and otherwise offered a conventional *vade-mecum* to the main towns and notables.[12] Meanwhile travellers, 'galloping topographers', wrote up their observations. Thomas Denton, a north-country perambulator, lifted substantial sections from the revised Camden when describing Ireland. Denton had visited only Dublin and its environs.[13] Typically, the visitors adopted the grids favoured by English topographers to classify what they saw in Ireland. The principal interest was in propertied dynasties. Inscriptions and armorial carvings offered unique information. Through heraldry incised on tombs and tablets, detailed genealogies could be constructed. Here the preoccupation of strangers and newcomers coincided with local traditions. The learned of Old Ireland valued and perfected the making of genealogical tables. The tradition persisted into the eighteenth century with such adepts as Charles Lynegar and Charles O'Conor of Belanagare. The latter might deprecate 'barren pedigrees, skeletons without meat and bodies without soul', but he compiled them.[14]

---

10 J. Davies, *A discoverie of the true causes why Ireland was never entirely subdued* (London, 1612). 11 Davies was reprinted in Dublin in 1664, 1733, 1751 and 1761, and reissued in London in 1747. 12 *The present state of Ireland* (London, 1673). 13 Thomas Denton, *A perambulation of Cumberland, 1687–1688*, ed. A.J.L. Winchester, Surtees Society, ccvii (2003), pp 513–50. Other accounts include those of J. Verdon in BL, Add. MS 41,769 and John Dunton, printed in E. MacLysaght, *Irish life in the seventeenth century*, 3rd ed. (Shannon, 1970), pp 320–90. 14 K. Simms, 'Charles Lynegar, the Ó Luinín family and the study of Seanchas' in T. Barnard, D. Ó Cróinín and K. Simms (eds), *A miracle of learning: studies in manuscripts and Irish learning: essays in honour of William O'Sullivan* (Aldershot, 1998), pp 266–83; R.E. Ward, J.F. Wrynn and C.C. Ward (eds), *Letters of Charles O'Conor of Belangare* (Washington, DC, 1988), pp 7, 151–2, 172–3, 235, 400–1.

Yet, for all the apparent similarities with the genealogical antiquarianism of Britain and continental Europe, the concern carried distinct resonances in Ireland.[15] Long and continuous settlement by particular families in England and Wales, proclaimed in the funerary monuments, surviving benefactions (both sacred and secular), and in mansions, contrasted with Ireland, where battered fragments attested to the overthrow of the once mighty. Thomas Dineley, associated with the lord lieutenant Ormond, treated his Irish itinerary much as he had his journey through the borderlands between Wales and England.[16] A second rambler, also in a viceregal entourage, Paul Rycaut, brought knowledge of the Levant to his view of Ireland.[17] Neither Dineley's nor Rycaut's tours of Ireland was published. It is unclear why they compiled them: in the hope that they might be printed or simply from the habit of systematizing otherwise diffuse impressions? Denton's caustic observation that, 'Ireland hath ever been accounted a land of wonders, tho the greatest wonder seems to be that such incredible stories should be told and so firmly believed as they are by the Irish to this day', may imply another motive. Precise reporting should replace romancing.[18]

Outside influences of a different sort strengthened the upsurge of interest during the 1680s in the topography and antiquities of Ireland. William Molyneux, the dynamo behind the Dublin Philosophical Society, oversaw initiatives to write a collaborative natural and civil history. Based on the county, this was again conceived as an Irish dimension of an English venture – Moses Pitt's Atlas. Questionnaires adopted the format of the English prototypes.[19] Results varied, according to the zeal and abilities of the locally-based contributors, and remained unpublished. The compilers memorialized incumbent property owners. In most cases, it was not the antiquity of their residence in the area that was advertised, but recent achievements, usually subsumed under the explanatory heading of improvements. Once more, the axiom of Davies, Boate and even Petty, the English as bringers of all benefits, was restated.[20]

The Dublin Philosophical Society emphasized the utility of its enquiries and activities. Its members experimented and speculated. They also observed,

---

15 T. Barnard, 'Aristocratic values in the careers of the dukes of Ormonde' in T. Barnard and Jane Fenlon (eds), *The dukes of Ormonde, 1610–1745*, pp 161–76; Barnard, *New anatomy*, pp 44–5. **16** The original is NLI, MS 392, printed in E.P. Shirley and F.E. Ball, 'Extracts from the journal of Thomas Dineley, esq, giving some account of Ireland in the reign of Charles II', *JRSAI*, iv (1856–7), pp 143–6, 170–88; v (1858–9), pp 22–32, 55–6; vii (1862–3), pp 38–52, 103–9, 320–38; viii (1864–6), pp 40–8, 268–90, 425–46; ix (1867), pp 73–91, 176–202; xliii (1913), pp 275–309. See also *The account of the official progress of His Grace Henry the first duke of Beaufort … through Wales in 1684* (London, 1888); Thomas Dingley, *History from marble*, ed. J.G. Nichols, Camden Society, 2 vols (London, 1867–8). **17** P. Melvin (ed.), 'Sir Paul Rycaut's memoranda and letters from Ireland, 1682–1687', *Analecta Hibernica*, 27 (1972), pp 125–82; S.P. Anderson, *An English consult in Turkey: Paul Rycaut at Smyrna, 1667–1678* (Oxford, 1989). **18** Denton, *Perambulation of Cumberland*, p. 515. **19** Hoppen, *Common scientist*, pp 155–6, 196–7, 200–1. **20** The bulk of the surviving returns are in TCD, MS 883.

and what interested them were natural and humanly-made phenomena. Moreover, the erstwhile director of the club, William Molyneux, embroiled himself in legal and political controversy. In order to argue his case about the constitutional position of the kingdom of Ireland *vis à vis* England, he familiarized himself with medieval records. Access to and interpretation of these arcane materials were assisted by a circle of learned kindred and acquaintances in Dublin.[21] Concurrently, his brother, Thomas Molyneux, became fascinated by the numerous remnants of Viking occupation. Danesforts were identified, often speculatively and inaccurately, across the island.[22] These relics were of interest in themselves as tangible reminders of an otherwise vanished era. They also fed theories about the Danish origins of distinctive features in Ireland, such as Christianity. In addition, the Vikings as conquerors and occupiers served as a surrogate for later interlopers. It was sometimes more diplomatic to expatiate on Danish misrule than on English.

Under such impulses, interest in the Irish past was deepening. In addition, and inspired partly by English examples, the tentative researches extended from the written to the wrought, built and wrecked. In Ireland, each quest encountered additional difficulties. A dislocated history of recent war, conquest and occupation destroyed much. Moreover, the conquerors justified their presence in terms of a cultural superiority. The corollary was that remnants of the indigenous culture associated with Gaelic and Catholic habits were to be eradicated because associated with inferiority and defiance. Only slowly did some suggest that materials from those worlds had merits that transcended the political confusion. An early instance was the Book of Kells. Pillaged during the Confederate Wars of the 1640s, it was deposited in Trinity College Dublin, the sole seminary of Protestant Ireland.[23] Although the most spectacular donation, it was not the only one. Since its foundation in 1592, the university had accumulated manuscripts and books, both purposefully and haphazardly. This early tradition strengthened under two provosts, Narcissus Marsh and Robert Huntington. Much of their interest focussed on booty salvaged or looted from the Near East. They hoped that these documents would aid the accurate elucidation of the Bible and early Christianity.[24] The provosts' catholic interests encompassed

---

[21] W. Molyneux to Bp A. Dopping, 14 Dec. 1696, Armagh Public Library, Dopping MSS 3/325; J.G. Simms, *William Molyneux of Dublin*, ed. P.H. Kelly (Dublin, 1982), pp 102–18. [22] Hoppen, *The common scientist*, pp 196–7; T. Molyneux, 'A discourse concerning the Danish mounts, forts and towers in Ireland' in G. Boate, *A natural history of Ireland in three parts* (Dublin, ?1726). Also S. Waring to T. Molyneux, 28 Jan. 1707[8], in BL, Egerton MS 1785, vol II, f. 144. [23] T.C. Barnard, *Cromwellian Ireland: English government and reform in Ireland, 1649–1660* (Oxford, 1975), p. 211; W. O'Sullivan, 'The donor of the Book of Kells', *IHS*, xi (1958–9), pp 5–7. [24] A.P. Coudert, S. Hutton, R.H. Popkin and G.M. Weiner (eds), *Judaeo-Christian intellectual culture in the seventeenth century: a celebration of the library of Narcissus*

material that might also illumine the earliest centuries of Christianity within Ireland. So it was collected and studied. It was part of an atmosphere of almost indiscriminate curiosity that led Marsh, Huntington and many of their favourite pupils to establish the Dublin Philosophical Society. Alongside that society, there flourished within Trinity College a theological discussion group, in which many of the same dons and clerics participated.[25] Neither the discussions nor the assembling of documents in the college library were innocent of confessional competitiveness. Marsh believed that facility in the Irish language might be acquired or improved by immersion in the ancient texts. Those thus equipped could then spread gospel truths among Irish speakers. Such hopes proved illusory. Nevertheless, a fillip was given to the saving and study of what had been in danger of destruction as a relic of superstition and primitivism.

III

First the imminence and then the actuality of war stopped the meetings of the Philosophical Society in Dublin, and dispersed its members. In 1692, its gatherings were resumed. Activists again received and reported curiosities. The wartime emergency had driven many from Ireland. The temporary exiles strengthened contacts with the erudite and inquisitive elsewhere. Once back in Ireland, they often directed their reports to the Royal Society of London, in whose *Philosophical Transactions* some were printed. The learned in Ireland knew of the advances that were being made in historical knowledge and method. Publications that might serve as models or stimuli, such as Montfauçon, were acquired and read. So, too, were the serials issued by the Royal Society of London and its counterparts in Paris and Leipzig. Correspondence and travel also kept the earnest in touch with innovations and controversies. It was, therefore, inevitable that the acrimonious exchanges between ancients and moderns should echo through Irish studies and closets, and maybe coffee-houses and taverns. Nevertheless, any recovery of lost knowledge in Ireland must differ from the quest in Britain or continental Europe. In particular, Ireland, having never been occupied by the Romans – except in the

---

Marsh (1638–1713), Archives internationales d'histoire des idées, 163 (Dordrecht, Boston and London, 1999); W. Horbury, 'Christian Hebraism in the mirror of Marsh's collection' in M. McCarthy and A. Simmons (eds), *The making of Marsh's Library: learning, politics and religion in Ireland, 1650–1750* (Dublin, 2004), pp 256–79. **25** T.C. Barnard, 'Enforcing the Reformation in Ireland, 1660–1704' in C. Gribben and E. Boran (eds), *Enforcing Reformation in Scotland and Ireland, 1550–1700* (Aldershot, 2006), pp 212–13.

1 Poor Clare nun and Franciscan friar from John Stevens, *Monasticon Hibernicum*, 1722

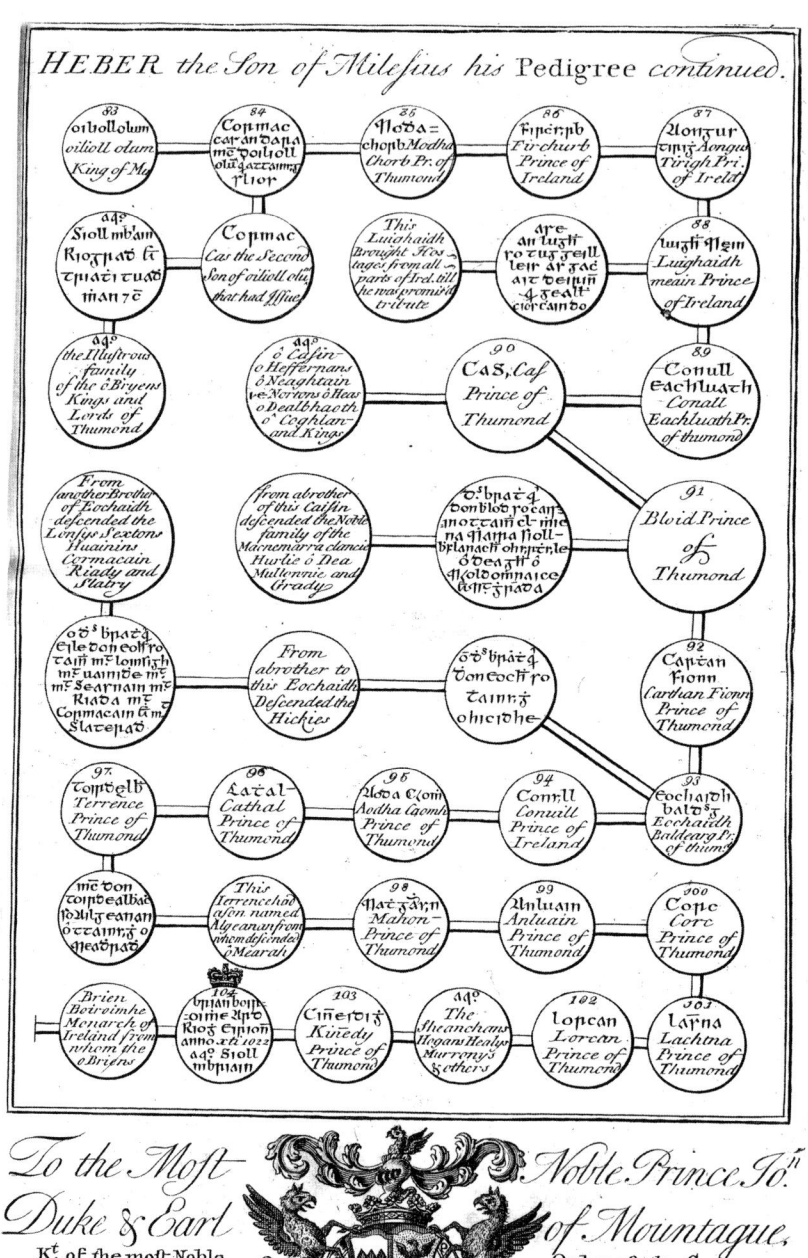

2 Arms of John, duke of Montagu, from Geoffrey Keating, *The general history of Ireland*, 1723

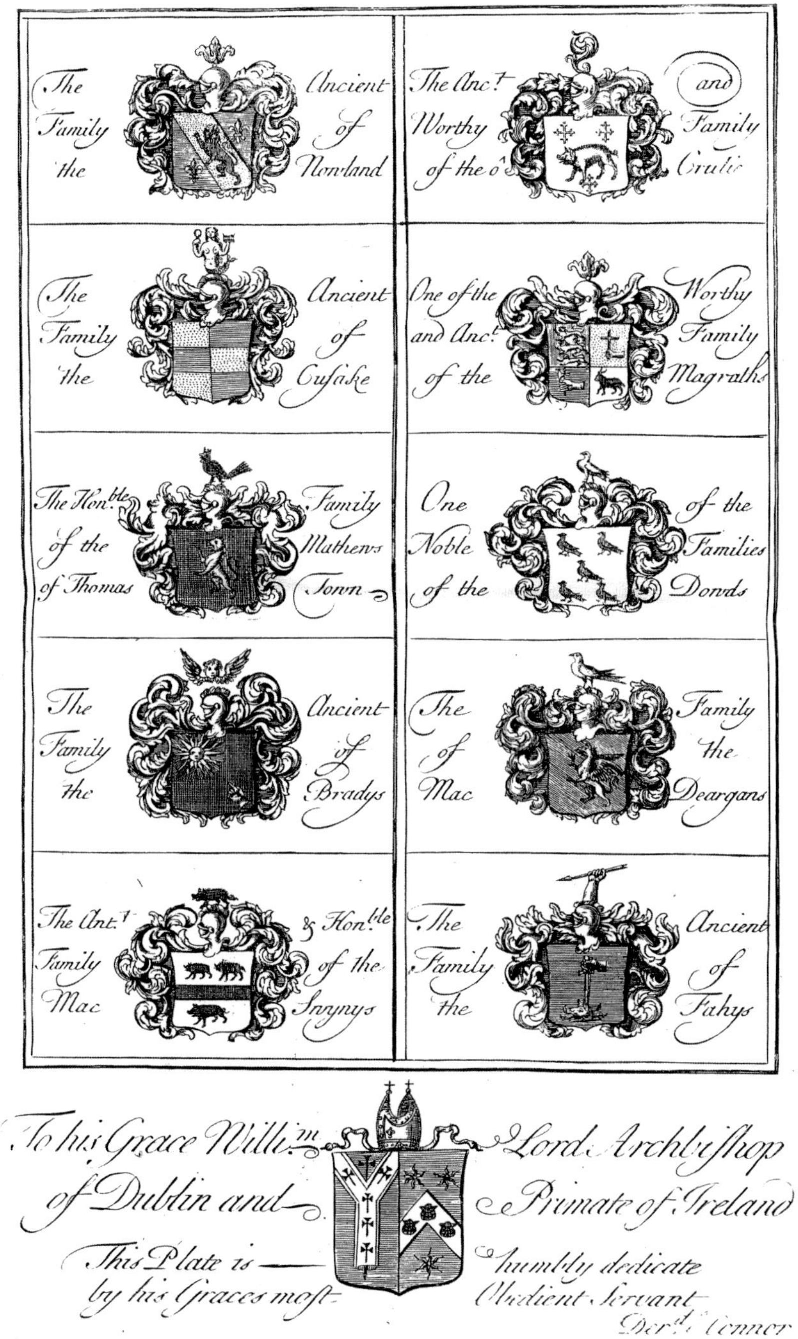

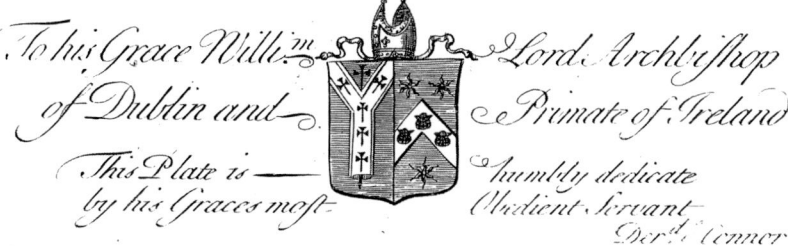

3 Arms of William King, archbishop of Dublin, from Geoffrey Keating, *The general history of Ireland*, 1723

4 Engraving after a drawing by Jonas Blaymires of Limerick cathedral from Walter Harris (ed.), *The works of Sir James Ware*, 1746

5 Jonas Blaymires, west end of St Patrick's Cathedral, Dublin, c.1737

6 Engraved portrait of Charles Smith, apothecary and historian, *c*.1750

7 Watercolour view from Burton House, County Cork, 1737

8 Kanturk Castle, County Cork, engraving, *c*.1740

9 Liscarroll Castle, County Cork, engraving, *c.*1740

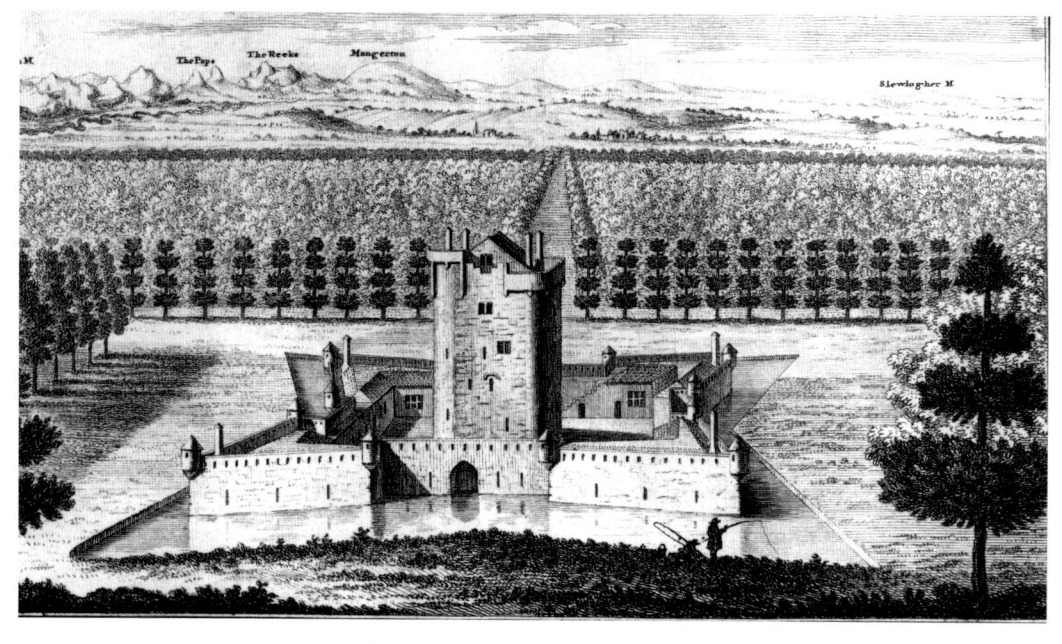

10 W.H. Toms, engraving of Lohort Castle, *c*.1738

11 Lohort Castle, County Cork, watercolour, *c.*1840

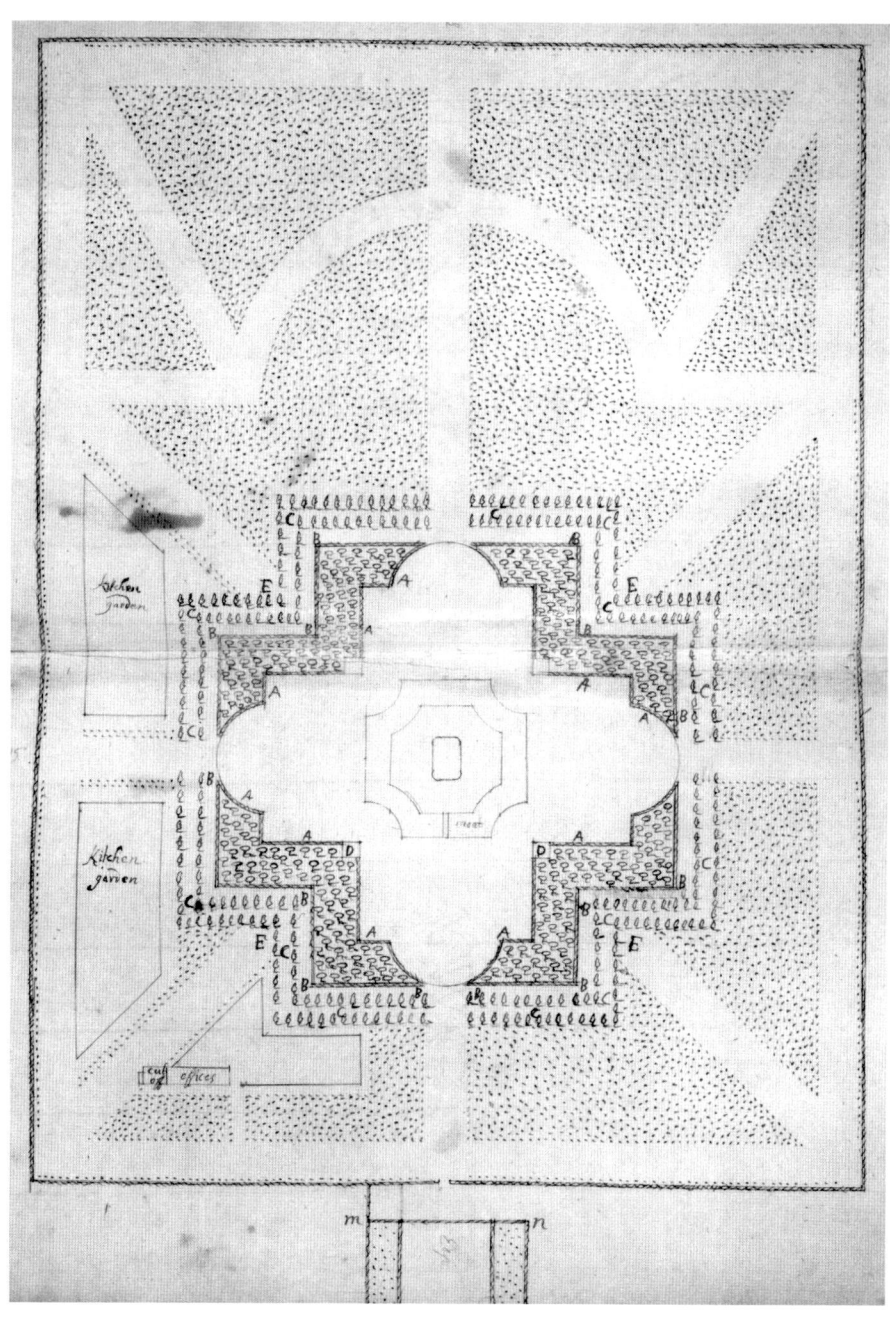

12 Charles Hay, garden design for Lohort, County Cork, 1742–3

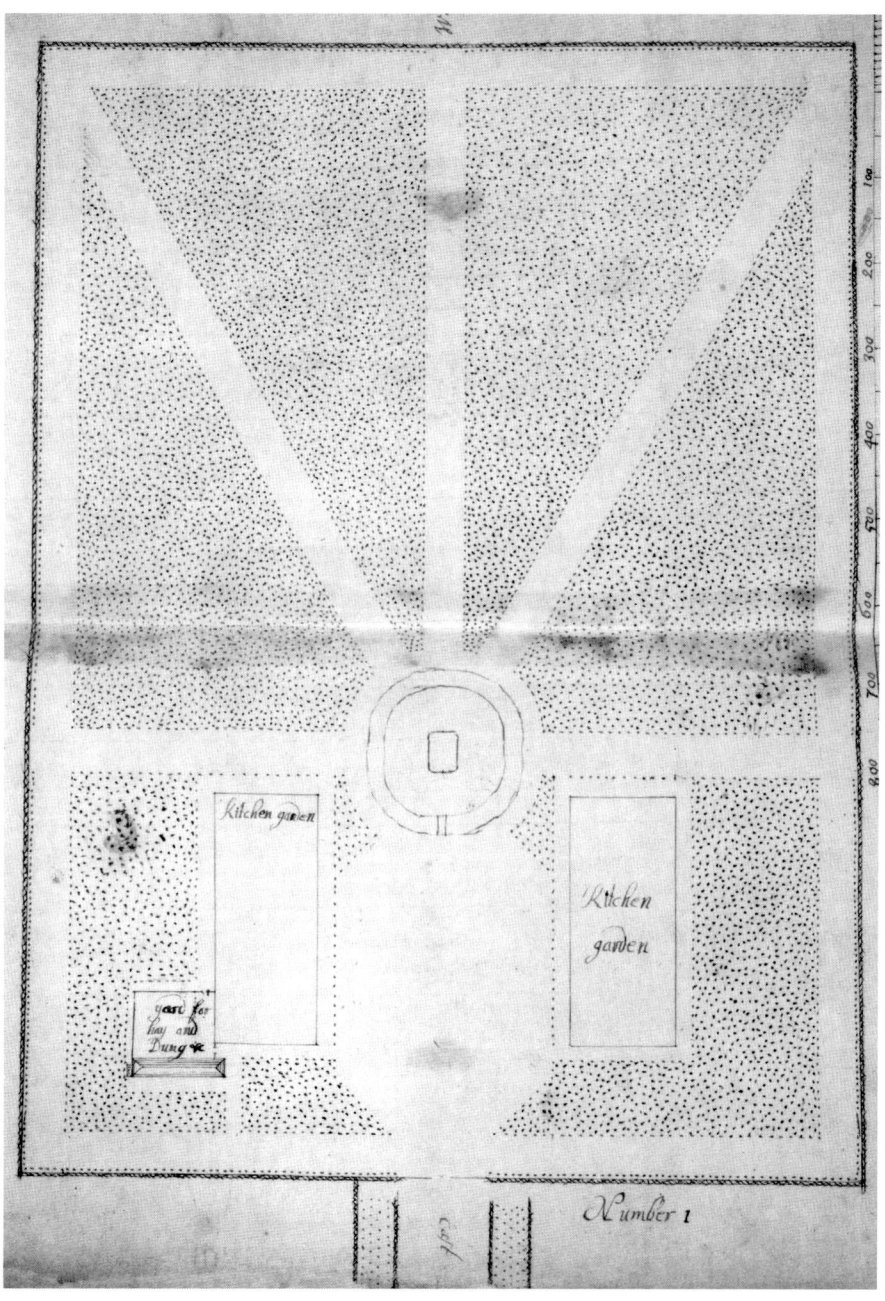

13 Charles Hay, garden design for Lohort, County Cork, 1742–3

14 Pair of chairs painted with armorials of earl and countess of Egmont, 1756

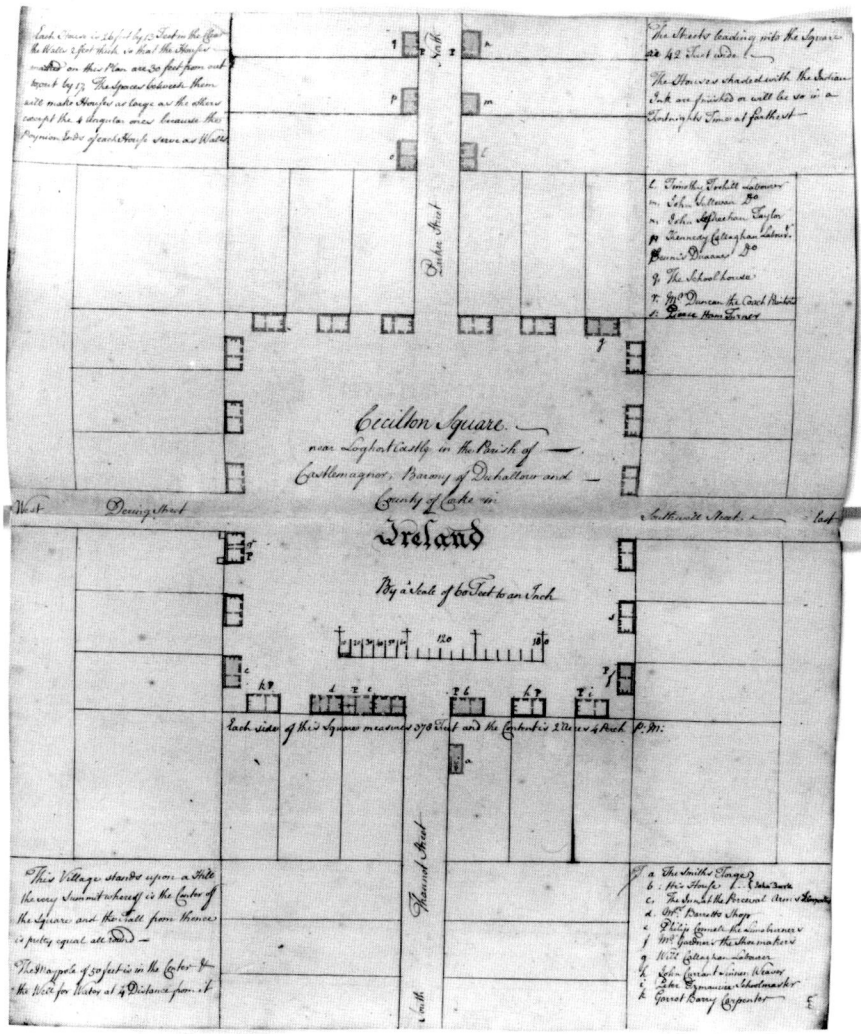

15 Plan of Cecilstown, County Cork, 1748

16 Engraving after Jonathan Fisher, canal between the lakes of Killarney, 1770

minds of a few imaginative speculators – offered a different progression from barbarity to civilization and then to decline. Other stages, intensely scrutinized by scholars elsewhere – druids, Danes, Saxons and Norman conquest – were relevant to the Irish experience. However, the raw and unfinished nature of Irish developments, with Catholicism remaining the confession professed by the majority of the population, imperfect assimilation to the institutional and cultural norms of lowland Britain, and the slow and uneven pace of economic invigoration gave the Irish past stranger meanings. Yet, it shared with the histories of its nearest neighbour, a value for investigators. If properly probed and reconstructed, the chronicle of Ireland offered lessons. According to stance – Catholic or Protestant, English or Irish – it furnished examples worthy of imitation (its early embrace of Christianity and the achievements that had turned it into a haven for the holy and scholarly) or of repudiation (nomadic ways, communal not individual rights to property, superstition and ignorance).

The fresh upheavals stimulated new histories. William King, a Church of Ireland dignitary in Dublin, having seen and suffered during the Jacobite ascendancy, justified the actions of the Irish Protestants in changing their ruler. With a clerical superior, Anthony Dopping, bishop of Meath, he had collected eyewitness testimonies to the humiliations and privations of the Protestants. If necessary these would have been incorporated into a record of sufferings to rival those that had appeared after 1641. Another clergyman narrated the military events.[26] The elder Sir Richard Cox pleaded for the restoration of English control over Ireland with an impressive parade of precedents. Cox was frank in urging William III and Mary II not to relinquish Ireland, 'one of the most considerable branches of your mighty empire'. Subordination to England brought to Ireland the 'streams of justice, peace, civility, riches and all other improvements', so that the Irish were 'beholding to God for being conquered'.[27]

King, soon to be consecrated bishop of Derry and then translated to the archbishopric of Dublin, hoped for a fuller treatment of the natural and civil histories of his country. In the event, King was too busy himself to undertake the task. Accordingly he looked to others, only to be disappointed. Another Church of Ireland bishop appealed for a 'good' natural history, believing that Ireland offered 'more curious matter to a wise observer' than any other European country.[28] In 1722, Archbishop King concluded that no one was inter-

---

[26] George Warter Story, *A true and impartial history of the most material occurrences n the kingdom of Ireland during the last two years* (London, 1691). [27] Cox, *Hibernia Anglicana*, i, sig. A3–[A3v]. [28] [F. Hutchinson], *A letter to a member of parliament, concerning the imploying and providing for the poor* (Dublin, 1723),

ested in making collections relevant to the natural history of Ireland, since the prevailing impulse was 'to make money and let the world jog on'.[29] Despite an almost habitual pessimism, King built up a formidable library, principally of printed books, but also some manuscripts, as a resource for any who attempted the daunting job of a history. Also, he paid for the transcription of medieval manuscripts. Some of the commissions had immediate and local functions: to assist the various legal battles that King waged against any who encroached on his jurisdictions as archbishop or sought to subjugate the kingdom of Ireland to that of England. Yet, his collecting contributed to an atmosphere in which, for whatever reason, relics from the past were cherished. Furthermore, King, who survived until 1729, retained the outlook that he had acquired first as an undergraduate and fellow of Trinity after the Restoration and then as a member of the Philosophical Society during the 1680s. Wide-ranging curiosity went with sharp awareness of intellectual currents beyond Ireland and anger at the constant disparagement of Ireland.

The 'entire and coherent history of Ireland', desired by the elder Cox and King, did not appear in their life-times.[30] A look at the attempts to supply the want simultaneously encourages and cautions. On the one hand, much activity was directed into producing and publishing such an authoritative account; on the other, several would-be chroniclers were frustrated. The frustrations arose only partly from the scale and complexity of the task. Despite professions to the contrary, interest among subscribers and readers was small. Five projects – those of Roderick O'Flaherty, John Stevens, Dermod O'Connor, Anthony Raymond and Walter Harris – reveal the varying fortunes of the historians.

IV

O'Flaherty, from the learned castes of Gaelic Ireland, had grasped the propitious moment of the Catholic James VII and II's accession in 1685 to offer a history favourable to the indigenous inhabitants, their religion and culture. *Ogygia* skilfully annexed the Stuart monarch to this world by elaborating on his ancient Irish lineage. Written in Latin, *Ogygia* was aimed at a British and European as well as an Irish readership. The bright morning of 1685 soon gave way to the defeat, exile and death of King James. O'Flaherty's fortunes sank with those of many of his co-religionists in Ireland. Undaunted, he hoped still to contribute 'to the illustrating of affairs conducing to the public good of my country'.

[29] Abp W. King to H. Maule, 26 May 1722, TCD, MS 750/7, 118. [30] Cox, *Hibernia Anglicana*, i, sig [b1v]–[b2].

Moreover, *Ogygia* had been challenged by other writers, eager to assert either Scottish or English over Irish claims to cultural primacy. O'Flaherty was impatient to answer the 'many late writers', such as Sir George Mackenzie, Edward Stillingfleet, William Nicolson and Dr Chamberlain, who, 'as strangers not well versed in this country have, some out of ignorance, others out of designed malice and envy committed most apparent gross solecisms by mispresentments of matters'.[31]

In the 1680s, O'Flaherty's learning had brought him to the notice of the Protestant virtuosi of the Philosophical Society. In particular, the Molyneux brothers had assisted him. Respect for O'Flaherty survived into the next generation. Samuel Molyneux, the son of William Molyneux and the reviver of the Society in Queen Anne's reign, took up O'Flaherty. Samuel Molyneux tried to organize the publication of O'Flaherty's sequel in which he vindicated *Ogygia*. O'Flaherty had himself negotiated with Cornelius Carter in Dublin to publish the book by subscription. Carter had proposed subscriptions of 30 pence each. Ninety-six would suffice to buy the paper for the publication. Carter would then divide the profits equally with the author. In 1708, O'Flaherty planned to go ahead on this basis, and sought the help of Molyneux in Dublin in having the subscription appeal printed.[32] Evidently, Molyneux scrutinized the costings more critically. Soon he reported to O'Flaherty that, in order to print the vindication in the same format as his adversary, Sir George Mackenzie's work, an advance of £26 would be required. Molyneux believed in the venture, reassuring O'Flaherty that he needed to sell only 100 copies to break even. However, he advised O'Flaherty to change his printer from Carter to Aaron Rhames. The ostensible reason was that Rhames would be cheaper, but Carter's predilections for Catholicism and unsavoury reputation may also have been factors.[33] In the altered political climate, Molyneux advised O'Flaherty to drop his original but now tactless dedication to King James. Since Molyneux was seeking subscribers among those in Dublin for the meeting of parliament, such circumspection was wise. For his part, O'Flaherty hoped to sign up subscribers at the Galway assizes. In the spring of 1708, he had to confess that he had failed to find any, and the case had not altered a year later. O'Flaherty voiced a forlorn hope that the proposal 'sped better with you there [in Dublin] among the gentry of the nation'.[34] It did not. Despite Molyneux's offer of a subsidy of £5, *Ogygia vindi-*

---

[31] R. O'Flaherty to S. Molyneux, 9 April 1708, Molyneux letter book, Southampton City Archives, D/M, 2/1. [32] R. O'Flaherty to S. Molyneux, 17 Dec. 1708, ibid. [33] M. Pollard, *A dictionary of members of the Dublin book trade* (London, 2000), pp 92–3. [34] R.O'Flaherty to S. Molyneux, undated [April 1708], 21 June 1709, Molyneux letter book, Southampton City Archives, D/M, 2/1.

cated waited until 1775 to be published. Then it benefited from the renewed controversies over the early history of Ireland and Britain, and had as its midwife Charles O'Conor, a passionate and judicious champion of Catholic Ireland. Moreover, interest in the earlier history of Ireland was now translated into a willingness of subscribers to advance money for the publication. Two hundred and sixty, rather than the ninety-six wanted by Molyneux, subscribed.[35] In turn, the readiness to pay towards the publication reflected more than just a larger group interested in Irish antiquities. The impresario, O'Conor, and the publisher, Faulkner, traded on O'Flaherty's connections in Connacht, and particularly with the port of Galway. By the 1770s, Galway and its environs contained prospering merchants and professionals willing to pay to be associated with the project.[36]

O'Flaherty's failure reminds both of the obstacles that faced the Catholic Irish in having writings published in Ireland and of a restricted demand for substantial books in early eighteenth-century Ireland. The original *Ogygia* had been published in London. Copies were shipped into Dublin, where they sold for a hefty seven shillings.[37] The price, coupled with the Latin of the text, put it beyond most. A slightly more cheering variant of O'Flaherty's experience is offered by an English Catholic interested in Irish antiquities. During 1722 *Monasticon Hibernicum* was published in London. It was a considerably expanded, although still modest, translation of a work in French by Alemand, issued originally at Paris in 1690. Its first composition and publication suggest opportunism at the moment when French armies were fighting in Ireland and hopes rose that Ireland would be returned to Catholicism. The translator who enlarged Alemand's text claimed he did so because the work was unknown in London and hard to come by even in Paris. Also, it was suggested that Alemand had few sources to hand, so that it was 'so easy to improve upon the undertakings of others, especially when they are foreigners'. The improver was John Stevens. A versatile writer, who translated Spanish as well as French works, Stevens had come to Ireland in the retinue of the lord lieutenant Clarendon in 1685. He returned to Ireland to fight during the Jacobite war. His interest in Iberian affairs probably began with his father who was part of the household of Charles II's Portuguese queen, Catherine of

---

[35] M. Keon to C. O'Conor, 20 Feb. 1772; C. Vallancey to same, 25 April 1772, 23 Jan. 1773; costs for printing *The Ogygia vindicated*, RIA, MS B i 2. [36] R. O'Flaherty, *The Ogygia vindicated*, ed. C. O'Conor (Dublin, 1775). [37] J. Malone, bill with Sergeant Dillon, 10 Oct. 1685, NLI, MS 40,898/4, item 2. Cf. *A catalogue of a choice collection of valuable books, in most faculties ... the library of the Reverend Doctor Nicholas Knight, deceased* ([Dublin, 1732[3]), item 40; *A catalogue of a choice collection of valuable books, in most faculties ... the library of the judicious Sir Henry Echlin* ([Dublin, 1730]), p. 52; *A catalogue of books, to be sold by the administrators of the Reverend John Nicolson ... being the library of the late Arch-Bishop of Cashel* (n.p, 1729), p. 43.

Braganza. Thanks to Clarendon and his kin, John Stevens was introduced into the circles that looked to the Ormondes. Indeed, in 1703, he dedicated a translation of a life of the Emperor Charles V to the second duke of Ormonde.[38] He retained links with Ireland that enabled him to persuade a few there to subscribe to his account of *Ancient abbeys*.[39] Having supplemented Dugdale's *Monasticon Anglicanum*, which included some Irish material, Stevens was emboldened to issue a separate volume on Ireland. It followed naturally from his English investigations. However, since Stevens was a professional writer, even (to some) a Grub Street hack, he may have aimed to profit from the rising English curiosity about Ireland. The wrangles over the recent Declaratory Act, which placed Ireland more firmly under British control, had once more brought Ireland to wider attention.

Stevens was a Catholic and keen to detail the many religious houses in Ireland. He also reviewed the evidence, culled primarily from Colgan, Ware and Ussher, which justified Ireland being known as 'the island of saints'. It was the uninterrupted history of monastic orders that Stevens wanted to tell. Where Alemand had tried to cash in on the upsurge of interest in Ireland within France, Stevens had in view an English readership. 'Ireland being so great an ornament of the imperial crown of England, every part of its history and antiquities is as proper reading for the English, as even for the natives of that country'. These differed little from the terms in which Cox had prefaced *Hibernia Anglicana*. Stevens, to add to the appeal of his work – essentially a gazetteer of religious houses organized county by county and by the several religious orders – had plates inserted. They illustrated the habits of the principal religious orders, both female and male, which, he contended, would be unfamiliar to most. By this device, the continuing – illegal – presence of the regular clergy was emphasized, and this at the moment when further draconian penalties against Catholic priests were in debate.[40] In addition, anxious Protestants in Ireland were scheming to have printed weighty volumes of anti-Catholic polemic. Many of the same subjects – larger versions of the same plates? – reappeared in the second volume of Harris's enlarged version of Ware in 1745.[41] The attractions of *Monasticon Hibernicum* were further increased by the inclusion of Herman Moll's 'pocket companion to the roads of Ireland'.[42]

38 D.F. Prudencio de Sandoval, *The history of Charles the Vth*, translated by J. Stevens (London, 1703), sig. [A2]. **39** M. Murphy, 'A Jacobite antiquary in Grub street: Captain John Stevens (*c*.1662–1726)', *Recusant History*, 24 (1998–9), pp 437–54; R.H. Murray (ed.), *The journal of John Stevens, 1689–1691* (Oxford, 1912), pp ix–xvii. **40** [John Stevens], *Monasticon Hibernicum* (London, 1722). Cf. S.J. Connolly, *Religion, law and power: the making of Protestant Ireland, 1660–1760* (Oxford, 1992), pp 282–9. **41** *The whole works of Sir James Ware concerning Ireland revised and improved*, 3 vols (Dublin, 1745), in BL, Egerton MS 1785, ii, ff. 273–318v. **42** It was dedicated to the earl of Cadogan, a soldier born in Ireland. The map would reappear in the 1723 London and 1726 Westminster editions of Keating.

How widely Steven's octavo *Monasticon* circulated in Ireland is impossible gauge. In 1726 and 1728 it was included in the extensive stock lists of two Dublin booksellers.[43] It was another in the Dublin trade, Ebenezer Rider, who prolonged its life by popularizing it. In 1735, Rider started a newspaper, the *Country Journal*. It was to appear three times weekly. Pride of place was given to the serialization of *Monasticon Hibernicum*. Rider introduced it with a tag: 'history being the most useful; as well as the most delightful branch of knowledge'. He hoped 'everybody will be pleased with this part of the history of Ireland'.[44] The practice of serializing histories, often in abridged forms, was common in English newspapers. It widened access to what had often started as costly and bulky publications.[45] Readers of the *Country Journal* were also treated to the reproduction of one of the engravings from the original *Monasticon*: of a habited Augustinian monk.[46]

Rider's resurrection of Stevens' text can be related to three of the Rider's other publishing enterprises and to the more general scene in Ireland. The year after the *Country Journal* began, Rider tested the water for the most ambitious historical publication to be projected in Dublin, an English edition of Sir James Ware's collected works. Rider published Ware's account of Irish writers, grandiloquently puffed as 'collected not only from the best books, and most authentic accounts we have in print, but also from several curious manuscripts and archives in the most eminent libraries in Europe'. Ware's name was not used, although, in essence, the compilation was a digest of his biographical dictionary.[47] Rider also plucked Sarah Butler's *Irish tales* from the shadows into which they had retreated, with a new edition. Finally, he issued an edition – the fifth – of Charles Forman's *A defence of the courage, honour and loyalty of the Irish nation*.[48] Forman, like Stevens, Butler and Harris, showed the Irish in flattering lights. Indeed, the *Irish writers* was prefaced with an intention to scotch the belief current in London, that 'Irishmen, coward and blockhead were synonymous terms, and signified one and the same thing'.[49] Rider's *Journal* survived for less than a year. Nevertheless his list, if inspired by commercial calculations, suggested an increased appetite for sympathetic versions of the Irish past.

---

43 *A catalogue of books newly arrived from England, Holland and France. To be sold by Smiths and Bruce, booksellers on the Blind-Key* (Dublin, 1726), p. 63; *A catalogue of books, sold by John Smith and William Smith, booksellers on the Blind-Key* (Dublin, 1728), p. 77.   **44** *The Country Journal*, 1/1, 5 June 1735.   **45** Sweet, *Antiquaries*, p. 311.   **46** *The Country Journal*, 1/5, 13 June 1735.   **47** *Historiographorum Aliorumque Scriptorum Hiberniae Commentarium: or, a history of the Irish writers* (Dublin, 1736).   **48** *The Country Journal*, 1 /2 and 3, 7 and 9 June 1735. For Forman, involved in the controversy over the Irish college in Paris, Collège des Lombards, *Oxford DNB* and L. Chambers, 'Rivalry and reform in the Irish College, Paris, 1676–1775' in T. O'Connor and M.A. Lyons (eds), *Irish communities in early modern Europe* (Dublin, 2006), pp 110–11.   **49** *Historiographorum Aliorumque Scriptorum Hiberniae Commentarium*, sig. A2.

Butler's *Irish tales* was first published in London in 1716. It is remarkable for several reasons. Ostensibly by a woman, it is a precocious historical novel.[50] Set during the Viking occupation of Ireland, it culminates in the battle of Clontarf of 1014. The message of the ending was unequivocal: 'thus did that warlike and ancient kingdom free itself from the tyranny of its mortal enemy the Danes'.[51] The topic of oppressive rule by invaders had a clear application to the present-day kingdom. Topicality was underscored by the date of first publication – in the aftermath of the Jacobite rising – and the author's name. 'Butler', whether genuine or fictitious, could only invoke the head of the tribe, James Butler, second duke of Ormonde, who had just fled into continental exile rather than renounce his allegiance to the deposed Stuarts. *Irish tales* also upheld Ireland's claim to have been an island of saints and scholars: 'Once Ireland was esteemed one of the principal nations in Europe for piety and learning'. The claim was buttressed by reference to the, as yet unpublished, history of Geoffrey Keating. Other points about *Irish tales* serve only to intensify its oddities. It purported to be a posthumous publication, the task of seeing it through the press in London undertaken by Charles Gildon, a Grub-Street hack with a Catholic past like Stevens, and a more unsavoury reputation.[52]

Someone in 1716 judged that there was a market for *Irish tales* linked with the resonant Butler name. Others, first in London and then in Dublin, believed it was worth reissuing in 1727 and 1735. An opportunist publisher in 1727 amended the title from 'Irish' to 'Milesian'.[53] Any explicit Jacobite agenda is improbable, but a hope of cashing in on rising interest in Ireland among both the dispossessed and the aggrieved incumbents can be argued. 'Milesian' and 'Ogygian' were adjectives that alerted the knowing to a distinctive approach to the Irish past.[54] By 1735, Rider may also have hoped that the Butler authorship would enchant buyers. Thomas Carte's massive three volume life of the head of the Butlers, the first duke of Ormond, had just been published and was attract-

50 P. Baines and P. Rogers, *Edmund Curll, bookseller* (Oxford, 2007), pp 50–1, regard 'Sarah Butler' as a pseudonym. Cf. R. Loeber and M. Loeber, *A guide to Irish fiction, 1650–1900* (Dublin, 2006), p. 218. 51 Sarah Butler, *Irish tales: or, Instructive histories for the happy conduct of life* (London and Dublin, 1735), p. 66; Ian Campbell Ross, '"One of the principal nations in Europe": the representation of Ireland in Sarah Butler's *Irish Tales*', *18th-century Fiction*, 7 (1994), pp 1–16. 52 P. Rogers, *Hacks and dunces: Pope, Swift and Grub Street* (London, 1980), pp 35–6. 53 A mss note on the BL copy of the 1716 London issue (pressmark: 1607/4314) suggests a 1719 issue of *Milesian Tales*. It is included in *A catalogue of books to be sold by auction for the benefit of the poor* (Dublin, 1729), lot 365. 54 In 1743, subscriptions were invited for Charles O'Conor's 'Ogygian Tales', 'a curious collection of Irish fables, allegories and histories', by the writer who would emerge as the leading Catholic historian of the day. O'Conor's tales never appeared. T. Contarine to C. O'Conor, 13 May 1743, 17 June 1743, 9 Dec. 1743; R. D[igby] to same, 14 Dec. 1743, 24 Jan. 1743; M. Reilly to same, 10 April 1761, RIA, MS B i 1; *Proposals for printing by subscription Ogygian Tales* (Dublin, 1743), in ibid.; Ward, Wrynn and Ward (eds), *Letters of Charles O'Conor of Belanagare*, p. 506.

ing considerable notice in Ireland. Carte's compilation had its place among a group of apparently objective explorations of seventeenth-century Ireland, usually, as in the case of Carte, through a major actor. However, these weighty publications of the 1730s and early 1740s did not create the interest, but merely cashed in on it.[55] More influential in originating the taste for learned disquisitions was the realisation in 1723 of a long-held ambition to publish Keating's *Foras Feasa ar Éirinn*.

Written in the 1630s, Keating's *Foras Feasa ar Éirinn* proved enduringly popular, as is attested by the numbers of hand-written copies that have survived. Later seventeenth-century writers, such as Peter Walsh and Cox, made use of it. In 1717, its essence was incorporated into Hugh MacCurtin's *Brief discourse in vindication of the antiquity of Ireland*. Striking, too, is the reference to Keating, still in manuscript, in Butler's *Irish tales*. The clearest signal of Keating's status as the text that could resolve the contestation between Catholic and Protestant historians in favour of the former comes with its publication in a lavish folio edition in 1723. So important was Keating's work thought to be that rivalry developed to be first with a printed version. The race went to a team in London. The text was translated and elaborated by an Irish exile, Dermod O'Connor.[56]

What has been pieced together of the genesis of and reactions to the publication presents numerous mysteries. At the same time, some strong themes emerge. Thanks to its wide circulation in manuscript, Keating's *History* had gained a totemic significance. Something of its reputation can be detected in a note in Richard Gough's copy of the 1723 Dublin printing. He and six other prominent English antiquaries had paid their subscriptions in February 1722. Another copy was ordered for the nascent London Antiquaries Society. Gough had been impressed by O'Connor, who showed him 'a fine vellum MS of it [Keating's History] in Irish'.[57] Gough, unversed in Irish, clearly fell for O'Connor's patter and for the prop that he had to hand.

The intrinsic merit of Keating's *History* might suffice to explain why it, rather than other projected treatments, was published with brassy fanfares. Keating confuted the disparagement of Ireland and its aboriginals begun by Giraldus Cambrensis in the thirteenth century and intensified in the seventeenth century with the accounts by English and Protestant partisans. Defenders of Catholic Ireland believed that if Keating could be brought to a wider readership, through

---

55 T.C. Barnard, '"Parlour entertainment in an evening": histories of the 1640s' in M. Ó Siochrú (ed.), *Kingdoms in crisis: Ireland in the 1640s* (Dublin, 2001), pp 20–43. 56 D. Ó Catháin, 'Dermod O'Connor, translator of Keating', *ECI*, ii (1987), pp 68–87; H.R. Plomer, 'Dermo'd O'Connor and Keating's *History*', *Irish Booklover*, iii (1912), pp 125–7. 57 Bodleian Library, Oxford: pressmark, Gough Ireland, 139. The other subscribers included Gale, Le Neve and Stukeley.

translation into English and print, then it would scotch critics. As well as the appeal of Keating's interpretation, the success of the publishing venture owed much to O'Connor's literary entrepreneurship. His skill in this regard is attested by Gough's response. Further evidence is afforded by the subscribers who were persuaded to underwrite first Dublin and then London editions of 1723. How far this success in attracting subscriptions can be attributed to O'Connor rather than to his backers and collaborators is uncertain. A rival asserted that O'Connor, known to be skilled in the Irish language and to be translating Keating, received 'a considerable offer for his history' which enticed him from Dublin to London.[58] Behind the successive London printings was the bookseller, Benjamin Creake.[59] The allegation that Creake initiated the project is undermined when he denounced O'Connor. Creake claimed that he had agreed to publish the work so long as O'Connor met the production costs. This was a common arrangement, but the physical ambition of *The History* imposed a heavy financial burden on O'Connor and the other promoters. To raise the cash, another customary method was used: subscription. It worked, as the printed lists of subscribers show. However, if Creake is to be believed, O'Connor embezzled the money that had been advanced: £300 in all. Creake was left to pay the printers, engravers and paper-suppliers. At least he had the printed sheets. The hope of recouping costs probably inspired him to revive sales by new issues, notably that of 1726 with a Westminster imprint and those of 1732 and 1738.

The proposed publication had been advertised in 1721. As well as agents in London, booksellers in Bath, Oxford, Cambridge and Edinburgh collected subscriptions.[60] England and Scotland yielded advances, but striking too is the ability to tap into the Irish market. Groups with strong local or familial ties can be discerned among the subscribers. For the 1723 Dublin issue there are clusters: for example, from Kilkenny and Carlow. Those from Kilkenny included the mayor (Richard Phillips), four aldermen and several other residents. The Carlow subscribers may have interested themselves because the dedicatee of the work, Lord Inchiquin, owned extensive property in and around the borough. The former Irish lord chancellor, the high Tory Sir Constantine Phipps, together with his son and son-in-law, subscribed. But so too did Hugh Smith, a hatter. In contrast, only three women were named as subscribers.

---

58 *A letter from Dr Anthony Raymond, to my Lord Inchiquin, giving some account of the monarchs and ancient state of Ireland* (Dublin, 1725), p. 4. **59** For Creake, see H.R. Plomer, G.H. Bushnell and E.R. McC. Dix, *A dictionary of the printers and booksellers who were at work in England, Scotland and Ireland from 1726 to 1775* (Oxford, 1932), p. 66. **60** *Proposals for printing by subscription the General History of Ireland*, printed in full in A. Harrison, *The Dean's friend: Anthony Raymond 1675–1726, Jonathan Swift and the Irish language* (Dublin, 1999), pp 108–10.

Oddly, the London edition of 1723 succeeded better than the Dublin issue. Perhaps the greatest coup was to have the prince of Wales and the archbishop of Canterbury head the subscribers. Further publicity occurred when a copy of the newly published text was presented to Prince George.[61] Somehow O'Connor and his associates had directed the curiosity or vanity of the elevated into a shabby world of scribes, hackney writers, translators and opportunists some of whom hailed from Ireland and knew its indigenous language. One from these circles involved in the Keating project was the versatile but disreputable John Toland.[62] Among the subscribers, but harder to detect, were the expatriate Irish, Catholics and Protestant, respectable and substantial, beavering in the professions and trades of London. One client from this group for O'Connor's services as scribe and antiquary was Maurice O'Connor, a successful lawyer. Counsellor O'Connor subsequently returned to Ireland, where he patronized Carolan and was friendly with Charles O'Conor of Belanagare.[63]

Equally striking are the many in Ireland persuaded to pay in advance for the English edition. Its format was more lavish. Unlike the Dublin printing, its title page was embellished with Irish type; the same type was also employed to print a two-page poem. Conspicuous are several O'Connors and O'Carrolls. It could be that the controversy excited by the original edition stirred interest in Ireland. But just how O'Connor – or Creake – managed to exploit it, and why he had not done so before, when the Dublin printing was on the stocks cannot be explained. There appear to be links, based on place, kinship or acquaintance, from which the project benefited, but which are now irretrievable. Who, for instance, had alerted Count O'Dwyer in Naples to the desirability of acquiring the book? Major Thady O'Mulrian, soldiering in O'Dwyer's regiment in southern Italy, also subscribed. So, too, did an Irish merchant in Seville, Edward Mulkiran.

Publicity, with the glamour of the prince of Wales's patronage, was the best advertisement. It is tempting to assign a role in effecting the introduction to the prince's secretary, Samuel Molyneux. Before he removed permanently from Ireland, Molyneux (as has been detailed) resurrected the Dublin Philosophical Society and worked – unavailingly – for the publication of O'Flaherty's *Ogygia Vindicated*. However, the likelihood that Molyneux did act as an intermediary is reduced by his not being listed as a subscriber to the *History*.[64] More innova-

---

61 Harrison, *The Dean's friend*, p. 118, citing C.E. Doble et al. (eds), *The remarks and collections of Thomas Hearne*, 11 vols (Oxford, 1885–1921), viii, p. 83. A map in the London edition – of the travels of the Scythians before they reached Ireland – was dedicated to the prince. **62** *A letter from Dr Anthony Raymond, to my Lord Inchiquin*, p. 4; D. Berman and A. Harrison, 'John Toland and Keating's *History of Ireland* (1723)', *Donegal Annual* (1984), pp 25–9. **63** Ó Catháin, 'Dermod O'Connor, translator of Keating', p. 75. **64** Nor is any copy of Keating apparently listed in *A catalogue of the library of the Honble*

tive as a tactic to entrap subscribers was the format of the volume. Indeed, it was central to the venture. O'Connor and his collaborators decided to endow the work with visual allure. Such an appeal was conspicuously lacking in O'Flaherty, for example. The embellishments of Keating were tenuously connected with his text. Keating had followed one well-established convention of the annalists in including often speculative genealogies for Brian Boru and other of the high kings. These were offered in tabular form through engraved plates. Ingeniously, the subscribers were linked to this world. Not only did they have their names printed in the conventional fashion; their coats of arms were shown in seven preliminary engraved pages in the 1723 Dublin edition. Two hundred and eighty-two of the 447 subscribers were gratified by this means. Some may not have been armigerous before. The device was calculated to conjure money from the vain as well as the bookish. Through an acquaintance in Dublin, Aaron Crossly, O'Connor would have known that the publication of Crossly's Irish peerage was in train. It too was calculated to pander to pride in lineage and standing.

The inclusion of the heraldic achievements in the preliminary pages of the printed Keating complicated and raised the costs of producing the volume. O'Connor himself had skills as a herald painter, so he may have drawn the blazons himself. But they had also to be engraved. The London version adopted a variant. Subscribers could pay extra to have full-page engravings of their heraldic achievements inserted. Only the grand, almost all peers, agreed and paid. Some might believe that their ancestry linked them with the contents of the tome. The translation was dedicated astutely to William O'Brien, earl of Inchiquin, who was represented as the lineal descendant of Brian Boru.[65] Most of the others who bought into O'Connor's scheme had Irish peerages and estates (Cork and Burlington, Orrery and Mountrath) or connections (the duke of Grafton, the lord lieutenant), but the willingness of the duke of Montagu to pay to be included is not so easily explained. In London it was considerably easier than in Dublin to arrange for the drawings to be made and engraved. The work was organized by Thomas Cluer, an experienced entrepreneur with a cheap print warehouse in London, and probably performed by Thomas Cobb.[66] These insertions, irrelevant to Keating's text, turned this edition into a vanity publication. Yet, it was a strange vanity in the minds of the English and anglicized to wish to push back a pedigree into the murky annals of Ireland. At the

Samuel Molyneux, Deceas'd ... ([London, 1730]) or in the remnant of Molyneux's collection inventoried in City of Southampton Public Libraries Committee, *A catalogue of the Pitt Collection* (Southampton, 1964). **65** See too *A letter from Dr Anthony Raymond, to my Lord Inchiquin*. **66** On Cluer, see T. Clayton, *The English print, 1688–1802* (New Haven and London, 1997), pp 7–8.

very least, it indicated that in aristocratic circles, Ireland was no longer synonymous with barbarism.[67]

The laggard scholars overtaken by O'Connor smarted at his triumph, and accused him of tricks. One aggrieved but knowledgeable contemporary dismissed the book as 'an heap of insipid, ill-digested fables, and the rest but very indifferently handled'.[68] Another, of the next generation, struggling to offer his own account of the Irish past, ridiculed O'Connor's effort as 'the grossest imposition that has ever yet been obtruded on a learned age'.[69] Such repining was predictable. Even so, the reasons for O'Connor's success in getting into print and his competitors' failure are worth pondering. As has been suggested already, the renown of Keating's history was so great that whoever printed it first would earn enviable dividends. O'Connor and his collaborators secured subscriptions from the educated and venerable of Old Ireland. They had the contacts and the gift of the gab to do this. At the same time, it is notable that this constituency, although weakened and uprooted, was prepared to pay towards the publications of 1723 and 1726. Some at least, prospering in London and continental Europe, had the wherewithal to buy into a scheme for which, thanks to O'Connor's silver tongue, they had a yearning.[70]

Others bent on gaining subventions for their proposed histories either showed less commercial acumen or belonged to smaller worlds. Among contemporary projects, that of the Church of Ireland vicar of Trim, Anthony Raymond, most closely resembled O'Connor's. Raymond, indeed, planning his own version of Keating, employed O'Connor as interpreter and transcriber. Raymond was understandably outraged when his employee absconded (he said) with materials that properly belonged to Raymond. Without O'Connor's linguistic and palaeographical skills, Raymond floundered. Furthermore, when he sought subscribers for his forthcoming history, he signed up only 168. They were drawn disproportionately from his fellow clergy. Undoubtedly, clergymen formed a large component among book-buyers and readers in early eighteenth-century Ireland. But for a subscription to succeed, it needed to broaden its appeal.[71]

---

67 Ó Catháin, 'Dermod O'Connor, translator of Keating', pp 75–9.   68 [T. O'Sullevane], *Memoirs of the right honourable the marquis of Clanricarde* (London, 1722), pp cxxiii–cxxv.   69 Charles O'Conor, *Dissertations on the history of Ireland* (Dublin, 1753), p. x; Ward, Wrynn and Ward (eds), *Letters of Charles O'Conor of Belanagare*, p. 263.   70 There is little overlap with the predominantly Catholic subscribers to C. Nary, *A new history of the world* (Dublin, 1720).   71 A. Raymond, *An account of Dr Keting's History of Ireland* (Dublin, 1723); A. Carpenter and A. Harrison, 'Swift, Raymond and a legacy', *Swift Studies*, i (1986), pp 57–60; B. Cunningham, *The world of Geoffrey Keating: history, myth and religion* (Dublin, 2000), pp 218–24; Harrison, *The Dean's friend*, pp 105–48; Ó Catháin, 'Dermod O'Connor', pp 68–87; [O'Sullevane], *Memoirs of Clanricarde*, pp cxxix–cxxv. The list of subscribers in *The Dean's friend* is incomplete; the full list from RIA, MS 24 G 11, pp 335–8 is printed in A. Harrison, *Ag Cruinniú Meala* (Dublin, 1988), p. 146. At least sixty-two were clergymen; maybe more, as there is uncertainty about the

O'Connor, reviled as a trickster, was also resented because his translation ruined the market for any other. His bungled version did not communicate Keating's message clearly and accurately. It had been hoped that a more widely available Keating would alter attitudes in and towards Ireland. Owing to the perceived and sometimes magnified inadequacies of the O'Connor rendering, this did not happen. Those still hopeful that histories could correct misconceptions and mistreatment had to shift their ground. In particular, they came to focus on countering the extremely damaging evidence of Catholic savagery alleged to be evident in and immediately after 1641. Proponents of the view that atrocities had occurred during the 1640s focused their attention on the depositions relating to the violence, many of which had passed into the collection of the bishop of Clogher, John Stearne, and then (in 1741) to Trinity College in Dublin. Catholics needed to chip away the thick varnish that obscured the authentic picture. At the same time as specific episodes obsessed the protagonists, attention was still paid to setting those episodes in plausible contexts.

Anthony Raymond had laboured to bring forth a history. Later in the eighteenth century, another clerical antiquary concluded that Raymond 'composed a great deal on the fabulous history of Ireland without throwing one ray of light on the subject'.[72] Raymond was too young to have been affected by the vibrant atmosphere of Trinity College and the Dublin Philosophical Society before 1688, but was washed by the second wave of enthusiasm in the 1690s. Later he was encouraged by Archbishop King. Raymond's animus against O'Connor contradicts the idea of happy cooperation among all engaged in the common endeavour of elucidating earlier Ireland.

Much less is known of the other two attempts during the 1720s to compile Irish histories. Yet they do contribute to the powerful impression of a quickening interest in scholarship. John Conry advertised his intention to publish an Irish history in 1724. Raymond knew of it and Bishop Nicolson duly paid his subscription.[73] Conry was reported by Nicolson to own the best surviving collection of Irish manuscripts, and indeed lent one to the bishop.[74] It has been suggested that Conry may have descended from the family of hereditary historians, the O'Mulconrys, and was accorded the accolade of 'Lord Chronologer of Ireland'.[75] Any prospect of bringing out Conry's history was scotched by O'Connor's version of Keating.

status of the fellows of Trinity. 72 E. Ledwich to J.C. Walker, 5 Sep. 1796, TCD, MS 1761/4, f.23. 73 W. Nicolson, account book, s.d. 4 March 1723[4], Cumbria County Library, Carlisle; Harrison, *The Dean's friend*, pp 140–2. 74 W. Nicolson, account book, s.d. 27 Nov. 1723, Cumbria County Library, Carlisle; cf. H. Maule to W. Wake, 4 June 1722, Christ Church, Wake MS 14/23; W. Nicolson, *Irish historical library*, pp 243–6. 75 Harrison, *The Dean's friend*, pp 141–2.

A second scheme was promoted by the Revd Nicholas Knight. A Dublin incumbent, Knight had been educated at Trinity College during the 1680s, when the successive provosts, Marsh and Huntington, encouraged historical researches. Tastes and approaches inculcated then may have come to belated fruition. In 1726, Knight issued a printed appeal for information 'to give the world a distinct view of the ancient and present state of Ireland'. He proposed to divide the material into four parts: natural history; ancient history; ancient religion; and the present condition of the kingdom. His acknowledged models were Ware, Ussher, Heylin, Chamberlain's surveys of contemporary Britain and Ireland[76] and Crossly's recently published *Peerage*.[77] The deficiencies of the last work emboldened Knight to invite peers to send corrections to Eliphal Dobson, who was presumably to publish the completed history. Knight also intended to bring the information in Ware's *Bishops* up to date. Knight's plan ended with his own death.[78] His scheme for amplifying Ware resembled what Harris would soon do; a more accurate peerage was undertaken by John Lodge during the 1740s.

It was hard for any individual to amass the materials necessary for such histories. Knight optimistically requested correspondents to communicate to him 'rarities of art and nature'. He, like several contemporaries with antiquarian leanings, collected an impressive library, including manuscripts (copies more often than originals).[79] About 1300 titles that had belonged to Knight were auctioned in 1733. Numerous historical works furnished models of how the subject had been tackled in other places or offered information about Ireland. Two recent publications looked especially relevant: Alemand's 'Monastical History of Ireland', lately published in Stevens' expanded version in London; and *Modern history, or, The present state of all nations*, published in Dublin in twelve volumes in 1724.[80] But also there were the staples of Ware, Ussher, Spenser, Hamner, Cox, Keating (in the 1723 translation for which Knight had subscribed), Borlase, Temple, Peter Walsh, O'Flaherty, and Thomas Massingham. In addition, Knight had picked up motley manuscripts. One was a copy of Sir Henry Piers's 'chorographical description of the county of Westmeath', which had been prepared in 1682 for William Molyneux's attempt to chart the antiquities and topography of Irish counties.[81] The same survey, maybe even the copy recently owned by Knight, interested another Church of Ireland cleric, James

---

[76] *Hiberniae Notitia* (Dublin, 1723) modelled on Chamberlain's regular compilations. [77] A. Crosly, *The peerage of Ireland* (Dublin, 1725). [78] *Whereas the Revd Nicholas Knight, D.D., has undertaken to give the world a distinct view of the ancient and present state of Ireland, in IV parts* (Dublin, 1726) [copy in Marsh's Library, Dublin]; *Alumni Dublinenses*, p. 473. [79] *A catalogue of a choice collection of valuable books, in most faculties ... the library of the Reverend Doctor Nicholas Knight, deceased* ([Dublin, 1732[3]). [80] Ibid., lots 24 and 901. [81] Ibid., lot 43.

Smythe, whose elder brother had recently established himself in Westmeath. Smythe felt that 'such a monument of antiquity would be valuable in a family'. Accordingly, he proposed that it be transcribed 'fairly and correctly'.[82] By this means, it could circulate although not published. Only in 1786 was it printed.[83] A second of Knight's manuscripts, relating to the rebellious earls of Essex and Southampton at the close of Elizabeth I's reign, seems to have been acquired first by a Dublin priest, then by a bookseller and late in the eighteenth century by William Ousley, an avid Irish collector. Ousley, initially an indiscriminate picker-up of Irish trifles, came to focus on Persian manuscripts and artefacts.[84]

Knight's was an ambitious – indeed over-ambitious – project, reminiscent of the cooperation promoted by Hartlib's friends in the 1650s and Molyneux in the 1680s. Efforts to render such a project practicable by assigning a county to an individual would be resumed in the 1730s. Whatever Knight achieved before he died has yet to be identified. Yet, his library shows how the dedicated could form a comprehensive collection of all that was relevant. But it was the very inadequacy of what was available in print that spurred on the inquisitive. Manuscripts, unpublished, often indecipherable and even unlocated, came to be venerated as more likely than jejune printed tracts to resolve the many mysteries and controversies of earlier centuries. Also, awareness of the potential of artefacts was dawning. These currents united in the next grandiose publishing scheme.

V

Catholics, hopeful of popularizing historical interpretations kinder to their forbears, placed perhaps extravagant faith in what a printed Keating would do. O'Connor's bungling queered the pitch for at least a generation. Even without the appearance of Keating, Protestants in Ireland were unhappy about a spate of publications, especially in the 1730s, that tilted against and sometimes unhorsed their favourite jockeys, notably Temple. Reissuing Temple was one strategy to counter the revisionists. Published first in London in 1646, his history of the Irish rebellion was reprinted several times, on some occasions surreptitiously.[85] The heat that the work could still generate was indicated by a note in a copy of the edition printed in Dublin in 1724. This alleged that it had been reprinted because 'very scarce', since the previous year, the duke of Liria (son of

---

82 Revd James Smythe to W. Smythe, 11 Nov. 1732, 5 Dec. 1732, NLI, formerly PC 449. **83** C. Vallancey (ed.), *Collectanea de rebus Hibernicis*, i (Dublin, 1786); P. Lefroy, 'Luke White, 1740–1824, printer and publisher of Piers' "Westmeath"', *Meath Archaeological and Historical Society*, vii (1980–1), pp 77–9. **84** Commonplace book of W. Ousley, NLI, MS 5905, p. 202. **85** London, 1646, 1679, 1746; Dublin, 1698, 1713, 1716, 1724; Cork, 1766.

the duke of Berwick and therefore grandson of James VII and II) had bought up all available copies 'to destroy the memory of so black a period'.[86] Similarly, the Quaker owner of a copy of the 1716 reprint of Temple annotated (probably in the 1730s) its title with 'too much forgotten by the Protestants of Ireland'.[87] This copy of Temple was conveniently bound with the 1713 Dublin edition of Archbishop King's *State of the Protestants*.[88] These authors concentrated on the turbulent seventeenth century.[89] However, both partisans and the disinterested longed for an authoritative account of earlier times. Their counterpart to Keating was another venerated writer from the seventeenth century, Sir James Ware. So, just as there was feverish activity to have Keating reprinted, there were similar efforts to translate and supplement Ware's principal compositions.

Ware's seemingly innocent antiquarianism in compiling long lists of the successive bishops of Irish dioceses and in detailing all writings of those born or working in Ireland was not devoid of didacticism. By showing the antiquity of Christianity and the strength of civility in the island, Ware might rout those who denigrated Ireland. But, like other Protestants, he was also fabricating a lengthy pedigree for the Church of Ireland and buffing up the reputations of many generations of immigrants from Britain. Ware's *Works* bulk large among the Irish historical publications in the eighteenth century. His *Antiquities* had been published first in 1654.[90] They contrasted tellingly with the overt utilitarianism of the contemporary Hartlib group, just as Ware's own royalism set him apart from willing collaborators with the usurpers of the 1650s such as Lawrence and Petty. Ware's reputation originated with his writings and his voluminous collections, especially of manuscripts. His standing grew steadily thereafter. A son exploited his parent's name and some of his library to write and publish inflammatory anti-Catholic tracts.[91] However, the full exploitation of Ware's learning began in Queen Anne's reign. Dublin, by far the largest and most affluent of the incorporated boroughs, instead of commissioning its own history opted in 1705 to subsidize (to the tune of £60) a re-issue of Ware.[92] It

---

86 J. Temple, *The Irish rebellion* (Dublin, 1724), copy in Marsh's Library, G.4.3.39. Liria subscribed to the 1723 edition of Keating's *History*. 87 J. Temple, *The Irish rebellion* (Dublin, 1716). This issue also contained King's *State of the Protestants*. 88 A copy of this double-decker fetched four shillings in 1746. *A catalogue of books, being the library of the late Philip Ridgate, esq., LL.D.* ([Dublin], 1746]), p. 17. 89 For the genre, see T.C. Barnard, '1641: a bibliographical essay' in B. Mac Cuarta (ed.), *Ulster 1641: aspects of a rising* (Belfast, 1993), pp 173–86, 223–8; T.C. Barnard, 'The uses of 23 October 1641 and Irish Protestant celebrations', *EHR*, 106 (1991), pp 889–920, reprinted in Barnard, *Ascents and descents*, pp 111–42. 90 J. Ware, *De Hibernia & Antiquitatibus eius, Disquisitiones* (London, 1654). 91 Robert Ware, *The examination of Faithful Commin Dominic fryar* ([?Dublin], 1679); R. Ware, *The reformation of the Church of Ireland* (Dublin, 1681); [R. Ware], *Foxes and fire-brands* (London, 1689); R. Ware, *Pope Joan* (London, 1689); W. Harris, *The history and antiquities of the city of Dublin* (Dublin, 1766), sig. [A2v]. 92 J. Ware, *The history*

was padded with lists of current office-holders, including mayors and sheriffs of the capital, which increased its attraction to Dublin ratepayers.[93] Soon, the 1705 edition was dwarfed by a scheme of Walter Harris.

Harris undoubtedly hoped to make money. But profit was not his sole motive in organizing a greatly amplified edition of Ware's works. Harris married into the Ware family, which, by the 1720s, was prominent in professional and affluent Dublin.[94] Marriage did not bring him any of Sir James Ware's own manuscripts. Indeed, many had left the island and entered the duke of Chandos's famed library. His bride did, however, give him a personal, almost proprietorial interest in the respected antiquary. In addition, Harris displayed ardour in defending and advancing the Protestant interest in Ireland. Civil and natural histories, based initially on the counties, were one tactic, inherited from the earlier promoters, but now – in the cases of Counties Down, Dublin, Cork, Kerry and Waterford – completed and published. Harris, like his precursors, recognized the necessity of collaboration. To this end, the interested were dragooned into the Physico-Historical Society, under whose auspices the local surveys appeared. He himself composed works in praise of the acknowledged founder of Protestant Ireland, William-Henry (more familiar as William III) and to trounce Catholic nay-sayers.[95] Another weapon in his armoury was Ware.

There were setbacks on the way to publication. The entrepreneurial Harris admitted this – one intended reprint had to be abandoned although subscriptions had been paid. His use of three different publishers for the three separate volumes also hinted at unhappy dealings.[96] Further troubles made him castigate the printer of another of his books.[97] The list of subscribers published in the second volume (in 1746) attests to the limited appeal of the work, or the limits of those to whom Harris could confidently apply. It is overwhelmingly a catalogue of worthies from the professions, clerical and lay, mostly living in Dublin. Of the 241 recorded subscribers, 102 were Church of Ireland clergymen. This was an even higher proportion than Raymond had attracted for his projected history. The subject matter of the volumes – succession lists of bishops and the

---

and antiquities of Ireland (London, 1705); J.T. Gilbert and R.M. Gilbert (eds), *Calendar of the ancient records of Dublin*, 16 vols (Dublin, 1889–1903), vi, p. 349. **93** Ware, *History and antiquities of Ireland*, sig. bbb[1v] –[bbb2v]. **94** Barnard, *Making the Grand Figure*, pp 221–2, 305–6, 338; Barnard, *New anatomy*, p. 48. **95** W. Harris, *Fiction unmasked* (Dublin, 1752); W. Harris, *A new history of the life and reign of William-Henry* (Dublin, 1747); E. Magennis, 'A "Beleaguered Protestant"? Walter Harris and the writing of *Fiction unmasked*', *ECI*, 13 (1998), pp 86–111. **96** In 1752, he advertised the three volumes as being still for sale – from him at his Clarendon Street address and from the leading booksellers, George Faulkner and Peter Wilson. He was now organizing subscriptions for another projected volume of *Hibernica*. W. Harris, *Fiction unmasked* (Dublin, 1752), advertisement, p [212]. **97** W. Harris, *Hibernica: Or, some antient pieces relating to Ireland* (Dublin, 1747), p. 147.

cathedral dignitaries – together with the illustrations were deliberately pitched towards these buyers. Many of the other subscribers were members with Harris of the Physico-Historical Society. This organization was crucial to the promotion both of the publication of Ware and of the series of county histories. It was to the president of the Society, Lord Newport, the lord chancellor, that Harris addressed his 'Essay on the defects of the histories of Ireland'.

The project had been preceded by another directed by Harris, for 'The genuine works' of Ware. Subscriptions had been collected, but no book appeared. Harris invited the earlier subscribers to transfer their investments to the new venture, which was announced early in 1739. The first volume, containing 170 sheets, was said to be printed already as far as page 304. The subscription was half a guinea, and the total price, £1 3s. 6d. An important attraction of the edition were the copper-plate engravings which accompanied it. They were to be issued separately, and would each cost an additional 4d. Bulky and expensive, the book expressed and catered to a growing feeling of patriotism among the Irish Protestants. Harris traded on the posthumous reputation of Ware, himself a member of a successful settler dynasty of the seventeenth century. Yet, Harris re-organized and greatly supplemented Ware's scanty original. He claimed to incorporate unpublished additions prepared by Ware himself that had come into Harris's own possession: a claim impossible to verify. The amount of fresh information to be added – 400 new articles –may explain the delay between the publication of the first and second volumes. In 1739, it was said that the second volume was in the press: it would have about 150 sheets and be illustrated with about thirty half-sheet copper-plates. It too could be reserved through subscribing half a guinea. The total cost would be £1 5s. In the event, the second volume was not published until 1746, and by a different publisher, Samuel Powell.[98] By then it had been further inflated so that 'The writers of Ireland' formed a separate and third volume. This instalment came out in 1746, from yet another printer, Alice Reilly.

Other evidence hints at Harris's opportunism and combativeness. Maybe, though, it was just those unlovable characteristics which enabled him to complete schemes mooted almost a century earlier. In parallel with bringing out *The works of Ware*, Harris oversaw – and indeed helped to write – the first published histories of Irish counties.[99] In conjunction with Cox, he adopted the tactic of Molyneux in the 1680s. Printed *Proposals* were circulated to the most promising counties in the hope that magistrates, grand jurors and other nota-

---

98 The imprint is 1745, but Harris's preface is dated 18 Jan. 1745[6]. **99** W. Harris, *The antient and present state of the county of Down* (Dublin, 1744); Harris, *The history and antiquities of the city of Dublin*.

bles gathered for the assizes would respond to the queries. The clergy of the established Church were also expected to assist. The information sought ranged over natural and humanly engineered features. As the publicity declared, all would contribute to full descriptions of 'the ancient and present state of the several counties of Ireland'.[1] That these enquiries were not simply backward-looking is demonstrated by the declaration of purpose from the Physico-Historical Society. Set up in 1744, with Harris as a leading force, it would oversee the collection, analysis and diffusion of the data.[2] The Society's professed aim 'is to procure proper collections for the natural and civil history of the several counties of this kingdom, whereby the many gross misrepresentations (a conscious or unconscious echo of O'Flaherty) it lies under may be removed, and a foundation laid for the improvement of the arts and sciences'. It was acknowledged that steps in these directions had already been taken under the auspices of the Dublin Society, chartered in 1733.[3]

The newer body was intended to complement, not to compete with, the senior society. Neither Harris nor Smith is recorded as a member of the Dublin Society. Among its distinctive contributions would be the survey of a variety of historical materials. Accordingly field-work would be combined with study of manuscripts, such as those of the 1641 depositions, recently deposited in Trinity College Dublin, and many formerly belonging to Sir James Ware that had been acquired by the duke of Chandos.[4] The directors of the Physico-Historical Society appreciated the importance of print in publicizing and sustaining its activities. Newspapers reported meetings; a brief account of its establishment and purposes was printed; the county histories were sponsored. Yet, like most of its predecessors, the society fell prey to the faddism of the smart. As early as 1747, there was worry that the society was in decline. One cause, it was thought, is 'the obscurity in which the society continues by not furnishing the public with such observations as might constantly be procured from persons of genius in this kingdom'. To remedy this, six-penny pamphlets of remarkable observations were proposed. 'Only such things as may be both interesting and instructive' were to be published.[5] It is arguable that the group suffered from the same problem that Harris encountered in his solo ventures. Just as writers in Ireland

---

1 Sir R. Cox to W. Harris, 3 and 17 Feb. 1740[1], k.I.II.14, Armagh; Minute book of the Physico-Historical Society, RIA, MS 24 E 28, s.d. 14 April 1744; Harris, *County of Down*, pp vi–xiv; *Proposals for collecting materials for publishing the antient and present state of the several counties of Ireland* ([Dublin], [1740]).
2 Harris, *Hibernica*, pp 136–7; M. Herity, 'The Physico- Historical Society and its precursor, "Hibernia", 1738–1752', *Studia Celtica Japonica*, 8 (1996), pp 65–85; E. Magennis, '"A land of milk and honey": the Physico-Historical Society, improvement and the surveys of mid-eighteenth-century Ireland', *PRIA*, 102, sect C (2002), pp 199–217. 3 RIA, MS 24 E 28, s.d. 4 Nov. 1745. 4 RIA, MS 24 E 28, s.d. 7, 15 and 28 May 1744, 1 Oct. 1744, 4 Feb. 1744[5], 10 Feb. 1745[6], 2 Feb. 1746[7]. 5 RIA, MS 24 E 28, s.d. 2 Feb. 1746[7].

bewailed how few would subscribe to, let alone buy, their works, so the fickle took up for a time and then dropped crazes like the Society. One disillusioned contemporary observed, 'it's more profitable to feed bullocks, wethers or the like active employments than muse on history, genealogies or such like exploded scribbling'.[6] At the same time, the communal endeavours were hampered by personal clashes. Harris fell out with Charles Smith, the member most active in completing the histories of Counties Waterford and Cork. Harris, claiming that he had contributed much material to the accounts, demanded the profits of half the edition. Colleagues urged Harris 'to make up the affair amicably', but he demurred. When Harris threatened to seek redress in the law courts, the Society had to impose a settlement. Harris's pursuit of his claim, together with the earlier promise from Cox that he would receive proper payment in any partnership, indicate a strong business sense, if not avarice.[7] Discord of this kind did not conduce to the realisation of an ambitious publishing programme.

Smith, an obscure apothecary from the Waterford port of Dungarvan, may have suffered from the social condescension as well as the irascibility of Harris. The latter, a graduate of Dublin University, was familiar with the Protestant élite of the capital. However, Harris knew the Irish provinces less. Smith subscribed to the expository and explanatory frameworks of the Protestants' cultural superiority that coursed through Harris's publications. At the same time, Smith traversed the terrain about which he later wrote. Better than the strident Harris, Smith combined the ancient and modern, the empirical and speculative.[8]

It is likely that Harris lost money on his own ambitious undertakings. Efforts were made to shift the unsold stock of *Ware* in the 1760s. Harris himself was indefatigable in searching for sponsorship. His self-appointed role as the historiographer for the Protestant interest in Ireland was eventually rewarded. In 1755, he petitioned parliament to fund the publication of a chronological history of Ireland. Thanks to the pleas of Harris's erstwhile collaborator, Sir Richard Cox, it was agreed to pay a maximum of £2,660 towards an edition of 750. Harris never completed the work, but himself received an annual pension of £100.[9] Moreover, his assertions about the importance of the documents that he had collected were believed. Again, the state intervened to buy the collection,

---

6 G. Dillon to C. O'Conor, 15 Dec. 1747, RIA, MS B i 1, 134–6.   **7** Sir R. Cox to W. Harris, 6 March 1740[1], Armagh; RIA, MS 24 E 28, s.d. 2, 9, 16 June 1746, 14 July 1746, 2 Feb. 1746[7].   **8** C. Smith to unknown, 10 June 1758, Royal Society of Arts, London, Guard Book 3/14; W. Fraher, 'Charles Smith, 1715–1762: pioneer of Irish topography', *Decies*, 53 (1997), pp 33–44. For less favourable opinions: M. Reilly to C. O'Conor, 6 June 1752, 16 Oct. 1755, RIA, MS B i 1; R. Ousley to Sir L. O'Brien, 7 April 1769, NLI, Inchiquin Mss, folder 2806.   **9** *Journals of the house of commons of the kingdom of Ireland* (Dublin, 1796), v, pp 233, 376; De Valera, 'Antiquarian and historical investigation', pp 80–3.

selling it to the Dublin Society as the fitting repository (the Physico-Historical Society having collapsed).[10]

Whether or not Harris exaggerated his losses, he did put into print three volumes of recondite and apparently accurate history. The edition of Ware entered scholarly libraries. Often owners inserted their own corrections and additions. Less sensational or partisan than Temple or King, through bulk alone it gained iconic status. Catholics were not so impressed, and questioned Harris's abilities and purposes. Charles O'Conor tartly commented that Harris 'has more mistakes than pages'.[11] The costs of producing the edition were considerably increased, but also its attractiveness, by the insertion of illustrations. This device, as has been seen, was adopted in *Monasticon Hibernicum* and the 1723 printings of Keating. It was also used by the Physico-Historical Society to add to the appeal of the histories of Cork and Waterford. However, Harris's scheme for plates in Ware surpassed any of the contemporary Irish ventures. The paradox of forwarding the improvement of Ireland through portraying the remnants of older civilizations was not lost on Harris and his illustrator. Plates were costly. They also caused further contentions: between Harris and the principal draughtsman who made the drawings from which the plates were engraved and printed.

In the first volume of Ware's *Works*, the cathedrals are depicted through engravings. Most of the plates were based on drawings made on the spot by Jonas Blaymires. This talented draughtsman had been despatched by Harris, not just to draw, but to stimulate interest in the project. Blaymires may not have been the most diplomatic publisher's representative.[12] In addition, he was seeking commissions for himself quite independent of whatever fee he was to be paid by Harris for his topographical views. Blaymires' encounters with the potentates who ruled over the provincial cathedrals – sometimes the bishop, sometimes the dean – revealed a general indifference to art and history among the clergy. Blaymires was an acute and amusing observer of both his animate and inanimate surroundings. Harris used his drawings but not his lively verbal descriptions of what he had seen. Yet, one owner of the published *Ware* was impressed enough by the insights of Blaymires to preserve his written account of drawing the nine churches of Clonmacnoise and the Romanesque cathedral at Clonfert in his copy.[13]

10 Minute book of the Dublin Society, s.d. 13 Aug. 1761, RDS; C. MacNeill, 'Harris: Collectanea de Rebus Hibernicis', *Analecta Hibernica*, vi (1934), pp 248–450. They are now NLI, MSS 1–19. **11** Ward, Wrynn and Ward (eds), *Letters of Charles O'Conor*, pp 38–9, 65–6, 113. **12** Generally on Blaymires, T.C. Barnard, 'St Patrick's cathedral in the age of Swift' in J. Crawford and R. Gillespie (eds), *The history of St Patrick's Cathedral, Dublin*, forthcoming; W.G. Strickland, *A dictionary of Irish artists*, 2 vols (Dublin, 1913), i, pp 68–9. **13** J. Blaymires to W. Harris, 7 Oct. 1738, preserved in J. Ware, *The whole works*, 2 vols (Dublin, 1764) in the office of the keeper of manuscripts, TCD.

Blaymires had a taste for the picturesque that verged on the romantic. It was certainly at variance with the frigid rationalism of the Church of Ireland prelates with whom he had to deal. At Killaloe, the bishop remonstrated that the artist had not done justice to the cathedral. Blaymires retorted that 'it is the exact portraiture of it', and asked, 'is it possible that I can draw a Venus from a broomstick'? In Cashel, the archbishop wanted Blaymires to delay until the modernization of the cathedral had been completed. Again, the draughtsman hoped that drawings could 'be taken before the alterations be made that the portraiture of the ancient building might still show what it was'. Bishops and deans commanded Blaymires to doctor his images. However, the scrupulosity of the antiquarian and the sensibility of the artist made him stick to his own preferences. At Cashel he was excited by the detail of Cormac's chapel as well as the dramatic situation of the church on the rock. At Kilkenny, Blaymires heard that the bishop wanted to demolish the round tower beside St Canice's. The illustrator's unusual aesthetic showed when he enthused over Holy Cross Abbey. He remembered that, 'the ivy upon several parts of the old walls has grown to a great height and it makes the whole to appear like a ruin in a wood, which affords a beautiful scene'.[14] Zealous improvers insisted on tidying the past, even its physical relics. But, bit by bit an insistence on accuracy, together with ideologies and aesthetics more appreciative of older attitudes, induced greater tolerance of the quirky survivals.

Dublin booksellers knew that the look of their wares could help sales. In 1742, it was proposed *An universal history* should be printed in eight folio volumes in Dublin. It was to include the same maps, cuts, copper plates as the London edition. 'engraven in the best manner, with improvements on the London edition'.[15] Even with these embellishments, it was predicted that the Dublin edition would cost half the price of the London original. Yet providing engraved illustrations of the quality in London printings taxed the talents and resources of operators in Ireland. Harris, for the first volume of Ware's *Works*, employed locals. For the second volume, however, eighteen engravings portraying members of different religious orders, both female and male, were inserted. Harris boasted that they were scraped 'by the best hands in Paris'.[16] These were the same images that had enlivened *Monasticon Hibernicum*. Harris conceded in his preface that 'the monastical state of Ireland' was not 'very acceptable to English readers'. To make it more palatable, he had re-ordered

---

[14] J. Blaymires to W. Harris, 19 and 30 Jan. 1738[9], 21 and 28 April 1739, 16 May 1739, 2 June 1739, Armagh Public Library, papers of the Physico-Historical Society, K.I.II.14. [15] Advertisement in *State letters of Orrery*, ii, p [446]. [16] *The works of Sir James Ware concerning Ireland revised and improved*, ii (Dublin, 1745[6]), preface.

Ware's original and added the illustrations. Were they designed to send *frissons* through nervous Protestants or simply seized upon as handy decorations in a grave tome?

Harris could claim to have improved Ware's slighter original. Towards the end of the century, one caustic but close reader alternated between admiring the edition as 'a great work', shrewdly calculated with its numerous anecdotes to sell well, and lamenting Harris's frequent interpolations of 'extraneous trash'.[17] Harris's liberties were justified by the uncertain state of his own finances and the service rendered to the larger Protestant interest in Ireland. Notwithstanding the considerable activity in exploring and describing Irish antiquities, authoritative information was hard to locate. In 1775, Gilbert White, the inquisitive parson from Selborne in Hampshire, bemoaned the absence of detailed studies of the mountains and fauna of Ireland. White did know that 'modern improvements in arts and agriculture' had occurred, thanks particularly to the judicious use of premiums administered by the Dublin Society. These advances were trumpeted in the county histories of Smith and Harris, and would soon supply the marrow of Arthur Young's printed *Tour*.[18] Nevertheless, White wanted an account of the manners of 'the wild natives, their superstitions, their prejudices, their sordid way of life'. Also, he imagined 'the noble castles and seats, the extensive and picturesque lakes and waterfalls, and the lofty stupendous mountains'. Ireland, it seemed, was to satisfy the growing taste for the primitive and romantic. The unimproved as much as improvements was worthy of notice.[19]

---

[17] M. Reilly to C. O'Conor, 18 Nov. 1749, 1 Oct. 1751, RIA, MS B i 1; E. Ledwich to H.T. Clements, 3 Dec. 1787, 13 July 1788, TCD, MSS 1461/2, ff 300–0v; 1461/3, f. 70. [18] A. Young, *A tour in Ireland*, 2 vols (Dublin, 1780). [19] Gilbert White, *The natural history of Selborne*, ed. W.S. Scott (London, 1962), p. 77.

CHAPTER FIVE

Improvement, imagination and antiquarianism in mid-eighteenth-century Ireland: the earls of Egmont and Lohort Castle, County Cork

A S HAS BEEN ARGUED, a zest for improvement gripped many in late-seventeenth- and eighteenth-century Ireland. Voluntary societies devoted to the task were formed; parliament voted funds for improving projects; individuals campaigned, chastised the lethargic and pushed themselves forward as improvers. Ardent improvers were often indifferent to, if not contemptuous of, relics from the past. The latter included social organization and primitive cultures which frustrated the full exploitation of the natural resources of the island. The belief that there were vast untapped riches led optimists in the 1650s and 1680s to survey the terrain accurately and apply the best techniques. Little in these attitudes and activities encouraged appreciation of unimproved landscapes or what survived from earlier eras. Ragged ruins were likely to be used to warn of the baleful impact of a superstitious and unreasonable religion as well as of the traits of the Gaelic Irish. Yet, the need to survey the kingdom minutely, often as a prelude to the confiscation and redistribution of property and to the more systematic use of natural assets, did cause older structures and curious features to be noted. In the minds of the zealous modernizers, the record was no more than a preliminary to condemning and razing the unwelcome reminders of previous and now discredited regimes.

Just as the desire in Ireland to implant fresh skills, develop new manufactures and to popularize more diversified crops was influenced by similar movements in England and Scotland, so there were signs in those neighbouring countries of a parallel impulse, which sometimes complemented and sometimes competed against the cult of improvement. This heralded a dawning awareness of the complexities and interest of allegedly dark ages, the productions of which had tended to be written off as superstitious and monkish. A symptom of the changing atmosphere was the rehabilitation of the term 'Gothic': from being entirely pejorative it was moving by the early eighteenth century into a friendlier light. Some now associated it with the robust independence of the Anglo-Saxons that had been corrupted and over-powered by the sinister insinuations of the Latins. The shifts in opinion were accompanied and accelerated by ingenious researches into and theorizing about the earlier inhabitants of England, Wales and Scotland.[1] Quickly enough the speculations and enquiries spread into Ireland. Identification and evaluation of the original inhabitants and first settlers generated controversy. These very disagreements stimulated closer study of the physical remains – in the shapes of manuscripts, artefacts and fragmentary buildings. In this overheated world of scholarship, the relics were valued as evidence that might solve the puzzles and as testimony to the accomplishment of previous generations.

An approach which did not instinctively dismiss the remnants from the centuries before 1689 at first sight looks to be the antithesis of the improving schemes that gained momentum from the same date. Yet, the relationship between the two – the one apparently backward-looking and the other assertively forward-thinking – was more complicated and less hostile than might be supposed, as the previous chapter has contended.[2] Here, an analysis of some projects on the estates of the Percevals in south Munster in the first half of the eighteenth century allows further nuances to be investigated.

II

The Percevals resembled other families, originating in England, which acquired large holdings during the Elizabethan and early-Stuart confiscations in Ireland. Through the profits of public office in Dublin, notably in the Court of Wards, they amassed substantial estates concentrated in the north of County Cork. They allied themselves by marriage and political cooperation with similar dynasties in Ireland, such as the Southwells. The Percevals, in common with their kindred and allies, although prominent and prospering in County Cork, never severed their connections with England. Indeed, the properties and links that they retained there were made more important by the disruptions of the 1640s and 1650s, and again during the alarms of James II's reign.[3] The Percevals,

1 C. Gerrard, *The patriot opposition to Walpole: politics, poetry and national myth* (Oxford, 1994), pp 108–49; S.J. Kliger, *The Goths in England: a study in seventeenth- and eighteenth-century thought* (Cambridge, MA, 1952); R.J. Smith, *The Gothic bequest: medieval institutions in British political thought* (Cambridge, 1986); G. Worsley, *Classical architecture in Britain: the heroic age* (New Haven and London, 1995), pp 175–95. 2 S. Piggott, *Ancient Britons and the antiquarian imagination* (London, 1989), pp 13–35; R. Sweet, *Antiquaries: the discovery of the past in eighteenth-century Britain* (London, 2004), pp 119–276. 3 Their earlier history can be traced in J. Adamson, 'Strafford's ghost: the British context of Viscount Lisle's lieutenancy of Ireland', in J.H. Ohlmeyer (ed.), *Ireland: from independence to occupation, 1641–1660* (Cambridge, 1995), pp 128–59; A. Clarke, *Prelude to Restoration in Ireland: the end of the Commonwealth, 1659–1660* (Cambridge, 1999), pp 176–7, 294–5, n. 11; D. Dickson, *Old world colony: south Munster, 1630–1830* (Cork, 2005), pp 11–12, 178–80, and figure 41; P. Little, *Lord Broghill and the Cromwellian Union with Ireland and Scotland* (Woodbridge, 2003), pp 26, 39, 40, 45, 49, 50, 201, 206; M. MacCarthy-Morrogh, *The Munster*

aware that the financial base of their position lay in Ireland, kept it in good repair. The heads of the family, advanced to the rank of baronets, were intermittently active in Ireland: they resided, both on the Cork estates and in Dublin. Also, they contributed to public life by sitting in parliament and serving on the Irish privy council. However, partly through the accidents of premature deaths and partly through the temperaments of successive heads of the family, the participation in Irish affairs was sporadic. In consequence, the Percevals evolved from Irish Protestant notables to Anglo-Irish grandees, only occasionally resident in Ireland. Like the senior line of the Boyles, earls of Cork and Burlington, the Pettys and the Southwells, the Percevals became absentees. Rare descents onto their Irish lands might mask but could not disguise the transformation.

Sir John Perceval sat in the Irish Commons as a knight of the shire for County Cork between 1703 and 1714. He was raised to the Irish peerage as a baron in 1715, advanced to viscount in 1723 and (in 1733) created earl of Egmont. After 1714, although he watched vigilantly over Irish affairs, both the welfare of his estates and the more general economic concerns of the island, he did so from a distance. He orchestrated campaigns to promote measures in the English parliament (in which he sat as member for Harwich from 1727 to 1734) that might benefit the trade and industry of Ireland and to thwart others that were expected to do damage. As a result of these activities, Perceval was regarded as a key figure in the Irish lobby that operated in and around Westminster.[4] He was helped by his wealth, standing and connections. In 1714, his Irish rental was totalled at £3,518; by 1737, it had risen to £5,567.[5]

Perceval's heir was bred up to show the same concern with the well-being of his Irish patrimony, which he inherited in 1748 when his father died. Young Perceval, another John and adorned with the courtesy title of Lord Perceval, was elected to the Irish parliament as member for Dingle in 1734. He also sat in the Westminster parliament until he was given an English barony in 1762.[6] Sharing many of his father's interests, he toured the Irish estate during 1731. In reacting to what he saw, he betrayed his enslavement to the reigning doctrine of improvement.[7] In particular, he was impressed by his father's agent, Richard

---

plantation: English migration to southern Ireland, 1583–1641 (Oxford, 1986), pp 81, 164–8, 281. **4** Lord Perceval to Abp W. King, 16 Feb. 1719[20], BL, Add. MS 47,029, f. 14v; same to earl of Abercorn, 25 Feb. 1719[20], ibid., ff. 19v–20; Lord Wharton to Lord Perceval, 17 Feb. 1719[20], ibid., f. 14v; F.G. James, 'The Irish lobby in the early eighteenth century', *EHR*, 81 (1966), pp 544–57; D.W. Hayton, *Ruling Ireland, 1685–1742: politics, politicians and parties* (Woodbridge, 2003), pp 244, 255, 266, 271; R. Sedgwick (ed.), *History of parliament: The Commons, 1715–54*, 2 vols (London, 1970), ii, pp 336–8. **5** *HIP*, vi, pp 49–50; GEC, *Complete peerage*, v, pp 28–9. **6** W. Taylor to Lord Perceval, 16 Sep. 1734, 1, 7 and 26 Oct. 1734, BL, Add. MS 46,982, ff. 67, 72, 75, 802; *HIP*, vi, pp 50–1; GEC, *Complete peerage*, v, pp 29–30. **7** J. Perceval to Lord

Purcell, and Purcell's fostering of the textile industry in and around Kanturk, otherwise 'a wretched place ... [which] if left to itself would immediately fall to ruin'. Perceval was taught that the profitability of the estate depended on the adoption of the improvements devised and recommended by Purcell and paraded before his impressionable young master.[8]

The younger Perceval, in responding to what he encountered, subscribed to another common view. The terrain seen in north Cork looked reassuringly familiar – like the west of England, where his family had lands. But Ireland needed sustained and intensive entrepreneurial intervention, if the fitful resemblances to industrious England were to last. His father agreed: 'tis certainly a fine country and wants only people and planting to be as beautiful as many parts of England'.[9] Such observations, together with their praise of Purcell's initiatives, marked out the Percevals as uncritical worshippers at the shrine of improvement. Yet, modernizing ambitions did not exclude an interest in the antiquities on the estate. This can be seen in attitudes towards the castles of Kanturk and Liscarroll, and schemes for the preservation and embellishment of Lohort Castle. Agents on the spot, responsible for implementing and (occasionally) initiating the projects, mimicked the attitudes of their masters. Accordingly, the enchantments of improvement competed with the allure of antiquities, association and atmosphere. A liking for the picturesque and romantic was kindled.

The first earl of Egmont, to the fore in promoting Irish manufactures and trade, immersed himself in apparently more arcane matters. Aggrieved when the holders of Irish peerages were shouldered aside in England, literally so in the procession at the wedding of George II's eldest daughter and the prince of Orange, he strove to demonstrate the rights of Irish peers, including himself, to appropriate precedence.[10] As well as devoting himself to the general issue of how the Irish peers as a group were to be treated, Egmont and his heir documented the antiquity and renown of their family. As the title of their earldom hinted, the Percevals believed that they were related to the earls of Egmont in the Low Countries, and through them with the venerable ruling families of Christian Europe, including Charlemagne.[11] Even before the first earl took up these questions, forbears had paid minute attention to their ancestry. Heralds were con-

---

Perceval, 1 and 4 June 1731, BL, Add. MS 46,982, ff. 95, 95v–6. **8** Same to same, 11 June 1731, 20 Aug. 1731, 28 Sep. 1731, BL, Add. MS 46,982, ff. 98, 104, 107–7v; T.C. Barnard, 'The cultures of eighteenth-century Irish towns' in P. Borsay and L. Proudfoot (eds), *Provincial towns in early-modern Britain and Ireland: change, convergence and divergence*, Proceedings of the British Academy, 108 (2002), p. 205. **9** Lord Perceval to J. Perceval, 19 June 1731, BL, Add. MS 46,982, f. 99v. **10** [J. Perceval], *The question of the precedency of the peers of Ireland in England* (Dublin, 1739). **11** BL, Add. MS 47,157.

sulted; pedigrees compiled; genealogical manuscripts collected and constructed; portraits of ancestors were copied and others were commissioned specially for distribution among kinsfolk and clients.[12] The obsession culminated in the composition by James Anderson (best known as a writer on freemasonry) of the annals of the dynasty. Egmont interfered in this work, *A genealogical history of the house of Yvery*, for which he himself amassed much information.[13]

Indicative of the distortions in the Yvery chronicle was its insistence that the first earl had declined an English peerage, when, in fact, he craved one.[14] The future second earl shared his father's delight in meddling in such matters. John Lodge, who was compiling a comprehensive *Peerage* to replace Crossly's defective compendium, was consulted about his discoveries in the Irish public records. In Dublin, Lodge was instructed to wait on Lord Southwell, a distant kinsman of Egmont, to communicate the errors that he had detected in *The house of Yvery*.[15] Lodge also helped in hunting for and copying documents useful in the second earl's disputes with neighbours and tenants in County Cork. In 1748, for example, Egmont, having just inherited his father's dignities, wanted to include among them the lordship of Duhallow. Deprecatingly, Egmont stated that 'it was looked upon as a feather of some ornament, and tho of very little use, I don't desire that in any time the smallest pretensions of my family should be weakened by my want of attention to them'. Lodge, whether ironically or not, complimented the Percevals on having in the earl 'a representative so careful and attentive to preserve all their rights'.[16]

Frenzied memorialization of this kind might be thought to smack of insecurities. At first glance, the Percevals' preoccupation can be taken as further proof of a trait common among the Irish Protestants catapulted to high positions and wealth as a result of the *bouleversements* under Elizabeth I and James VI and I. Yet, none of the Egmonts' contemporaries within the Irish peerage, such as the

---

12 For example: Sir R. Southwell to Sir J. Perceval, 23 Feb. 1682[3], BL, Add. MS 47,151, f. 255v; same to G. King, 2 Sep. 1689, ibid., f. 258; R. Downing to E. Lloyd, 26 Oct. 1686, ibid., f. 269; W. Hawkins to R. Tisdall, 14 May 1698, ibid., f. 231; W. Perceval to Lord Perceval, ibid., f. 287; W. Perceval to Lord Perceval, 19 Feb. 1739[40], ibid., Add. MS 47,008B, f. 60; same to Lord Egmont, 16 Aug. 1748, ibid., f. 91; Egmont to W. Perceval, 3 Nov. 1748, ibid., f. 99v; W. Cooley to Egmont, 2 Sep. 1748, ibid., Add. MS 47,006, f. 53. For surviving family portraits, see N. Figgis and B. Rooney, *Irish painting in the National Gallery of Ireland*, i (Dublin, 2001), pp 389–93.   **13** J. Anderson to Lord Perceval, 1 April 1738, BL, Add. MS 47,013A, f. 62. Owing to Anderson's death, the history was finished by William Whiston.   **14** W. Cooley to Lord Perceval, 21 May 1742, BL, Add. MS 47,004A, f. 61; Anderson, *House of Yvery*, ii, p. 407.   **15** W. Cooley to Lord Perceval, 24 Dec. 1741, 25 June 1743, BL, Add. MS 47,004A, ff. 21, 86; Rev. K. Perceval to same, 23 Oct. 1742, 21 Dec. 1742, 5 Feb. 1742[3], 14 June 1743, 17 Oct. 1747, BL, Add. MS 47,008B, ff. 19v, 20, 21, 25, 44; J. Lodge to Lord Perceval, 7 Aug. 1742, 9 Sep. 1742, 9 Oct. 1742, 2 Nov. 1742, 23 Dec. 1742, ibid., Add. MS 47013B, ff. 66, 71, 77–9, 84–5, 108–9; BL, J. Lodge to same, 3 May 1743, BL, Add. MS 47,004A, ff. 82–3.   **16** Egmont to J. Lodge, 19 Sep. 1748; J. Lodge to Egmont, 1 Oct. 1748, BL, Add. MSS 47,009B, ff. 45, 51v; 47,014A, f. 144.

Blundells, Boyles, Cootes, Southwells and Temples, pursued these antiquarian issues so passionately. The quest led the Percevals to buy an important collection formed by the herald, St George. Yet, pedigrees and heraldry constituted only one element in multifarious memoranda and transcriptions. Even a cursory analysis of his surviving papers discloses a man interested equally in the future and the past. The Percevals' antiquarianism, making voluminous collections of heraldic and genealogical papers and commissioning a history to demonstrate his membership of the ancient European aristocracy, had practical uses. It assisted, for example, when the second earl of Egmont strove to uphold his rights to a manorial jurisdiction against the incursions of others in north Cork, such as the St Legers of Doneraile and the Barrys at Castlelyons.[17] In addition, the first earl was a compulsive diarist, annalist and reporter; he intervened on behalf of Irish trade and fostered settlement in Georgia.[18]

A sharper impulse to demonstrate the antiquity of the Percevals may have arisen in 1737 when Egmont married his son into the English peerage, in the shape of the Cecils, earls of Salisbury. The Salisburys professed admiration for the family into which their daughter had married and its devotion 'to the noble purposes' for which life was given.[19] The Cecils had risen above the obscurity of their origins within the yeomanry and washed away any grubbiness from their profiteering from the sixteenth-century Court of Wards. The Percevals could reasonably hope to obscure their own unscrupulous use of the Irish Court of Wards in their enrichment and gentrification. Certainly the preamble to his patent as an Irish baron, granted by George I, described Perceval as 'descended from an house of the most remote antiquity who under the standard of William Duke of Normandy, our great ancestor, first entered England'.[20]

The Percevals' claims to a venerable past were embodied impressively in their Irish properties: the castles of Kanturk, Liscarroll and Lohort. A revival of interest in these ancient piles seems to have coincided with the marriage and then succession to the earldom and estate of the first earl's heir. At least in the case of Lohort, the interest expressed both the personal and practical. If the formidable bastion silenced detractors tempted to impugn the Percevals as upstarts, it might also protect the Percevals' dependants from physical attack.

17 Perceval to H. St Leger, [May 1748], [draft], BL, Add. MS 47,009B, f. 37; W. Cooley to Lord Egmont, 30 Sep. 1748, ibid., Add. MS 47,006, f. 66v; T. Barnard, *The kingdom of Ireland, 1641–1760* (Basingstoke, 2004), pp 106–8. **18** His published diaries include D.W. Hayton (ed.), 'An Irish parliamentary diary from the reign of Queen Anne', *Analecta Hibernica*, 30 (1982), pp 99–149; M.R. Wenger (ed.), *The English travels of Sir John Percival and William Byrd II: the Perceval diary of 1701* (Columbia, 1989). See too: J. Ingamells, *A dictionary of British and Irish travellers in Italy, 1701–1800* (New Haven and London, 1997), pp 757–8. **19** Lady Salisbury to Lord Perceval, 25 Feb. 1736[7], BL, Add. MS 47,013A, f. 35. **20** Anderson, *House of Yvery*, ii, p. 408.

Continuing unsettledness fortified the defensive purpose of the structure. At the same time, the eagerness to preserve and indeed improve the fifteenth-century stronghold suggested a dawning appreciation of what was customarily dismissed as barbaric and Gothic. The tower at Lohort could never be divorced from an earlier and uncouth age in which the native Irish and Catholics had menaced families like the Percevals. The castle reminded of a heroic age of martial prowess among the Protestant settlers of Munster. Lohort was drawn and engraved for a plate included in Anderson's annals. The caption recorded some of the heroic events that the fortress had witnessed. With rumours of invasions and uprisings on behalf of the exiled Stuarts in the 1740s, it was feared that the 1640s had come again. Lohort was to serve as the centre of resistance in a potentially hostile countryside. Such defensive functions, however, intertwined with the decorative look of the structure.

In Munster, the Percevals' dependants deferred to their landlords' whims. In 1740, a Cork tenant congratulated the earl, 'none but one of your lordship's lively imagination and good taste could have foreseen that grandeur and beauty' in Lohort. The recently ordered renovation and innovation rendered the qualities of the castle 'apparent to every one'.[21] Elsewhere, independent of prompting from absentees, a few in Ireland were savouring relics of times before the settlers of the sixteenth and seventeenth centuries wrought their improvements.[22] Those involved with Lohort during the late 1730s and 1740s aimed to please their largely absent masters. They did so by expressing opinions in which were united the cults of improvement and the picturesque. Accordingly, their plans and thoughts serve as a register of contradictory aesthetic impulses in the 1730s and 1740s. Furthermore, as a site known to neighbours and visited by strangers, Lohort may have helped to spread notions of the picturesque into Ireland. Most notable among the recorded visitors in this period is George Berkeley, the bishop of Cloyne, who stayed there in 1750. His party included a music master, Thomas Prior (reckoned 'a great patriot on this side of the water'), and a drawing master, Thomas Mitchell. The last was retained to teach William Berkeley, the bishop's promising son. The precocious boy sketched the south-east prospect of Lohort.[23] Young Berkeley was only the latest of several who had been so beguiled by the scene as to paint or draw it. It

---

[21] R. Brereton to Lord Perceval, 11 Nov. 1740, BL, Add. MS 47,009A, f. 66v. [22] T.C. Barnard, 'Art, architecture, artefacts and Ascendancy', *Bullàn*, 1, no. 2 (1994), pp 17–34. For a divergent interpretation, see K. Whelan, 'Reading the ruins: the presence of absence in the Irish landscape' in H.B. Clarke, J. Prunty and M. Hennessy (eds), *Surveying Ireland's past: multidisciplinary essays in honour of Anngret Simms* (Dublin, 2004), pp 297–328. [23] W. Cooley to Lord Egmont, 4 Sep. 1750, BL, Add. MS 47,006, ff. 76–6v. For William Berkeley's talents: A.A. Luce and T.E. Jessop (eds), *The works of George Berkeley, bishop of Cloyne*, 9 vols

was too the region from which Edmund Burke hailed, and may have incubated his ideas on the sublime and picturesque. In addition, the presence at Kilcolman of Edmund Spenser's castle valued more as interest in Spenser's poetry revived.[24]

III

Lohort was not the Percevals' principal seat even when they lived regularly on their County Cork estates. An impressive house – Burton – was built early in the 1670s on a new site near Churchtown. Burton House was widely regarded as the exemplar of correct modern classicism, then still rare throughout Ireland.[25] The premature deaths of two owners, the third and fourth baronets, followed by the devastation of the Williamite War, left Burton a ruin. Repairs made the stables habitable for the fifth baronet, the future first earl of Egmont, but his lengthening absences meant that it received scant architectural attention and lost its status as the paradigm of modernity in County Cork.[26] Talk of impending visits by the earl or his heir justified sporadic repairs. But the house had to compete for spending against the family's English residences – in London, Somerset and Kent – and with other houses on the Irish holdings. By the 1740s Burton was let to the local clergyman, Robert Brereton, a distant cousin. Brereton lived in the clearly capacious offices adjoining the ruined house.[27] Even so, the family fussed about the look of the place. A watercolour painted in 1737 recorded the man-made plantations shading into the distant mountains. The very facts that the painting had been made and was then pre-

(London, 1948–57), viii, pp 285, 300, 304. **24** On Burke, see L.M. Cullen, 'The Blackwater Catholics and County Cork society and politics in the eighteenth century' in P. O'Flanagan and N.G. Buttimer (eds), *Cork: history and society* (Dublin, 1993), pp 535–84; F.P. Lock, *Edmund Burke: volume I: 1730–1784* (Oxford, 1998), pp 91–124; on Spenser, see T. Barnard, 'Edmund Spencer, Edmund Spenser and the problems of Irish Protestants in the eighteenth century' in Barnard, *Ascents and descents*, pp 290–305. **25** T.C. Barnard, 'The political, material and mental culture of the Cork settlers, c. 1650–1700' in Barnard, *Ascents and descents*, pp 52, 54, 56, 60, 71; Barnard, *Making the grand figure*, pp 43, 173; R. Loeber, 'Irish country houses and castles of the late Caroline period: an unremembered past recaptured', *Quarterly Bulletin of the Irish Georgian Society*, xvi (1973), p. 31, frontispiece, plate 8. But see, too, the more modest ground plan in BL, Add. MS 47,157, loose at f. 52. **26** Edward Southwell recorded about 1719 only 'park wall, garden fruit, situation, plantations, strong walls', yet was able to stay the night. Journals of Edward Southwell, Beinecke Library, Yale University Library. See too W. Taylor to Sir J. Perceval, 22 Aug. 1710, BL, Add. MS 46,964B, f. 28; R. Loeber, *A biographical dictionary of architects in Ireland, 1600–1720* (London, 1981), p. 41. **27** W. Cooley to Lord Perceval, 11 Nov. 1743, 14 Sep. 1744, BL, Add. MSS 47,004A, f. 134; 47,004B, f. 117v; Egmont to R. Purcell, 28 June 1748, ibid., Add. MS 47,034, f. 5; survey of Egmont's estates, c.1760, ibid., Add. MS 47,049, ff. 16v–17; Anderson, *House of Yvery*, ii, p. 327; W.M. Brady, *Clerical records of Cork, Cloyne and Ross*, 3 vols (Dublin, 1863–4), ii, pp 74, 246; Luce and Jessop (eds), *Works of George Berkeley*, viii, p. 266.

served carefully in the family suggested an aesthetic interest in the place.[28] Egmont took exception when a cabin was built on the avenue, once the great beauty of Burton. In the mansion, there survived a 'large parlour or drawing room' and a 'fine bed-chamber', together with two turrets. From the contemporary description, neither seemed especially commodious. Indeed, the second turret was deemed suitable 'for such 2nd hand gentry as one would not care quite to disoblige and yet could not without injury sink so low as to accommodate them in the house'.[29]

The Percevals owned houses older than Burton, notably the castles at Kanturk and Liscarroll. Kanturk Castle, more grandiose than Lohort, was not regarded as a suitable seat for the family. By the late 1730s, it was being cannibalized, with some of its magnificent fireplaces removed for use elsewhere.[30] Yet, Egmont chose to have *The house of Yvery* illustrated with engravings of Kanturk, Liscarroll and Lohort. Drawn and engraved specially for the publication, they better evoked a chivalric past than the wrecked domestic buildings at Burton.[31] The plate of Lohort published in 1742, based on a meticulous drawing, was engraved and printed in London by W.H. Toms.[32] The portrayal of Lohort, no less than the text of Anderson's *House of Yvery*, may owe as much to imagination as to accurate observation. In particular, the tower of the castle is shown surrounded by a fortified octagonal enclosure, in its turn projecting into a moat. These features invested the place with a military character that echoed the designs of Vauban and those sketched in Irish contexts by the first earl of Orrery, Wibault and Thomas Phillips.[33] Throughout the discussions of how to improve the setting of the castle, the octagon is emphasized. Plantings were designed to echo and reproduce the form. Octagonal defences reappear in a second published view of the castle: that supplied by Egmont for Smith's *History of Cork*, which appeared in 1750. It is a more modest structure than the one recorded by Toms. A third piece of evidence, a plan of the castle and its

28 BL, Add. MS 47,009A, f. 27. **29** R. Brereton to Lord Perceval, 7 April 1747, BL, Add. MS 47,009B, f. 15v; W. Cooley to Lord Egmont, 12 Aug. 1748, ibid., Add. MS 47,005B, f. 46. **30** J. Hickey to either Lord Egmont or Perceval, 18 Aug. 1740, BL, Add. MS 47,007, f. 1. **31** Anderson, *House of Yvery*, ii, facing pp 192, 217, 336. Also for Liscarrol, see Dickson, *Old world colony*, p. 36, figure 9. **32** BL, Add. MS 47,009A, f. 27; W. Cooley to Lord Perceval, 17 July 1743, BL, Add. MS 47,004A, f. 92. It seems probable that Toms was related to John Toms, one-time vicar of Kinsale, whose progeny looked to the Southwells for help. The probability is increased by the fact that in London, he specialized in nautical scenes (a taste harking back to Kinsale), although he did also produce topographical prints. Journals of Edward Southwell, s.d. 13 Aug. [*c*.1719], Beinecke Library, Yale UL; Barnard, *New anatomy*, p. 199; T. Clayton, *The English print, 1688–1802* (New Haven and London, 1997), pp 114, 140–1, 150–1, plate 169. John Boydell was apprenticed to Toms: James Raven, *The business of books: booksellers and the English book trade* (New Haven and London, 2007), p. 253. **33** D.J. Griffin and S. Lincoln, *Drawings from the Irish Architectural Archive* (Dublin, 1993) pp 24–6; Loeber, *Biographical dictionary of architects in Ireland*, p. 41; E.P. McParland, *Public architecture in Ireland, 1680–1760* (New Haven and London, 2001), pp 138–41.

plantations in 1744, has only a circular moat and no hint of the defensive octagon.[34] This configuration accords better with a surviving but undated pen and wash sketch.[35] The octagon reappears in a vignette of Lohort included in an engraving of the Somerset seat of Enmore, devised by an English herald between 1762 and 1770. It derives from Toms's earlier representation, and has no particular claim to verisimilitude. Liscarrol, also illustrated, was embellished with an angular fortification.[36] If no 'octagon' was ever built in the moated space at Lohort, an outer enclosure of the demesne at Lohort is labelled 'a part of the octigon'. Anxiety was also voiced about preserving 'the octagon ditches' and the spaces between them, suggesting that they were earthworks at the perimeter of the Lohort demesne.[37]

Despite the successive representations of Lohort as an impressive piece of military architecture, the portrayals reflected aspiration not actuality. Throughout the years between 1737 and 1752 (the time of Perceval's Cecil marriage), the repair and refurnishing of the castle and the re-ordering and re-planting of the grounds absorbed the future second earl and operatives on the spot. A gardener, Charles Hay, was despatched from England.[38] He drew at least nine variant designs for the gardens and park. They conformed to the styles current in Britain. Areas of formal and geometric planting, through which vistas, rides and walks were cut to command distant prospects, were juxtaposed against patches of studied wildness. Constant throughout the schemes is the wish to exploit the natural beauties of the landscape, of which the distant Mount Hillary was the most conspicuous. Striking features might be invested with extra drama with more planting or by constructing buildings that would catch the eye.

It is possible that Batty Langley, an English designer of garden buildings and author of architectural manuals provided sketches for some proposed additions to the Lohort demesne. Langley had sought the support of Perceval for a planned book on Gothick buildings in England. Langley's prospectus spoke of depicting 'all the most venerable ancient castles and other private Gothick buildings in this kingdom [England], wherein such parts that are defaced by devastation, time, &c, will be restored (as near as can be done) to their primitive purity so as to illustrate and perpetuate to posterity the native simplicity,

---

34 'This ye plan of the plantation as it stands at present, June 28 1744', BL, Add. MS 47,007, f. 135. **35** W. Laffan (ed.), *Painting Ireland: topographical views from Glin Castle* (Tralee, 2006), p. 36. **36** Mowl, 'Enmore Castle', figs. 6–8. **37** BL, Add. MS 47,007, ff. 144–5; R. Purcell to Egmont, 9 April 1752, ibid., Add. MS 47,003, f. 118; *Archaeological inventory of County Cork. IV: North Cork*, part 2 (Dublin, 2000), p. 529. Mr Mowl makes the unsupported and implausible suggestion that it had been constructed late in the 1630s in anticipation of the rising of 1641. 'Enmore Castle', p. 106. **38** C. Hay to Lord Perceval, 10 March 1742[3], BL, Add. MS 47,007, f. 84v.

strength and elegancy of that grand mode of building'.[39] Langley's strong links with freemasonry were shared with Anderson, the chronicler of the house of Yvery, and may explain how Langley came to the Percevals' notice.[40] Evidently he supplied drawings for ornaments to the Percevals' estates, including a bridge at Lohort.[41] In so far as the second earl's taste for the Gothic has been noticed, it has been derided: his lumbering approach contrasted with the sprightliness of Horace Walpole.[42] However, he may deserve more credit as a precocious patron of the style, through his use of Langley, and then through his attempts to introduce the mode into Ireland.

Mundane considerations frustrated the most striking plans. Hay, perceived as an interloper, was soon at loggerheads with the agent (and his wife), who lived in the castle. The Percevals' agent at Lohort, William Cooley, having given himself a crash course on the latest theories about gardening (the 'physico-philosophical' approach), was soon criticizing Hay's ideas and advancing his own.[43] Confident in his command of current fashion, Cooley advised Lord Perceval, 'let the serpentines flow ever so winding, at least when they terminate, the eye should be entertained with some object'. He proposed existing landmarks as eye-catchers: 'a wood, a hill, an obelisk, a church, building, castle, etc.' But new eye-catchers were also needed. A building on Doneraile Hill would have 'all the appearance of state and magnificence'.[44] In the schemes, first of Hay, then of Cooley, the castle served as the constant backdrop. The subordinates on the spot, prodded and pestered by Egmont, reported their strenuous efforts to enhance the martial and picturesque qualities of Lohort. In the context of furnishing the castle, it is revealing that Cooley wished to commission 'Gothick oak chairs'.[45] No less than his master, he was a precocious admirer of the Gothic in the appropriate setting.

Much in the reports throughout the 1740s related to mundane repairs. The building must be made staunch: first against the weather; then against possible depredations by locals. Boys stole the leaded lights from the windows; cracks were blamed on the pounding given the place by Sir Hardress Waller in 1650.[46]

---

39 B. Langley to Lord Perceval, undated, BL, Add. MS 47013B, ff. 119, 123, 125; B. Langley, subscription proposal, ibid., Add. MS 47013B, f. 121. **40** H.M. Colvin, *A biographical dictionary of British architects, 1600–1840*, 3rd edn (New Haven and London, 1995), pp 597–8; E. Harris, *British architectural books and writers* (Cambridge, 1990), pp 262–80; A. Rowan, 'Batty Langley's Gothic' in G. Robertson and G. Henderson (eds), *Studies in memory of David Talbot Rice* (Edinburgh, 1975), pp 197–215. **41** W. Cooley to Lord Perceval, 29 March 1745, 12 April 1745, BL, Add. MS 47005A, ff. 29, 36. **42** Mowl, 'Enmore Castle', pp 103–19. **43** C. Hay to Lord Perceval, 22 Dec. 1743, BL, Add. MS 47,007, f. 122; W. Cooley to same, 7 Sep. 1744, 14 Jan. 1745[6], BL, Add. MSS 47,004B, f. 112; 47,005B, ff. 4v–5. **44** W. Cooley to Lord Perceval, 14 Jan. 1745[6], 1 Jan. 1747[8], BL, Add. MSS 47,005B, f. 5v; 47,006, f. 1. **45** Same to same, 26 July 1746, BL, Add. MS 47,005B, f. 72. **46** Same to same, 21 Sep. 1744, 5 Oct. 1744, BL, Add. MS 47,004B, ff. 121, 131.

Beyond the tower, the moat and retaining walls required attention. Cooley set out aims succinctly in 1741. He played on Lord Perceval's known susceptibilities. 'Nor is the castle, however people may affect to put you out of conceit with it, unworthy the dignity of a nobleman. There is something of a solemn majesty in every article of it, and tho it has been so rudely butchered instead of repaired, it wants very little were the windows and water settled to receive your lordship and family'. He suggested that it would appeal to Lady Perceval, being 'surrounded with beauteous prospects, fine spacious rooms, a sporting country abounding in game and in short every other blessing, except trees and artificial gardens'.[47] Inventories confirm that the interior was elegantly furnished. It included a library in which were shelved Philip Miller's *Gardener's dictionary*, a treatise on *The timber tree improved*, and a manual that allowed the Egmonts to be seen in context, Anthony Collins's *Peerage*.[48] The 'study' was hung with engraved views of Venice, Westminster Abbey, Rokeby House (Yorkshire) and Melton Constable in Norfolk.[49]

With the interior of the castle in reasonable order, Cooley set about supplying the missing trees and formal gardens. Soon, in a pattern often repeated among the functionaries on large estates, Cooley fulminated against the defective workmanship and poor aesthetic judgement of the mason entrusted with repairs.[50] Another of the Percevals' correspondents in Ireland commented on the 'genius and desire of this nation for improvements as well as the want of ability to put them into execution'.[51] At Lohort, ornamental gardens were laid out and trees planted. A canal was dug; 500 feet long and ten to twelve feet wide, it looked 'very handsome from the west of every room'. Within eighteen months, the water had turned stagnant.[52] Less easily resolved was how to elaborate on the octagonal enclosure. Cooley declared early in 1745 that all future improvements 'should be made to correspond with this expansive octagon, so that the four cardinal vistas of the plantation will answer the four cardinal ope[ning]s of the octagon'.[53]

Cooley bragged of his swift mastery of gardening, surveying and architecture. Soon he was quoting Sir Henry Wootton's architectural writings, citing

---

[47] Same to same, 4 Dec. 1741, BL, Add. MS 47,004A, f. 20. [48] Evidence of the use of Miller's *Dictionary* is in W. Cooley to Lord Perceval, 28 Oct. 1743, 15 June 1744, 7 Sep. 1744, 23 Oct. 1744, BL, Add. MSS 47,004A, ff. 128–8v; 47,004B, ff. 75, 112, 137v. [49] Catalogues of books, the kitchen and goods at Lohort, 24 Dec. 1741, 28 Jan. 1741[2], 14 Oct. 1742, BL, Add. MS 47,004A, ff. 21–2, 25v, 73–4v. [50] W. Cooley to Lord Perceval, 8 June 1742, BL, Add. MS 47,004A, f. 66; J. Hickey to same, 18 Aug. 1740, 1 Jan. 1740[1], 24 June 1746, ibid., Add. MS 47,007, ff. 1, 5v, 75. [51] J. Hellewell to Lord Perceval, 16 Nov. 1741, BL, Add. MS 47,009A, f. 111. [52] W. Cooley to Lord Perceval, 7 Sep. 1744, 5 Jan. 1744[5], 17 Dec. 1745, 17 June 1746, BL, Add. MSS 47,004B, f. 114v; 47,005A, ff. 5, 120–20v; 47,005B, f. 52v [53] W. Cooley to Lord Perceval, 5 Jan. 1744[5], 1 March 1744[5], 21 Aug. 1747, BL, Add. MSS 47,005A, ff.1v–2, 19–20; 47,005B, f. 122.

François Blondel and referring to Michelangelo's dome of St Peter's in Rome – the latter perhaps tangential to the needs of Lohort.[54] Later, he would suggest as a model the elliptical arches on which the Treasury Buildings in London were supported. Cooley's schemes, rather than the more ambitious ones of the designer Shaw and the professional gardener Hay, were adopted. Cooley asserted that 'in a few months', he had 'done your lordship more real service than all the gardeners or architects yet employed in that way'.[55]

IV

The antiquity of Lohort, communicated through engravings, supported the Percevals' claims to inclusion among the ancient aristocracies of continental Europe. In the Irish context, it had a more recent history that received unusual publicity in the 1740s, perhaps because it was thought relevant to current dangers. The pioneering history of Cork by Charles Smith, published in 1750, included engravings of Kanturk and Lohort, not of the modern houses dotted over the county. Egmont himself had supplied the illustrations on which the plates were based. Smith's *Cork*, sponsored by the youthful Physico-Society in Dublin, subscribed to the same mixture of modernity and antiquarianism evident in the Percevals.[56]

Smith, consciously advertising the achievements of the English and Protestant minorities in Ireland, linked the anxious 1740s with the turbulent 1640s. He insisted that only the first earl of Cork had done more than the first Sir Philip Perceval, Egmont's forbear, to resist the uprising of 1641.[57] Possible foreign landings – first by the Spaniards, then by the French in league with the Stuart pretender, Charles Edward – on the long and secluded coasts of the south-west and west were rumoured. These might then trigger uprisings of Catholics. Unease worsened in a region severely affected by famine in 1740 and 1741. Yet, Egmont's informants in the locality disagreed about the threat. The entrepreneurial Purcell in Kanturk urged vigilance. He regarded the Irish Catholics as 'our natural enemies' and felt that 'every papist would be a spy for the enemy'.[58] Early in 1744, when the government issued proclamations to round

---

54 Presumably F. Blondel, *Cours d'architecture enseigné à l'Académie Royale* (Paris, 1675). A second edition was published in Paris in 1698. 55 W. Cooley to Lord Perceval, 14 June 1745, 18 July 1746, 1 Jan. 1747[8], BL, Add. MSS 47,005A, f. 65v; 47,005B, ff. 63v–4; 47,006, f.1. 56 R. Brereton to Lord Perceval, 28 March 1748, BL, Add. MS 47,009B, f. 32; W. Cooley to Egmont, 28 Oct. 1748, ibid., Add. MS 47,006, f. 72v; Rev. K. Perceval to same, 5 Jan. 1750[1], ibid., Add. MS 47,008B, f. 52; W. Perceval to same, 15 Jan. 1750[1], ibid., f. 121v; Emily Boyle, countess of Cork and Orrery (ed.), *The Orrery papers*, 2 vols (London, 1903), ii, p. 39. 57 R. Purcell to Egmont, 2 Jan. 1748[9], BL, Add. MS 47,002B, ff. 111v–12. 58 R. Purcell to Lord Perceval, 13 April 1744, 17 May 1744, 7 March 1745[6], BL, Add. MSS 47,001B, ff. 61v, 117; 47,002A, f. 27. Cf.

up Catholic priests, he stationed two Protestant guards – a glazier and bailiff – at Lohort. Cooley, resident in the castle, believed that the action was unduly alarmist.[59] However, he area was further unsettled when one of its most important figures, the earl of Barrymore, owner of nearby Castlelyons, was arrested on suspicion of Jacobitism. Barrymore, it was said, was 'perfectly revered among the common Irish ... and might in 10 days have 20,000 well-made, stout young fellows at his heels'.[60] By the autumn of 1744, Cooley had grown more edgy. He recommended that any new gardener for Lohort be given the title of constable, castellan, castle-keeper or warden. He believed that such a measure would prove 'a standing check to the popish insolence in this country', while also appealing to the Percevals' taste for medievalizing.[61]

The Young Pretender's successes in Scotland in 1745 and early 1746 scared Protestants in rural Ireland. Traditional defences, notably the militia, were revived.[62] During an earlier alert in 1715, Perceval demonstrated his forwardness. He enjoined equal care on his agents and tenants in 1745. Lohort, as a place of strength, protected by a moat, provided an ideal place for the officers and men of the troop to assemble and train. If the strength of the fortification fitted it for the emergency, its atmosphere was charged with the sufferings and heroism of previous generations of Irish Protestants. As the caption to the plate in Anderson's *House of Yvery* reminded, Lohort had been held in 1641 by Sir Philip Perceval with 150 men, only to be surprised by the Irish in 1645, but was recaptured in 1650 by Sir Hardress Waller.[63] The letter sent by Waller to the Speaker of the Westminster parliament, and soon published, was now quoted to emphasize that Lohort was 'a place of great strength'.

Reminders were timely. At the height of the panic over the Pretender, the Percevals' chief agent conceded that 'there are not very many amongst us who remember the cruelties and barbarities practised by the papists in the former civil wars in this country, yet we have all of us a just sense of what we are to expect if they should become our masters'.[64] Both the twenty-third of October (the anniversary of the day in 1641 when the Protestants had been delivered from a plot to surprise Dublin Castle but when an uprising had begun) and the

Luce and Jessop (eds), *Works of George Berkeley*, viii, pp 269–70. **59** W. Cooley to Lord Perceval, 17 Feb. 1743[4], BL, Add. MS 47,004B, f. 19v; R. Purcell to same, 9 and 27 March 1743[4], BL, Add. MS 47,001B, ff. 53v, 59v; J. Brady, *Catholics and Catholicism in the eighteenth-century press* (Maynooth, 1965), pp 71–3. **60** W. Cooley to Lord Perceval, 24 Feb. 1743[4], 17 March 1743[4], BL, Add. MS 47,004B, ff. 22–2v, 31. **61** W. Cooley to Lord Perceval, 26 Oct. 1744, BL, Add. MS 47,004B, f. 142v. **62** R. Purcell to Lord Perceval, 30 Aug. 1745, 1 and 8 Oct. 1745, 16 Dec. 1745, BL, Add. MS 47,001B, ff. 127, 146–6v, 148, 170. **63** C. Smith, *The antient and present state of the county and city of Cork*, 2 vols (Dublin, 1750), i, plate vi, facing p. 297. **64** R. Purcell to Lord Perceval, 8 Oct. 1745, BL, Add. MS 47,001B, ff. 148–8v; W. Cooley to same, 15 Sep. 1745, 11 Oct. 1745, BL, Add. MS 47,005A, ff. 97, 106–6v.

fifth of November prompted grim ruminations in 1745. Cooley retailed recollections of how before St Ignatius's Day in 1641[65], Catholics had been instructed to go nowhere without their rosaries. He noted, 'our priest and friars, which now much abound, have been known for years to preach in these parts, contenting themselves barely with saying mass, yet they are grown very vigilant of late, preaching frequently and earnestly entreating that none go without their beads, the distinguishing marks of true Catholics'. The priests' behaviour was felt to presage a fresh massacre.[66] Rumours circulated later in 1745 that the local Catholics would rise on the first of November. The Protestants hastened into the nearest towns, and there kept watch throughout the night. Although the predicted massacre did not occur, history enjoined continuing watchfulness. Percevals' tenants were to celebrate the anniversary of deliverance from the Gunpowder Plot by repairing to Kanturk.[67] Meanwhile Cooley turned to the past for guidance as to how to meet the present menace. He pored over the earl of Orrery's *Art of war*, a copy of which Perceval had despatched to him. Orrery's manual, much concerned with fortifications, drew on his experiences as a commander in south Munster during the Confederate War of the 1640s and might show Cooley how best to utilize the defences at Lohort.[68]

For many of the Percevals' tenants, the musters at Lohort amounted to convivial breaks from routine rather than re-enactments of the privations a hundred years before. Nevertheless, until the reassuring news of Cumberland's defeat of Charles Edward at Culloden reached north Cork, fears mounted. In this atmosphere the defensive rather than ornamental functions of the castle were stressed. The inscription on the engraving of Lohort included in Smith's *History of Cork*, varying the caption that had appeared in *The house of Yvery*, underscored this point. Before that a tract printed in Cork warned of the dangers.[69] Cooley and Purcell made the same argument. Because of the numerical majority enjoyed by the Catholics, 'we [the Protestants] ought at all times to be on our guard against them'. Cooley declared it 'both amazing and shameful to see what a sottish indolence prevails upon the Protestants on this occasion'. He blamed their dependence for income on their herds of cattle, making 'them dread the rabble and rather court than govern them'. Purcell railed against 'the stupidity of some and the worldliness of others, who think Ireland will be attacked only after England is reduced'.[70] Yet, Purcell, once the alarms had ended and facing the business of

---

65 17 October. **66** W. Cooley to Lord Perceval, 11 Oct. 1745, BL, Add. MS 47,005A, f. 106v. **67** R. Purcell to Lord Perceval, 5 Nov. 1745, BL, Add. MS 47,001B, f. 158. **68** W. Cooley to Lord Perceval, 5 Feb. 1745[6], BL, Add. MS 47,005B, ff. 12–12v; R. Boyle, earl of Orrery, *Treatise on the art of war* (London, 1677). **69** *Seasonable advice to Protestants; containing some means of reviving and strengthening the Protestant interest* (Cork, 1745); Smith, *Cork*, i, facing p. 297. **70** W. Cooley to Lord Perceval, 11 Oct. 1745, BL, Add. MS

running the estate successfully, adopted a more indulgent policy towards the Catholics. He strove, like others in his position, to distinguish the well-affected from the potential insurgents. By the autumn of 1746, he was once more recommending Catholics for tenancies of the Percevals' farms.[71]

V

As the apprehensions abated, so the Percevals reverted to a more measured view of the place. In 1748, the new Lord Egmont offered a kinsman accommodation at Lohort whenever he was in the vicinity. Self-effacingly, he called it merely 'a small and old habitation', which, nevertheless, with its varied views, would please the sensitive. In much the same spirit, lodgings there were offered to – and accepted by – Bishop Berkeley and his party in 1750.[72] In the more relaxed circumstances after 1746 the owner continued to play up varying associations and effects at Lohort. A concern to make it the focus of a carefully manipulated and re-ordered landscape persisted. Ideas about how best to heighten particular aspects – both physically and emotionally – often seemed at variance with conventional ideas of improvement. Yet improvement was still the term with which the projectors dignified the assorted schemes for the area around the castle.

The camaraderie that had briefly prevailed in 1745–6, probably in a rather contrived way, was to be prolonged by making the place the setting of chivalric rituals. In October 1745, at the height of the security alert, 129 men had mustered at the castle. Those who had equipped themselves with uniforms were treated to dinner by the officers. The troopers expected 'to be made drunk'. Some had lingered until two in the morning, becoming a danger to themselves as they descended the stone stairs.[73] As Cooley tartly observed, service in the militia 'is like all other amusements, shy to be obtained at first but afterwards as quickly followed as tobacco, cards or any other'.[74] Tenants commissioned as officers in Egmont's militia troop were dragooned into a military brotherhood which would continue to assemble in the castle. Something akin to a chapter or lodge was planned, in which each officer would have a seat – custom-made and painted with his own armorial bearings. Cooley worried whether 'they will be showy enough in mantling and feathering'.[75] The scheme soon ran into prob-

47,005A, f. 106v; R. Purcell to same, 7 Jan. 1745[6], 7 March 1745[6], ibid., Add. MS 47,002A, ff. 8–8v, 27. **71** R. Purcell to same, 16 Oct. 1746, 2 and 19 Feb. 1746[7], 2 March 1746[7], BL, Add. MS 47,002A, ff. 66v, 86v, 93, 99. **72** Lord Egmont to W. Perceval, 4 Aug. 1748; W. Perceval to Egmont, 13 Aug. 1748, BL, Add. MS 47,008B, ff. 85–5v, 90v. **73** R. Purcell to Lord Perceval, 22 Oct. 1745, BL, Add. MS 47,001B, ff. 154–4v. **74** W. Cooley to Lord Perceval, 17 June 1746, BL, Add. MS 47,005B, f. 50v. **75** W. Cooley to Lord Perceval, 26 July 1746, 1 April 1747, 25 Sep. 1747, BL, Add. MS 47,005B, ff. 72, 95, 127; R. Purcell to same, 28 Sep. 1747,

lems. Several officers lacked coats of arms. Invention – 'false heraldry' – made good the want. But then the herald-painter engaged to undertake the work proved unequal to the job. Instead, the versatile Cooley displayed an unexpected proficiency in simulating 'the Old English character' in which the blazons were to be rendered. He boasted that the finished articles looked 'mighty well'.[76] The armorial display on the chairs prefigured that on a set of Windsor chairs, some of which have survived, that Egmont commissioned and had painted with his own and second wife's heraldry.[77] Heraldic display was not a foible unique to the newer Protestant settlers: it was shared by members of the Irish Catholic diaspora.[78] For the initiates of the troop, the meetings at Lohort may have been accepted as a local variant of the kinds of association increasingly familiar from Masonic lodges and other groups designed for Protestant solidarity, such as the clubs in nearby Mallow and Youghal. Egmont himself seems to have been inspired more by his researches into the chivalric fraternities of medieval Europe and orders of knights, like the garter, with their quarters at Windsor. The value of Lohort as the embodiment of a noble past was further revealed when, in 1770, Egmont's second wife – a Compton, the English earls of Northampton – was granted a peerage in her own right. The title that she chose was Baroness Arden of Lohort Castle, in County Cork.[79]

The choice brings us back to the ways in which the Percevals conceived and used their Irish possessions to forward their ambitions. Thanks to ample revenues, they supported lives away from Ireland. Like other absentees – Boyles, Pettys, Southwells and Temples – they never forgot that the main source of the wealth necessary to buy an elevated manner of living was Ireland. Accordingly they stayed alert to prospective and actual threats, and – more than most in their situation – exerted themselves to counter and contain them. The chronology of renewed involvement suggests the role of marriage. The identity of the bride of the heir, the future second earl of Egmont, was at once an indicator of the ascent of the Percevals into the heights of English society and an incentive to further interference in Ireland. She was a Cecil. Her family, like the Percevals, had leapt from relative obscurity to prominence, but rather more spectacularly, so that by the 1730s they were regarded, except by the most exacting genealogists, as the true alloy of the aristocracy. Maybe, the Percevals, sensitive still to the supposed and actual slights to the Irish peerage to which they belonged,

---

ibid., Add. MS 47,002A, f. 125. **76** W. Cooley to Lord Perceval, 1 April 1747, 21 Aug. 1747, 18 March 1747[8], BL, Add. MSS 47,005B, ff. 95, 125; 47,006, f. 10. **77** *Antiques Trades Gazette*, 26 June 2004. **78** For example: P. O'Flanagan and J.C. Walton, 'The Irish community in Cadiz', in Clarke, Prunty and Hennessy (eds), *Surveying Ireland's past*, pp 375–7. **79** GEC, *Complete peerage*, i, p. 190; v, p. 30.

hoped to impress the supercilious English. Lohort was a plausible accessory in the elaboration of a medieval lineage. Further homage was to be offered: it took the elaborate form of the expansion of a settlement close to Lohort and its being renamed as Cecilstown.

The sponsorship by proprietors of model towns was a well-established method of improvement in sixteenth- and seventeenth-century Ireland. By the mid-eighteenth century, such initiatives were less common, but not unknown.[80] The townships were calculated to benefit the economy, strengthen the Protestant interest, promote urbanity and civility, and introduce the distinctive political and cultural values associated with England. Cecilstown was designed to achieve these ends. Yet, it was a modest venture. Cooley hoped originally that he could people thirty-two cottages, which would soon increase to fifty. Organized around a square with a maypole, there would be a Southwell Street and the inn was to be named 'The Perceval Arms'. The women would be given employment through the cultivation and spinning of flax: the culture which seemed to have boosted the fortunes of many other proprietors.[81] A neighbour, Hayes St Leger from Doneraile, proposed that instead of defensive works around the castle, houses for linen workers should be erected. The project 'would increase profits and Protestants, and so be better than any modern defence'.[82] Subsequently only twenty-four householders were listed, six of whom were Protestants. Ten of the dwellings were cabins or cottages, each let for an annual rent of ten shillings. Six more substantial houses were also noted. Their tenants included an inn-keeper (Protestant), who rented the most valuable property for a yearly £2, an armourer, shoemaker and female shop-keeper. In the next stage of development it was planned to build six more houses for prospective Protestant tenants. The intended occupiers would be a motley crew – a schoolmaster, horseman, stone-mason, carpenter, gardener, linen weaver and herald-painter. Some would bring useful skills, represented already among the existing inhabitants by three wool-combers. This was very much in keeping with the manufactures in the district encouraged by Purcell. A further boost was given when the Linen Board awarded subsidized flax seed and spinning wheels to the Percevals' venture. Here, too, Purcell offered an example: of him, it was said no person in the county has 'so keen a taste for that sort of improvement'.[83]

---

[80] B.J. Graham and L.J. Proudfoot, *Urban improvement in provincial Ireland 1700–1840* (Athlone, 1994). [81] W. Cooley to Lord Perceval, 27 April 1744, BL, Add. MS 47,004B, f. 46; plan of Cecilstown, [9 Sep. 1748], BL, Add. MS 47,009B, ff. 43v–4. [82] W. Cooley to Lord Perceval, 13 July 1744, BL, Add. MS 47,004B, f. 89v. [83] E. Harborne to W. Cooley, 28 April 1747, BL, Add. MS 47,005B, f. 107; W. Cooley to Lord Perceval, later Egmont, 13 March 1746[7], 8 May 1747, 13 Aug. 1751, ibid., Add. MS 47,005B, ff. 89, 105; 47,006, f. 99.

Other residents would cater to the more specialized requirements of the estate, and especially to the schemes for the castle and its environs. Shaw, the gardener, having worked on improvements for gentlemen in the neighbourhood, had offered his services – at a high price – to the Percevals.[84] The heraldic artist, James Duncan, originally from London, but more recently in trade in Cork city, had been brought into the countryside by the enterprises of Egmont.[85] Patrick Clahisy, the resident stone mason, rose most exuberantly to the Percevals' instructions. He had improved a house design by adding 'hewn stone, rustic quoins, a cornice and a pediment with an ox eye window in the centre of it and a pedestal on the pitch of it for an ornament or figure to stand on'. The building was further enriched with a cut-stone door-case, window sills and arched surrounds. The aim was to give the other tenants 'a pattern' in the 'modern taste' of architecture.[86] As with the castle, so with Cecilstown, most of the extravagant schemes remained on paper. Clahisy even had trouble quarrying the marble that Egmont requested from north Cork for the embellishment of Enmore.[87]

The settlement seems to have been reconstructed to a regular plan, around a modest square: more modest that originally intended. Cecilstown through its name reminded of the Percevals' alliance with the Cecils. Fewer tenants arrived than had been hoped. Just as the more populous township of Kanturk had been ceded earlier to Purcell in order to stimulate its economy, so Cecilstown was later rented to Cooley. The latter soon tired of the investment. By 1751, Captain George Brereton, son or brother of the rector of Burton, and another local landowner, John Longfield of Longueville near Mallow, bid to take over the tenancy.[88] Brereton was favoured with a lease, but he did not persist in the project for long. Instead, Samuel Tarrant rented the demesne and was permitted to live in the castle.[89]

The Percevals' attention to the minutiae of improvement on their distant Irish holdings fluctuated. On occasion, they derided the bulk of the tenantry. The second earl believed that 'slovenly management of land' prevailed in Ireland 'more than in any part of Europe'. He singled out for particular contempt, 'a strange stupidity of the Irish to be so fond of crab quicks upon the

---

84 W. Cooley to Lord Perceval, 24 June 1748, 12 Aug. 1748, BL, Add. MS 47,006, ff. 25, 38. **85** Inhabitants of Cecilstown, c. 1746, BL, Add. MS 47,006, f. 44. **86** P. Clahisy to Egmont, 3 April 1752, BL, Add. MS 47009B, f. 151v. The handwriting of this letter suggests that it was written – and maybe composed – by someone other than Clahisy. **87** R. Purcell to Egmont, 19 and 26 Aug. 1751, 3 and 27 Feb. 1751[2], 1 June 1752, 6 Nov. 1752, BL, Add. MS 47003, ff. 24v, 44v, 95, 102v, 128, 153. **88** G. Brereton to Egmont, 22 March 1750[1], 21 June 1751, 25 Oct. 1751, BL, Add. MS 47,009B, ff. 103, 122, 148–9; J. Longfield to G. Brereton, 4 March 1750[1], ibid., f. 100. **89** Survey of Egmont's estate, 1752, BL, Add. MS 47,050A, ff. 16, 21v; survey of Egmont's estate, c.1760, ibid., Add. MS 47,049, ff. 53v–4, 55v–6.

false notion of making cider out of their hedges'.[90] Towards those thought meritorious, the Percevals met obligations punctiliously. Brereton was preferred to the living and given a tenancy of Burton; legal business was put the way of a kinsman, William Perceval, who was also offered lodgings at Lohort; civilities were accorded to Bishop Berkeley, a long-standing friend of the Percevals; Cooley's quest for a salaried post in the revenue was assisted by his employer.[91] In return, the Percevals expected loyalty from their dependants.

VI

Cooley bore much of the heat of the action around Lohort. After 1748, as he reflected on his experiences, disillusion, even depression, set in. Egmont, as pernickety as other absentee proprietors, reproved Cooley for not writing often enough and in sufficient detail. In replying, Cooley allowed a little of his isolation and irritation to escape. 'To reside in this inhospitable castle almost secluded from humane society and absolutely from conversable for near three months' made him mope. He confessed he had 'little heart to write when one has so little to say'. The endless variations on the theme of improving Lohort and its environs were almost exhausted. No longer did he portray Lohort as an asset and ornament to the Percevals, but rather, if they were to keep it up, as a tax.[92] He dwelt on the drawbacks: a canal cut through the bog stagnated; the trees were destroyed by cattle; and walls of the castle leaked. Farce supervened in 1751 when the rickety bridge that spanned the moat collapsed under the weight of a fat maid-servant.[93]

By then it was rumoured that Cooley wanted to quit Egmont's service and the district. Others, such as George Brereton, were hopeful of taking over. Brereton used a tactic to which competing agents were prone, and disparaged his rival, Cooley's, stewardship. The former told Egmont of the air of neglect and disorder that hung over the castle and its environs. Cooley's wife, whose temper had earlier disturbed the gardener Hay, left. She turned out to be bigamously married to Cooley. In her place, Cooley installed two 'whores' (an apparently obligatory detail in such denunciations), who were allowed the run of the castle. Flax and potatoes grew in the formal beds: profit was now put before ornament. There had long been suspicions that Cooley charged the

---

90 Egmont to W. Cooley, [1748], BL, Add. MS 47,034, ff. 4, 6v.   **91** W. Cooley to Lord Perceval, 21 May 1743, 25 June 1743, 17 Feb. 1743[4], BL, Add. MSS 47,004A, ff. 85, 86; 47,004B, f. 19v; Lord Egmont to W. Cooley, [1748], ibid., Add. MS 47,034, f. 2v.   **92** W. Cooley to Egmont, 17 July 1748, BL, Add. MS 47,006, f. 32.   **93** Same to same, 17 July 1748, 5 July 1751, BL, Add. MS 47,006, ff. 31–3, 84v.

Percevals for work done on his own behalf, and was vague in his reports on the progress of improvements.[94] Cooley's eventual nomination (in 1748) as collector of the hearth tax at Navan in County Meath may briefly have distracted him from Egmont's affairs.[95] However, Cooley's performance in the collectorship throws doubt on his diligence and, indeed, honesty. Having solicited for the appointment for several years, he was dismissed within a year, owing to his unauthorized absence and unwarranted detention of some of the receipts.[96] The speed with which the revenue commissioners in Dublin disciplined their wayward employees contrasts sharply with the laxity with which many agents were supervised, especially by absentee landowners such as the Percevals. Yet, for all his shortcomings, Cooley survived as a favoured employee. Brereton tried hard to discredit him, but failed.[97]

In 1747, Cooley had assured Lord Perceval that 'a general spirit prevails in this kingdom, whether propagated by the Dublin Society or by whatever other means, of being the foremost in improvement. Everybody is ambitious of taking the lead according to the fancy that is most fashionable and one would hardly believe that the making of a man in these days a trustee of the linen manufacture is a very great gratification to an Irish member of parliament of a good fortune'. Cooley's evaluation prefigured the comments of a judge who toured much of the country late in the 1750s. It suggested the possible impact of the Dublin Society. Some in Munster felt that the Dublin Society was 'too remote from us'. To overcome that drawback, prominent Protestants in County Limerick tried to form their own group, into which a few tenants and neighbours of the Percevals were drawn.[98] Then, in the 1740s, the Physico-Historical Society was established to supplement the work of the Dublin Society. Egmont's kinsman, the Revd Kane Perceval, was active in the second body, compiling a propagandist account of its achievements. He may have encouraged his absentee relative to forward its programme.[99] Certainly Egmont did so, by lending two plates depicting his

---

94 Egmont to W. Cooley, before 28 June 1748, [July 1748], BL, Add. MS 47,034, ff. 2v, 6; same to R. Purcell, 3 Oct. 1748, ibid., Add. MS 47,034, f. 20; G. Brereton to Egmont, 22 May 1750, 21 June 1751, 25 Oct. 1751, ibid., Add. MS ff. 74, 103, 122; R. Purcell to Egmont, 3 Oct. 1751, ibid., Add. MS 47,003, f. 49.   **95** Egmont to W. Cooley, [1748], [July 1748], BL, Add MS 47,034, ff. 2v, 7; T. Brian to same, 10 Sep. 1748, ibid., Add. MS 47,006, f. 63; Egmont to R. Purcell, 28 Sep. 1748, BL, Add. MS 47,002B, f. 68; T. Brian to same, ibid., Add. MS 47,002B, f. 79v. For a comparable quest: Barnard, 'Edmund Spencer, Edmund Spenser and the problems of Irish Protestants in the eighteenth century', pp 290–305.   **96** Revenue commissioners minutes, s.d. 9 Sep. 1748, 13 Oct. 1748, 10 July 1749, 23 Jan. 1750, 30 June 1752, PRO, CUST 1/45; 1/46; 1/47; 1/48; 1/51 (I am grateful to David Fleming for these references); R. Purcell to Egmont, 18 March 1750[1], BL, Add. MS 47,003, f. 9v.   **97** G. Brereton to R. Purcell, 8 April 1760, BL, Add. MS 47,003, f. 178.   **98** *An essay to induce the gentlemen of the county of Lymerick to form a society for the improvement of tillage by English husbandry, and to encourage arts and manufactures* (Dublin, 1735), p. 16. They included William Freeman, John Lysaght and Sir Matthew Deane.   **99** W. Cooley to Lord Perceval, 21 Aug. 1747, 28 Nov. 1747, BL,

properties to illustrate Charles Smith's survey of Cork, which was sponsored by the Physico-Historical Society. By this device, his importance within the locality of Cork was proclaimed, just as it had been by other publications, such as Anderson's *Yvery*, to larger audiences outside Ireland.

This upsurge of public spirit and curiosity converged with more pragmatic calculations as how best to advance rents. The combination goes far to explain the burst of activity on the Percevals' holdings in north Cork. Nevertheless, other factors probably commended the schemes. Severe famine, and local, national and indeed international dangers added urgency to strengthening the Protestant and English interest in Ireland. These threats invested the history and present condition of Lohort with topical relevance. Then, too, more personal forces made an impact: the marriage of the heir, the settlement of part of the estate on him and the likelihood that he and his bride would visit the district. Moreover, the Percevals, both father and son, were fascinated by heraldry, pedigrees and antiquities and exhibited a lively interest in current politics and trade. Lohort offered an obvious focus for their assorted projects, both practical and ideological.

Soon enough, Egmont's interest in remote Lohort weakened. The lessening enthusiasm was reflected in, and may indeed have been influenced by, Cooley's switch from optimism to gloom. In 1748, the agent reported that 'all manner of improvement seems now to be at a stand'. Landlords with fewer resources than the Percevals were averse to burying their money in improvements.[1] Others, although approving improvements, held aloof from the societies. Bishop Berkeley, hailed by Smith as a model of the improving proprietor and well-known to the Percevals, abstained from the Physico-Historical Society, declaring, 'I wish them well but do not care to list myself among them.'[2]

Agents in Ireland were not impervious to their masters' crazes. The need to ingratiate themselves with employers, the financial well-being and good order of the estate, and the tedium of a reclusive life all added to the attractions of experiment and innovation. Cooley surrendered to the enthusiasm, and equipped himself intellectually and technically as an improver. For a season, his ardour matched and occasionally surpassed that of the Percevals. How far it was

---

Add. MS 47,005B, ff. 125, 139; [K. Perceval and P. Read], *An account of the rise and progress of the Physico-Historical Society* [Dublin, 1745]; E. Magennis, '"A land of milk and honey": the Physico-Historical Society, improvement and the surveys of mid-eighteenth-century Ireland', *PRIA*, 102, sect C (2002), pp 199–217. **1** W. Cooley to Lord Perceval, 21 Aug. 1747, 5 Oct. 1747, 29 July 1748, Add. MSS 47,005B, f. 125, 128v; 47,006, f. 35v; J. Kelly (ed.), *The letters of Lord Chief Baron Edward Willes to the earl of Warwick, 1757–62* (Aberystwyth, 1990), p. 95; R.J.S. Hoffman (ed.), *Edmund Burke, New York agent, with his letters to the New York Assembly and intimate correspondence with Charles O'Hara*, Memoirs of the American Philosophical Society, 41 (Philadelphia, 1956), pp 281–2. **2** Luce and Jessop (eds), *Works of George Berkeley*, viii, pp 285–6; Smith, *Cork*, i, p. 139.

a pose adopted to please his employers is hard to gauge. Equally difficult to ascertain is the frequency with which agents guided their masters and mistresses into novel ventures designed to enlarge the amenities and profits of their places. Whether of their own volition, or to humour exigent landlords, subordinates such as Cooley familiarized themselves with the latest crazes but also reflected on the characteristics and needs of their localities. Lohort embodied historical and martial episodes which, in relaxed times, could be cherished. Cooley and others entered fully into the schemes of the Percevals, and may have introduced their own distinctive insights. Without patrons and money, the likes of Cooley, no matter how much they were attracted to the picturesque, could realise few of their plans.

Cooley's paymaster, the second earl of Egmont, shifted his energies and spending into other projects. There were thoughts of transforming Mount Pleasant, his conventionally classical house, at Charlton in Kent into 'Tunbridge Castle'.[3] Grandiose in conception, battlemented and moated, it prefigured Enmore in Somerset. Enmore, purchased early in the 1750s, displaced any Irish scheme in the earl's affections. The house at Enmore was rebuilt on a gargantuan scale to designs by Egmont himself. To finance the purchase, he sold some lands in north Cork: a telling sign of the shift in the focus of the family's ambitions from Ireland to England.[4] At Enmore, a liking for fortifications was again evident: in this setting, of paste-board. The seventy-room structure boasted embattled square towers and semi-circular turrets at the entrance, together with a dry moat.[5] Here, Egmont gave full rein to his medievalizing enthusiasms, and so the north Cork properties were neglected. The intermittent attention that was directed onto the Irish holdings shed unexpected light on the otherwise obscure castle at Lohort. The Percevals chose to keep, repair and publicize it. If, as is suspected, elements of fabrication were introduced, they were further evidence of an antiquarianism which the Percevals fostered in provincial Ireland during the 1730s and 1740s.

---

[3] BL, Add. MS 47013B, f. 74. See also, ibid., ff. 66v–7. [4] Survey of Lord Egmont's estate, 1752, BL, Add. MS 47,050A, ff. 15v, 25v–6. [5] Dunning (ed.), *Victoria county history: Somerset*. VI, pp 38–9; Mowl, 'Enmore Castle', pp 103–19.

CHAPTER SIX

The worlds of an improving Galway squire: Robert French of Monivea, 1716-79

ROBERT FRENCH WAS PRAISED in his own day for his 'most notable undertaking' of improvements on the Monivea estate in eastern Galway. More recently he has been celebrated as 'the foremost modernizer west of the Shannon'.[1] He exemplifies several developments which continue to puzzle and divide historians: the conversion of pre-Reformation settlers to Protestantism, and its implications; the relative importance of the several worlds of estate, neighbourhood, Ireland and Great Britain to those intermittently active in all; the contrary or complementary impulses among members of the Irish elite towards Anglicization and integration into the British political, cultural and religious systems, and, at the same time, towards a livelier sense of Ireland's distinctive needs and of their own Irishness. French can be used to probe these issues, especially if aspects of his career which tend to be treated discretely – in the locality, Dublin and the wider world, or the cerebral and utilitarian – are reunited. By allowing the apparently trivial to jostle for attention with the conventionally weighty, something of his outlook may be retrieved. French has sometimes been regarded as the epitome of the improving squire.[2] This investigation, while not intended to lower his high reputation, like some that precede it, hints at ambivalences.[3]

II

The Frenches were one of the Anglo-Norman tribes that colonized Galway city. By the late seventeenth century, they and their connections ramified through the west and midlands, where seventeen of their principal residences have been

---

[1] Arthur Young, *A tour of Ireland*, 2 vols (Dublin, 1780), i, p. 386; L.M. Cullen, *The emergence of modern Ireland, 1600–1900* (London, 1981), p. 27. [2] The model study is D.A. Cronin, *A Galway gentleman in the age of improvement: Robert French of Monivea, 1716–79* (Dublin, 1995). [3] Like Denis Cronin's investigation, mine rests on the surviving papers of the Frenches of Monivea, most of which are in NLI. At present they are summarily listed and their arrangement in numbered envelopes (cited hereafter as E) provisional. I am greatly indebted to Catherine Fahy, Tom Desmond and Pat Sweeny for help with the collection.

located.⁴ The branch seated at Monivea plausibly professed devotion to 'the English interest' during the turmoil of the seventeenth century. This loyalism may have eased the Frenches' treatment during the Cromwellian Interregnum, and eventually – in 1677 – assisted them back to their lands.⁵ Increasingly, though, professions of devotion to the English crown were negated, at least in the opinion of the authorities, by the Frenches' continuing Catholicism. In the wake of James VII and II's defeat, the penal laws threatened the Catholic descendants of the Anglo-Normans, such as the Frenches, with loss of lands and livelihood. In 1704, Patrick French, eventual inheritor of Monivea, entered the Middle Temple in London. Clearly he was intending to qualify himself for the legal profession which for so long had been the preserve of the able sons of the Anglo-Irish and which was so helpful to the protection and enlargement of an Irish estate.⁶ However, in 1707, long-standing efforts to debar Catholics from practising the law were intensified by a statute that required of barristers communion according to the rites of the established Church of Ireland. Young Patrick French, having invested considerable effort in and time to his training, returned to Dublin in the same year. There he completed his legal education. Within two years he had apparently vaulted the barrier which would have excluded him from his intended calling, by conforming to Protestantism.⁷

This step, whatever material calculation or agonizing lay behind it, facilitated French's social as well as professional ascent. It started a process of assimilation which would be completed within the family well before the eighteenth century had ended. In 1713, Patrick French married a daughter of the Protestant bishop of Elphin, Simon Digby, one of whose houses – at Abert – made him a close neighbour. The Digby alliance introduced French into a powerful network of Protestants which straggled from Galway through the midlands to the Pale and Dublin, and on into the English aristocracy; it also exposed him to a sophisticated culture which sometimes buttressed, but more often subverted,

---

4 P. Melvin, 'The composition of the Galway gentry', *Irish Genealogist*, vii (1986), p. 81. 5 Safe conduct from C. Coote, 29 March 1652; certificate from C. Coote, 2 May 1656; agreement of 9 July 1686; certificate from H. Bankes, 25 July 1691, NLI, MS 2745; *Burke's Irish family records* (London, 1976), p. 410. 6 Patrick French to Patrick French, 15 Oct. 1703, NLI, French Mss, E/2; E. Keane, P.B. Phair and T.U. Sadleir (eds), *King's Inns admissions papers, 1607–1687* (Dublin, 1982), p. 179; T.C. Barnard, 'Lawyers and the law in later-seventeenth-century Ireland', *IHS*, xxviii (1993), pp 256–82; D.F. Cregan, 'Irish recusant lawyers in politics in the reign of James I', *Irish Jurist*, new series, v (1970), pp 95–114; D.F. Cregan, 'Irish Catholic admissions to the Inns of Court, 1558–1625', ibid., pp 306–20; *The case of Denis Molony* (?Dublin, 1698); *The state of the case of Denis Daly and Edmund Malone, esq.* (?Dublin, c.1695). 7 Legal case-book of Patrick French, NLI, MS 4917; Barnard, 'Lawyers and the law', pp 264, 273, 279–81; C. Kenny, 'The exclusion of Catholics from the legal profession in Ireland', *IHS*, xxv (1987), pp 351–2; T.P. Power, 'Conversions among the legal profession in Ireland in the eighteenth century' in D. Hogan and W.N. Osborough (eds), *Brehons, serjeants and attorneys: studies in the history of the Irish legal profession* (Dublin, 1990), pp 153–7.

that of his older kinsfolk like the Burkes, Dalys and Blakes. His wife brought a portion of £600, which, when combined with his own earnings at the bar, financed a campaign of physical improvements.[8]

A few years earlier, his French grandfather had lamented how family quarrels and public upheavals had caused 'the mismanagement of an estate and large stock these twenty years past'.[9] Quickly Patrick French repaired the worst ravages and sketched a pattern of concern that his son, Robert, would copy. New standards of comfort and civility, encountered perhaps during his recent stays in London or Dublin, were signalled by the sashing of seven windows in the ancient tower house of Monivea. (Soon enough they were broken.) Only in the later 1730s would the grand Kildare mansion of Carton be modernized with the insertion of sash windows. By 1753, this novelty had become common enough to appear in the gardener's house at Monivea. Before 1720, a 'cupola' or wooden lantern lent a raffish air to the otherwise antiquated structure. Rooms were plastered and panelled, and, by 1722, the house was adjoined by its 'pleasure garden'.[10] Meanwhile furniture had been bought in Galway or sent from Dublin; garden seeds were procured in Galway, Loughreagh and Portumna. A further sign of metropolitan sophistication percolating into the provinces was the despatch from the capital of two canopied beds, two brass candlesticks and a teapot (of an unknown material).[11] Since Jane French, Patrick's wife, had been surrounded by splendour in her childhood, her tastes may explain much of this activity.[12]

Notwithstanding these embellishments, Monivea remained a modest place, taxed in 1723 for only four hearths. By 1734, the establishment included a butler (paid £35 p.a.), three other male servants, 'Mary the cook', a dairy woman, a kitchen maid, an old nurse and her grand-daughter. Nine others, all but one with Irish names, and each allowed house, garden and three collops, were designated as 'sergeants', hinting at services and tenures of an archaic but not entirely obsolete military origin.[13] Jacobite invasion scares periodically alarmed the district and may have necessitated defensive strategies. In 1742, Patrick French, possibly prompted by his wife and their maturing children – one of whom had lately mar-

---

8 Draft marriage articles of Jane Digby and Patrick French, 1713, NLI, French Mss, E/26; inventories of Lackan and Abert, ibid. **9** Patrick French, senior, to Robert French, senior, 14 Jan. 1698[9], NLI, French Mss, E/1; draft will of Patrick French, senior, c.1700, ibid., E/67. **10** Account of 1710–11, pp 18, 70, NLI, French Mss, E/24; R. French, account book, ibid., MS 4918, p. 414. For sashing at Castle Durrow and Carton, bill of William Campion, 14 March 1733[4], ibid., MS 11,468; M. Ledwidge to W. Smythe, 6 Jan. 1738[9], ibid., PC 436. Sash-windows spread from continental Europe to Whitehall about 1670 and are recorded in Dublin by 1700. C.O'Brien to Sir C. Wyche, 25 April 1700, NA, Wyche Mss, 1/1/172; H.J. Louw, 'The origins of the sash-window', *Architectural History*, xxvi (1983), pp 49–72. **11** Accounts, 1715; accounts of Theobald Butler, 1717–18; accounts of Ferdinand Kelly, 29 Sep. 1722, NLI, French Mss, E/24. **12** Inventories of Abert and Lacken, NLI, French Mss, E/26; Barnard, *Making the grand figure*, pp 129, 163. **13** Accounts of Oliver Darcy, 1722, NLI, French Mss, E/26; accounts of Patrick French, 1733–9, ibid., E/84.

ried a brother of the architect and painter, Francis Bindon – added more ambitiously to the house. Thereby its accommodation was doubled.[14]

This bare summary shows how Patrick French had taken in hand his neglected inheritance. Attentive stewardship and methodical accounting were merely two of the habits dinned into Robert French by his father. The senior French exploited the timber on his lands, felling and selling some, but planting more. He raised black cattle which were sent to the local markets of Cooltragh, Loughreagh, Kilconnel, Aughrim, Tobberbracken and Banagher. But sheep were the staple crop. In 1734, the flocks numbered 2,475; by his death, ten years later, they had increased to 5,436.[15] French, the vigilant accountant, having reviewed his sales of wool and hops, wrote, 'expenses of selling in Dublin considerable, ergo, sell at home in the future'.[16] This brisk approach was further disclosed when he complained about loafers among his tenants: 'you know I never like such idle, vain persons … In short, we have the fate of meeting treacherous and ungrateful people. The girls are idle, slutty, gadding abroads, and never spin a thread of yarn.' He vowed, 'tho this is hard, there is no keeping insolvent tenants; nor should we be managed by combining tenants'.[17]

In later seventeenth- and eighteenth-century Ireland, a profession, notably in the law or established Church, but even within the army, could be combined with the active direction of an estate. Which activity, the professional or agricultural, required the more time or supplied the more money no doubt varied from individual to individual. Patrick French continued to practise in Dublin and on the local circuits. Yet it is unlikely that his fees approached his rental of £1,228 p.a. during the 1730s[18] Legal acumen, mastering settlements, entails and leases, and service as a trustee expanded the local opportunities for acquisitions and enrichment. So, for example, an aged kinsman, who lived on an island in Lough Corrib, summoned Patrick French and unloaded onto him numerous ancient documents and deeds, 'being of no use to him', but of great potential for the wily barrister.[19] Sometimes he lent it on mortgage: as a favour to relations and patrons; more commonly, to increase his possessions. By 1734, he reckoned that he had advanced almost £3,000 in this way.[20] Also, earnings from the law, as hard to collect as landed rents, added to the cash that French could deploy.

14 Patrick French to Jane French, 24 April 1742, NLI, French Mss, E/6; marriage articles of Elizabeth French and Nicholas Bindon, 18 Sep. 1740, ibid., E/117; ibid., MS 4918, p. 2. **15** Accounts of Patrick French, 1733–9, NLI, French Mss, E/84; list of stock sold, 1744, ibid., E/27. **16** Accounts of Patrick French, 1733–9, NLI, French Mss, E/84; undated deposition about Patrick French, ibid., E/76. **17** Patrick French to Jane French, 25 April 1742, NLI, French Mss, E/6. **18** Accounts of Patrick French, 1733–9, NLI, French Mss, E/84; memorandum about death of Bp S. Digby, after 1720, ibid., E/73; John Digby to Digby French, 11 Oct. 1746, ibid., MS 19,821. **19** Memorandum of 18 May 1743, NLI, French Mss, E/67. **20** Accounts of Patrick French, 1733–9, NLI, French Mss, E/84.

III

The traditions of his lineage combined with the conventions of the new Protestant world that he had joined in the education of his sons. Robert French, the elder, was sent to Trinity College, Dublin in 1734. He was allowed £50 or £60 annually. If Robert progressed to Oxford, the yearly allowance would be raised to £70. Instead, the youth followed his father to the Middle Temple in 1736 and then to the King's Inns in Dublin in 1742. A second boy, destined for ordination, also entered Trinity, followed by spells at Christ Church in Oxford and in London.[21]

Robert French inhabited a provincial environment already improved by his energetic and ambitious father. The experimentation with new crops, such as potatoes, cabbage and flax, the planting of oaks and evergreens, even the redirection of the river in an effort to drain the bog, would be unremarkable in an era when improvement was the rage, were it not that Robert French's public reputation centred on his zeal and originality as an improver. He readily acknowledged how much he owed to his father's example. In addition, he learnt from the earlier mistakes. Harder to unpick is the tangled skein out of which Robert French's public and private personae were woven. If his paternal pedigree reached back into a seemingly archaic and still Catholic society, his father and other of the Frenches who had converted (such as the French Park line) swiftly mimicked the behaviour of the emerging Protestant ascendancy.[22]

Similar values were transmitted through the female line. Both Robert French's mother and her brother, John Digby of Landenstown, County Kildare, exerted benign but decisive influences. Of Jane French, it was said that none could better 'plant and cultivate the principles of virtue and religion in young minds'.[23] The young French passed much of his adolescence in the company of his uncle, John Digby, and corresponded with him over the nature of 'perfect happiness'.[24] Digby showed how high spirits and charm could combine with

---

[21] Accounts of Patrick French, 1733–9, NLI, French Mss, E/84; Patrick French to Jane French, 25 April 1742, ibid., E/6; William Smythe to Ralph Smythe, 29 Oct, 1751, ibid., PC 445/28; G.D. Burtchaell and T.U. Sadleir, *Alumni Dublinenses* (Dublin, 1935), p. 309; J. Foster, *Alumni Oxonienses ... 1715–1886*, 4 vols (London, 1888), ii, p. 496; Keane, Phaire and Sadleir (eds), *King's Inns admission papers*, p. 179. [22] For the Castle French branch, John D'Alton, *Memoir of the family of French* (Dublin, 1847), pp 22–5. One member, Robert French, another lawyer, became a justice of Common Pleas in 1761. In general on the assimilation of such families: L.M. Cullen, 'Catholics under the penal laws' *ECI*, i (1986), pp 23–36; L.M. Cullen, 'Catholic social classes under the penal laws' in T.P. Power and K. Whelan (eds), *Endurance and emergence: the Catholics in Ireland in the eighteenth century* (Dublin, 1990), pp 57–83; K.J. Harvey, *The Bellews of Mount Bellew: a Catholic gentry family in eighteenth-century Ireland* (Dublin, 1998); D.A. Fleming and A.P.W. Malcomson, *'A volley of execrations': the letters and papers of John FitzGibbon, earl of Clare 1772–1802* (Dublin, 2005), pp xv–xlviii. [23] J. Digby to W. Smythe, 17 March 1726[7], NLI, PC 445/13. [24] R. French to Abigail French, 3 Feb. 1736[7], NLI, MS 19,821; Lord Athenry to P. French, 7 June 1738,

powerful piety and a concern with civic and private virtues. As a contemporary cooed, 'he joins in the most insinuating manner, the strictest principles of religion with the softest and most polished manners of a gentleman'. Digby asserted that his favourite maxim was 'to extract joy and merriment from all occurrences of life'. He recommended a Virgilian retirement, happy in 'the narrow bounds of my fields and garden'; he declared that he took 'no joy in getting beyond that circle'. Yet he adored dancing and when host to his young French relations confessed how they had lived 'in a rare, rattling way'.[25] He consciously subscribed to an Addisonian ideal of politeness and civility. In addition, he endorsed many of the values of the civic humanists and 'true Whigs'. These beliefs were all underpinned by both a practical and almost mystical Christian faith. Accordingly, while Digby – and his nephew French after him – relished the material world, he retained and acted in obedience to the unaffected piety of his father, the bishop. In his instructions to his young French charges, Digby upheld the superiority of the spiritual and moral over the transitory pleasures of the terrestrial world. He distilled his philosophy into one that obeyed scriptural precepts, both by doing good to others and through striving for self-perfection. He consistently urged activism even when appearing himself to sink into rural quietism.[26]

Later, Robert French in his will, probably unconsciously echoed his uncle's credo when he enjoined his own offspring to observe gospel commands.[27] By this time, in the 1770s, French, through a similar blend as Digby's of public spiritedness and independence of mind and behaviour, attracted comparable plaudits as a paragon of benevolence. The importance of Christian thinking to these attitudes was great. The embrace of an almost evangelical pietism by the convert Frenches continued in the conduct of Robert French's eldest daughter. In turn, she married Sir Lucius O'Brien, and thereby strengthened the current of Protestant activism in another formerly Catholic dynasty, the O'Briens.[28]

IV

Robert French, born in 1716, inherited Monivea with 6,110 acres in 1744. Over the next four and a half years, this patrimony yielded a yearly average of £587

ibid., French Mss, E/48; J. Digby to Mrs King, 24 Oct. 1738, ibid., MS 8472/4; ibid., MS 4919, ff 79v, 81. **25** J. Digby to W. Smythe, 23 Jan. 1733[4], 17 March 1736[7], 26 Dec. 1741, 4 Dec. 1746, NLI, PC 444/5 and /13; TCD, MS 5096. **26** J. Digby to R. French, 29 Dec. 1737, NLI, MS 19,821; TCD, MS 5096; Johnston-Liik, *HIP*, iv, pp 55–6. **27** J. Digby to R. French, 11 Oct. 1746, NLI, MS 19,821; will of R. French, 14 Feb. 1778, ibid., French Mss, E/128; R. French to Sir L. O'Brien, 25 June 1771, ibid., Inchiquin Mss, folder 2789. **28** TCD, MS 5096; Johnston-Liik, *HIP*, v, pp 372–5; G.O'Brien, *These my friends and forbears: the O'Briens of Dromoland* (Whitegate, 1991), pp 78–82, 86.

p.a. The rents were supplemented by sales of sheep and wool worth £1,758. These totals were markedly lower than his father's rent receipts in the 1730s. As well as harsh conditions during the 1740s, the son may have seen the yield reduced by his predecessor's neglects and by charges on the estate to maintain siblings and his widowed mother.[29] Marriage brought an infusion of much-needed money: a portion of £3000 came with his bride, Nicola Acheson. In 1749, the father-in-law added a further £1,000. Finances improved as French managed the property more aggressively. He switched to different crops. He encouraged the making of linen by attracting a skilled bleacher and weavers. In time, he sponsored the building of a model village. These represented substantial investments and the benefits were slow to materialize. Between 1748 and 1761, his annual income, exclusive of his earnings from the law and the profits of the demesne, averaged £1,369; between 1762 and 1768, £1,650; and after 1768, £2,367. Until the 1760s, the totals hardly exceeded those enjoyed by his father (see appendix, p. 166). Furthermore, by the late 1760s, heavy borrowing, combining with the effects of recession, suggested that behind the public perception of prosperity and success, French's fortunes were more precarious.[30]

After 1744, French divided his time between the country and Dublin: a pattern followed by many of the gentry with comparable responsibilities and incomes. At first, while still unmarried, he left a sister to housekeep at Monivea, delegated affairs there to a brother, and himself appeared only in vacations or when on the Connacht circuit.[31] Soon enough, in 1746, marriage – to a daughter of Sir Arthur Acheson of Market Hill near Armagh – changed his ways. The alteration was most marked in his Dublin life, but Monivea was affected. The house was redecorated, refurnished and then enlarged, in accordance with the tastes of his wife and the needs of a growing family and bigger staff.

Even before his wedding, Robert French was imprinting himself on the old mansion. His purchases – a mahogany dining table, breakfast and card tables, delft ware, glasses, porcelain cups, saucers and teapot – told of a newer fashions with which his parents' antiquated belongings no longer tallied. They also reflected an inclination to entertain.[32] The last impulse may be no more than a natural gregariousness. But the expansiveness could tell of French's awakening political ambitions. More costly works at Monivea followed his marriage. The parlour was smartened with a marble chimney piece and mahogany panelling.

29 Marriage articles of N. Acheson and R. French, 3 April 1746, NLI, French Mss, E/118; P. French, accounts, 1733–9, ibid., E/84; ibid., MS 4918. **30** NLI, MS 4918, pp 300–2; marriage articles of Anne French and Lucius O'Brien, 24 May 1768, ibid., French Mss, E/127; Arthur French to R. French, 25 Feb. 1772, ibid., MS 2745; case of Jeremy French, 11 Dec. 1807, ibid., E/52. **31** NLI, MS 4918, p. 2; D. French to R. French, 14 April 1747, ibid., French Mss, E/6. **32** NLI, MS 4918, pp 2, 3, 7, 8, 202–20; 4919, ff 74–5.

Christopher Constans in Dublin soon supplied a further two chimney pieces. A sumptuous bed of crimson stuff damask arrived, and French's own room acquired modish elegance with six walnut chairs, two matching stools and an armchair, for which needlework covers were then embroidered.[33] Much, but not all, was sent from Dublin: seat furniture, fabrics, extra glass, silver, porcelain (either from the orient or the European continent) and bright Rouen earthenware, currently favoured by the Irish gentry for use on their tables.[34] Carpets came: 'Turkey', 'Scotch', 'Swedish', 'Palempoe' and for the stairs.[35] The utilitarian covering of oiled cloth was made in, and for, the house.[36] Another novelty, spreading from Dublin, was to line the walls of two rooms with 'stamped paper'.[37] One chamber now functioned as a library.[38] At a more modest level, but again indicative of new refinement, six oyster knives were acquired.[39]

As a bachelor, French had spent little more than £100 on Monivea; now, in the early years of marriage between 1748 and 1754, he paid out over £450. Thereafter, spending returned to more modest annual totals, inflated only when an expensive harpsichord (£35) told of parental indulgence. Novelties were also sampled. China, 'Liverpool ware' in 1760, white ware and a set of 'yellow ware' were ordered for the service of meals. These represented lighter and cheaper ceramics invented by astute manufacturers in England to woo fickle consumers. The Frenches' purchases showed how the fashions set in Britain quickly penetrated the Irish provinces.[40] French estimated that between 1744 and 1767 he

---

33 NLI, MS 4918, pp 204, 206, 207, 218. **34** Barnard, *Making the grand figure*, pp 131–3. **35** NLI, MS 4918, pp 202, 207, 218, 219; Barnard, *Making the grand figure*, pp 105–6; C. Gilbert, J. Lomax and A. Wells-Cole, *Country house floors, 1660–1850* (Leeds, 1987), pp 37–47, 89–91. **36** NLI, MS 4918, p. 207. Gilbert, Lomax and Wells-Cole, *Country house floors*, pp 101–5. For the earlier use in Dublin: *A catalogue of the china ware and linen, of the late Henry Ingoldsby, Esq.; deceas'd to be sold by auction at his late house in Mary-Street … the 8th day of December, 1731* (Dublin, 1731). **37** NLI, MS 4918, p. 205; T. Barnard, 'The artistic and cultural activities of the Caldwells of Castle Caldwell, 1750–1783', *IADS*, x (2007), pp 90–111; Barnard, *Making the grand figure*, pp 92–4; A.K. Longfield, 'History of the Dublin wall-paper industry in the 18th century', *JRSAI*, lxxvii (1947), pp 55–62; A.K. Longfield, 'The manufacture of "raised stucco" or "*papier maché*" papers in Ireland, c.1750–70', ibid., lxxviii (1948), pp 55–62; D. Skinner, 'Flocks, flowers and follies some recently discovered Irish wallpapers of the eighteenth century', *IADS*, vi (2003), pp 11–19; D. Skinner, 'Irish period wallpapers', *Irish Arts Review Yearbook*, 13 (1997), pp 52–61. **38** NLI, MS 4918, p. 207. Rooms styled as libraries were common among the English aristocracy but still rare in Ireland at this date. T. Barnard, 'Libraries and glazed bookcases in eighteenth-century Ireland: additional evidence', *18–19th Century Fiction Newsletter*, 13 (1999), pp [4–6]; M. Girouard, *Life in the English country house* (New Haven and London, 1978), pp 179–80; P. Thornton, *Seventeenth-century interior decoration in England, France and Holland* (New Haven and London, 1978), pp 303–15. **39** NLI, MS 4918, pp 121, 202. Consumption of oysters in eighteenth-century Ireland is well attested; the making of oyster knives is not. L.A. Clarkson and E.M. Crawford, *Feast and famine: of food and nutrition in Ireland, 1500–1920* (Oxford, 2001), p. 46; M.L. Legg (ed.), *The Synge letters: Bishop Edward Synge to his daughter Alicia, Roscommon to Dublin 1746–1752* (Dublin, 1996), pp 87, 344; P.V. Thompson and J.J. Thompson (eds), *The account book of Jonathan Swift* (Newark and London, 1984), p. 266. **40** Barnard, *Making the grand figure*, p. 100; M. Berg, *Luxury and pleasure in eighteenth-century Britain* (Oxford, 2005), pp 46–153; K. Boney, *Liverpool*

spent £864 equipping Monivea. Averaged over the entire period, it amounts only to a modest yearly £37. The average hides the high spending of the early years. Nevertheless, it reinforces an impression of elegant comfort rather than ostentation. Occasional articles betray the quirks of the owner: a telescope, his inquisitive mind; paintings, as of Belisaurus, his place in a circle which, if not among the most avid collectors in mid-eighteenth-century Ireland, consistently interested itself in the visual arts.[41]

A mystery is how much French himself attended to the appearance and running of the country house once he was married. The mansion was further enlarged in the mid-1750s, probably to designs by Francis Bindon, a relation through marriage.[42] Already much of French's attention and spending was focused on the land around his house. Later, in the 1770s, when he was feted as model improver, French proudly listed what he had contributed to the well-being of the estate. He continued the tradition of vigorous intervention in which his father had also been active. By applying theory, observation, perseverance, experiment and flexibility, he drained much of the bog, increased yields of potatoes, rye and rape and introduced hitherto unknown trees, such as beech and elm. His practical skills are hinted out in his purchase of mathematical instruments and mathematical lessons.[43]

He singled out three particular innovations as the basis for the sustained improvement of Monivea.[44] First was the cultivation of flax. It had been grown, dressed, spun and woven at least since the 1720s, but only on a small scale and the product was mainly bandle linen for the use of the household. From the 1740s, French sponsored more intensive cultivation and specialized and commercial manufacture. An employee, sent into the north of Ireland to learn the trade, was subsequently appointed as overseer; a bleacher was lured from a green in Belfast; a spinning mistress was also engaged in 1748.[45] French, as well as procuring expert practitioners, built flax mills and a bleach-yard with a

porcelain (London, 1957); Maurice Hillis, *The Liverpool porcelains*, Northern Ceramic Society, occasional paper, I (1985), pp 8–13; N. McKendrick, 'Josiah Wedgwood and the commercialization of potteries' in N. McKendrick, J. Brewer and J.H. Plumb (eds), *The birth of a consumer society: the commercialization of eighteenth-century England* (London, 1982), pp 100–45; Peter Walton, *Creamware and other English pottery at Temple Newsam House, Leeds* (Bradford and London, 1976), pp 7–15, 67–77; L.M. Weatherill, *The pottery trade and north Staffordshire 1660–1760* (Manchester, 1971), pp 76–95. On the local alternatives: Peter Francis, *Irish delftware: an illustrated history* (London, 2000). **41** This may have been a copy of Salvator Rosa's *Belisaurus*. **42** Irish Architectural Archive, 22.73 P1 and P2; NLI, MS 4918, pp 3, 7, 8; D. Fitzgerald, the Knight of Glin, 'Francis Bindon (*c*.1690–1765)', *Quarterly Bulletin of the Irish Georgian Society*, x (1967), pp 3–36. **43** NLI, MS 4919, f. 79v. **44** NLI, MS 4918, pp 328–9, 500–1, 504, 582; Young, *Tour*, i, pp 369–87. **45** Patrick French, accounts, 1733–9, NLI, French Mss, E/84; indentures of 9 Oct. 1751, 23 Feb. 1757, 14 Oct. 1765, ibid., E/119, E/50, E/125; ibid., MS 4918, pp 52, 190, 316–20, 590; Young, *Tour*, i, pp 385–6.

green. Such initiatives, encouraged by the Linen Board and the Incorporated Society, were costly. By 1755, he calculated that he had spent £1147 13s. 6½d. on the undertakings, and as yet had received only £785 5s. 8½d: a loss of more than £360. The highest cost was the construction of the bleach yard, estimated at £538.[46] Towards the end of the 1760s, French changed the basis of operations. The original undertaker was allowed to continue the work on his own account, but only on condition that he kept every weaver on the estate employed. By 1776, Monivea boasted 276 houses, with ninety-six looms and 370 spinning wheels.[47] Thanks to leases with inducements, French had attracted proficient weavers: some migrated from Eyre Court in County Galway; others may have come through the suasions of his father-in-law in County Armagh.[48]

French, like numerous other landlord outside Ulster, benefited from the southward and westward spread of the skill in and demand for linen. General trends undoubtedly favoured him. However, his venture flourished – at least for a time – when those of other proprietors in the midlands (such as the Smythes of Barbavilla in Westmeath) and the west soon foundered.[49] French insisted on leasing only small plots to the weavers, who remained 'mere cottagers in a town without any land except a cabbage garden'. These operatives, unable to double as farmers, depended on the market for numerous staples.[50] Such interdependence of the farmers and manufacturers worked well until a slump in 1770 depressed the demand for linen and raised agricultural prices. This check startled French into reconsidering the economy of Monivea. Painfully aware of how vulnerable Irish commerce remained to the policies of Britain and to the instabilities of international trade, he repented of enslavement to a doctrine of industrial investment. About 1770, he reflected that the 'only manufacture which can never be carried too far' was 'the cultivation and improvement of the earth'. Henceforth he proposed to concentrate on 'plough and manure [rather] than on population and necessary manufactures'.[51] In practice, the linen industry had revived by the middle of the 1770s, so French was dissuaded from any radical review of his estate strategies.

46 NLI, MS 4918, pp 52–5, 390–1. 47 NLI, MS 4920, p. 121; Young, *Tour*, i, p. 386. 48 NLI, MS 4920; indentures made between 1754 and 1775, ibid., French Mss, E/122, E/123, E/125, E/126, E/128, E/131; HMC, *Various collections*, vi, p. 98. 49 W.H. Crawford, 'Development of the County Mayo economy, 1700–1850' in R. Gillespie and G. Moran (eds), *'A various country': essays in Mayo history, 1500–1900* (Westport, 1987), pp 72, 75; W.H. Crawford, 'Drapers and bleachers in the early Ulster linen industry' in P. Butel and L.M. Cullen (eds), *Négoce et industrie en France et en Irlande aux XVIIIe et XIXe siècles* (Paris, 1980), pp 113–20. For the Smythes' disappointments: J. Brush to W. Smythe, 30 Nov. 1741, 7 and 19 April 1742, 22 May 1742; draft letter of W. Smythe, 12 Jan. 1754, NLI, PC 449; J. Cooley to W. Smythe, 3, 10, 20 and 24 Feb. 1750[1], 10 and 31 March 1751, 28 Feb. 1756, ibid., PC 446. 50 Young, *Tour*, i, pp 386–7. 51 H. Archdall to R. French, 17 Oct. 1772, NLI, French Mss, E/6; R. French to Sir L. O'Brien, *c*.1770–2, ibid., Inchiquin Mss, folder 2788.

The lease had long been used as a principal instrument through which a landlord could reshape his locality. French, like his father before him and countless contemporaries, appreciated its potential. Conventionally enough he inserted into many tenancies requirements to build houses of lime and stone, with chimneys; to plant orchard and coppice trees; to hedge and ditch; and to reclaim or fertilize mountain and bog. The owner might supply materials and remit rent. In contrast, penal rent increases awaited those who defaulted on their tenurial obligations.[52] More personal to French was his belief in relatively small lots leased to weavers, carpenters and masons. Furthermore, the holdings granted to tenants – between twenty and 130 acres rather than the customary 200 to 500 acres – was his preference. He opposed the grant of large tracts, often to partnerships of villagers, since too many families then tried to wrest a living. Even so, he did not wholly abandon the practice: the mountain of Derrygllissane was let to twenty-two partners; similarly Ballynacregg and Knockaniver were leased to the villagers.[53] The length of tenancies varied. Usually they were for either twenty-one or thirty-one years or for three lives.[54]

French, in his care of the inheritance, showed personal strengths. He readily forsook crops such as apples and hops that failed; he experimented with novel techniques; he acted flexibly towards tenants. Despite the other calls on his time, he oversaw the entire enterprise. At the same time, he trained up subordinates to whom particular tasks could be deputed, but never relinquished overall direction. Even when enjoying a jaunt with his wife in England, he sketched unusual agricultural appliances and accessories, and compared the methods of cultivation there with those he knew in Ireland.[55] At home, notwithstanding a predisposition to equate Protestantism with industriousness, and to prefer Protestants as tenants, he was prepared to rent Cregboy to Daniel Kelly and his partners without any formal lease, 'as they are not qualified', presumably because Catholics. Normally methodical, he would occasionally let lands 'by parole', rather than with a written lease.[56] This sensitivity to circumstances – either of individual tenants or ecological and economic conditions – while integral to French's success, meant that the venture depended dangerously on his acumen and assiduity. Knowing this, he had tried to put his affairs on a more secure footing by transferring his interest in the linen business to his overseer. But such stratagems could not shield the estate against neglect during the minority or absence of his heirs.

---

52 NLI, MS 4919. **53** NLI, MSS 4919, 4920; Cronin, *Galway gentleman*; Young, *Tour*, i, p. 388. **54** NLI, MSS 4919, 4920; ibid., French Mss, E/122–131. **55** NLI, MSS 4918, pp 245, 280–1, 328–9; 7375. **56** NLI, MS 4920.

Monivea also felt the impact of French thanks to his zest for and patronage of physical improvements. Scarcely had his father been buried than he had workmen digging a drain through the bog in order to divert the course of the river. Such schemes, costly in labour and time, slowly reclaimed land, improved productivity and indeed, when publicized, won a gold medal from the Dublin Society.[57] These projects, together with new building, regularly employed tenants. French's annual bill for labour rose from £146 in 1747–8 to £670 by 1771.[58] Specialists like surveyors, carpenters and masons were attracted into the district. One carpenter, Benjamin Johnson, first busy about the modernization of the mansion in 1747, progressed to be a builder, designed and erected the parish church in the 1760s, and would be sent to French's son-in-law in County Clare to construct a flax mill.[59] Not the least of French's accomplishments, developed over the years, was to identify and nurture talent in underlings. Furthermore, he wished to retain the skilled in his service. A prime example were the Macales, like the Frenches themselves long-established in the locality, and related to the Catholic dynasties of Blake, Burke and Donnellan. Already in 1744, Richard Macale was looking after the livestock on the estate and thereafter he remained with French. By 1769 when Macale made his will he could describe himself as a 'gentleman'. He was disposing of the sizeable estate 'with which it hath pleased God to bless my industry'. He also remembered his landlord as a friend.[60] Meanwhile, in 1752, Macale's son, James had been entrusted with French's linen manufactory. In 1769, the younger Macale, now described as a linen draper of Galway, took it over completely.[61] James Macale accumulated an impressive collection of farms and lands, leased from several proprietors, and had £1500 in cash to invest on behalf of his dependents. He was also farming the tithes of the vicarage of Athenry, worth £500 annually.[62] French, for his part, treated the young Macale as a friend and nominated him to manage the family farms after his own death.[63] The Macales thrived thanks to the opportunities offered by the Frenches. Other tenants improved their circumstances more modestly than the Macales, but improve them they did.

Physical alterations advertised what French had spent and accomplished. The tower house at Monivea, though it retained its rugged core, was extended – prob-

---

57 NLI, MS 4918, pp 40, 245–6; R. French to Sir L. O'Brien, 25 June 1771, ibid., Inchiquin Mss, folder 2789; Young, *Tour*, i, pp 369–81. 58 NLI, MS 4918, pp 364–6. 59 D. French to R. French, 14 April 1747, NLI, French Mss, E/6; indentures, 28 May 1759 and 17 Oct. 1767, ibid., E/123, E/126; R. French to Sir l. O'Brien, 25 June 1771, ibid., Inchiquin Mss, folder 2789; surveys, ibid., French Mss, E/97; ibid., MS 4918, pp 132, 316–20, 416; J. Ainsworth (ed.), *The Inchiquin manuscripts* (Dublin, 1961), p. 312. 60 D. French to R. French, 14 April 1747, NLI, French Mss, E/6; will of R. Macale, 23 May 1769, ibid., E/51; NLI, MSS 4918, p. 218; 4919, f. 125v. 61 Draft will, undated, NLI, French Mss, E/152; indenture, 27 Dec. 1760, ibid., Inchiquin Mss, folder 2788; ibid., MS 4920, s.v. Gortkerine. 62 Accounts for tithes, 1767–8, 1770–9, NLI, French Mss, E/28, E/29; agreement for tithes, 27 Sep. 1777, ibid., E/52. 63 R. French, will, 14 Feb. 1777, NLI, French Mss, E/128.

ably to Bindon's drawings – in a style of classical symmetry. A second, smaller house at Corrondoe was rebuilt in the same idiom.[64] In 1752, French secured the grant of a weekly Saturday market and two annual fairs, and provided the market house with beam and scales.[65] A charter school was opened on land donated by French, and soon the provincial nursery of the Incorporated Society was attracted to the village.[66] He spent £338 on the church, consecrated in 1767. Publicly French regretted the lack of more Protestant churches and urged their construction, since 'it will ornament our country and is the best method to improve the people's morals'.[67] A similar belief in the intimate link between moral and material welfare inspired his loud advocacy of the charter schools. In parliament, indeed, he argued that the aims of the movement, 'to increase the Protestant religion and to train up the children of the poor to labour and industry are the most acceptable services that can be done to this kingdom'.[68] For French at Monivea, as for so many other landowners who subsidized the schools, the institutions promised to deliver into the neighbourhood a larger supply of docile youngsters equipped to weave, labour or serve in the house. Defenders of the protestant interest, under siege by the 1770s, applauded the strenuous landlord whose investment demonstrated the causal links between industry and Protestantism. Monivea blazed like a beacon in a naughty, Catholic world. As Arthur Young observed on his Irish visit, 'the general religion is Catholic, but about Monivea chiefly Protestant'.[69] Earlier, in 1759, Primate Stone had commended French for inducing 'a far greater number of the old inhabitants to conform to the established religion, the consequence of which has been that there is now a face of industry, sobriety and decency in that district unknown to any part of the province'.[70] French was held up as an exemplar, partly because such efforts were rare in Connacht and also because he himself proved how those of papist stock could be assimilated to the values of a Protestant and English Ireland. In the event, he was imitated by few neighbours, no doubt because of the great costs and strains.

V

Monivea was one of several worlds in which French moved. Upbringing, education and profession all led French to ride the circuits offered by kin and

[64] NLI, MS 4918, pp 284–90; Irish Architectural Archive, Dublin, 22/73, P1 and P2. [65] Grant of fairs and market, 1752, NLI, French Mss, E/64; ibid., MS 4918, pp 8, 414. [66] Indenture, 1 Feb. 1758, NLI, French Mss, E/123; lease to the Incorporated Society, ibid., E/120; ibid., MS 4918, pp 102–3. [67] R. French, draft speech to the House of Commons on behalf of The Incorporated Society, c.1770, NLI, French Mss, E/83; ibid., MSS 4918, p. 416; 4919, f. 67; TCD, MS 5225, p. 97. [68] French, draft speech, NLI, French Mss, E/83. [69] NLI, MS 4918, p. 272; Young, *Tour*, i, p. 387. The Society did not regard the school, with forty pupils, as one of its successes. TCD, MS 5225, p. 315. [70] PRONI, T 2915/7/1, quoted in Cullen, *Emergence*, p. 197.

acquaintances. Following his father, he intended to combine a legal career with supervision of the estate.[71] Even in the early days of his stewardship, he did not treat Monivea as a rural refuge for retirement, contemplation and privacy. A taste for sociability obliged numerous purchases for the Galway residence. Quickly French's local position stirred the hunt for public duties. In 1745, he contested the by-election for the parliamentary seat for the county. His comparative youth, coupled with the low standing of his line of the family in the county hierarchy, made this bid over-bold. His father, when named in the 1726 commission of the peace for County Galway, had been placed second to last. In 1746, Robert French was the last to be listed in the Galway commission.[72] What tempted French into this premature foray is unclear. Vanity and ambition are possible explanations. Another is that he represented particular opinions or a particular group within the county. The unsuccessful intervention cost him dearly: over £1,320.[73] In 1750, he my have considered a fresh contest, but soon receded from it.[74] However, in 1753, he returned to the electoral fray. He was now more securely established and better known in the area, and was allied with another candidate, Charles Daly. French and Daly, seen as representatives of 'the convert interest', were elected. Identified with the controversial court politics of Archbishop Stone and the lord lieutenant, Dorset, Daly and French survived an attempt to have them unseated on petition. French estimated that the election had cost him £1,009 10s. 2d: modest spending when compared with the costs of some county elections of the 1750s and 1760s. In 1768, for example, French's son-in-law, Sir Lucius O'Brien, spent £2,000 to be returned for County Clare. From 1753, French sat continuously in the Dublin parliament, retreating in 1761 from County Galway to the Leitrim borough of Carrick-on-Shannon and then, from 1768 to 1776, sitting for Galway city.[75]

French's public role happily united his concern with the well-being of his neighbourhood with that of the larger communities of Ireland and Britain. In addition, it catered to his activist philosophy. More practically, it obliged his presence in Dublin. While still a bachelor at the bar, he lodged in rooms, attended by two men servants. An agreeable routine, with moderate sums

---

[71] NLI, MS 4919, f. 64. [72] Commissions of the peace, 15 March 1725[6], 6 Nov. 1745, NLI, French Mss, E/62; ibid., MSS 4918, pp 2, 209; 4919, f. 65. Nevertheless, Patrick French had been elected MP for County Galway in 1713. Ibid., MS 4919, f. 64; *HIP*, iii, p. 248. [73] Martin Kirwan to Jane French, 21 March 1748[9], NLI, French Mss, E/62; ibid., MS 4918, pp 2, 209. [74] NLI, MS 4918, p. 6. [75] NLI, MS 4918, p. 6; *HIP*, ii, pp 239–41; iii, 6–7, 249–51; J.S. Kelly, 'The politics of "Protestant Ascendancy" in County Galway' in G. Moran and R. Gillespie (eds), *Galway: history and society* (Dublin, 1996), pp 245–50; A.P.W. Malcomson, *John Foster: the politics of the Anglo-Irish ascendancy* (Oxford, 1978), pp 300–1, 332; D. O'Donovan, 'The money bill dispute of 1753' in T. Bartlett and D.W. Hayton (eds), *Penal era ad golden age: essays in Irish history, 1690–1800* (Belfast, 1979), pp 59–60.

wagered at cards, tickets for the occasional concert – including *Messiah* after Christmas 1745 – and assemblies, the odd convivial evening in the tavern or with the Bull's Head Club, was rapidly replaced with the regime of a married man.[76] His father had been content to rent rooms in the capital: first in Ross Lane; then in Skinner Row.[77] The advance of the family within a single generation, measurable in the contrast between his mother's marriage portion of £600 in 1713 and his own wife's – of £3,000 – was reflected too in the Dublin accommodation now required.

A house north of the river, in still fashionable Mary Street, was rented from a Galway acquaintance, William Ormsby, for £61 p.a.[78] Immediately it was subjected to heavy spending. Eleven brass hearth grates, removed by Ormsby, had to be replaced. The chimneys were rebuilt to stop them from smoking. A coach and horses were bought; more servants were hired. The first year of keeping house in Dublin, from December 1746, involved the heaviest outlay of any year during French's life. Dublin expenses accounted for 35 per cent of his recorded spending for the year. In the Dublin total – of £668 – more than half went on non-recurrent items, such as the structural repairs, buying a coach, furnishings and utensils. Thereafter, Dublin life never cost him more than £440, or about 27 per cent of yearly spending. It could rise suddenly with exceptional demands – repairing or replacing the coach, doctors' fees, inoculating children, his wife's funeral. Spending when in Dublin fluctuated. The length of time passed there varied sharply. The meeting of parliament, every second year, necessitated more prolonged stays than in the alternate years. When French stayed only briefly in the city, Dublin expenditure fell to as little as 10 per cent of his annual budget.[79]

The patterns also altered with the stages of family life. Twice in the 1750s the Frenches established themselves at Mallow, newly popular as an Irish spa. These visits were probably an attempt to restore Nicola French's declining health.[80] The greater elaboration of the Galway and Dublin households reflected the influence of Nicola French. Her death in 1762, together with the departure of older children, explained the contraction and simplification of French's habits.[81] Between 1758 and 1767, French followed a practice common among other gentry who came to Dublin for the parliamentary winters by renting lodgings on an *ad hoc* basis. These modest arrangements meant that outgoings in Dublin

---

76 NLI, MS 4919, ff. 64v–7, 77. **77** J. Gibbs to P. French, 8 Feb. 1716[17]; Bp S. Digby to same, 29 April 1719, NLI, French Mss, E/4; Francis Furlong to same, 25 Jan. 1730[1], ibid., E/5. **78** NLI, MS 4918, pp 602–3. **79** NLI, MS 4918, pp 120–5. **80** NLI, MS 4918; Barnard, *Making the grand figure*, p. 340. **81** The apparently uxorious French wrote three years after her death, 'my ever dearest Nicky until we met again, thou amiable, affable, sensible companion and friend … thou most affectionate wife and tender mother'. NLI, French MS 4918, p. 14.

never amounted to more than 20 per cent of the total expenditure for the year. In 1767, French again took a Dublin house of his own, paying an annual £100. This measure was in preparation for the marriage of his daughter; so too was the costly equipment of the place. The wedding took place in the house.[82] (See Appendix, p. 166.)

In tricking out the Mary Street house, as at Monivea, it is impossible to disentangle French's from his wife's contributions. Many of the items recently bought for Monivea had their counterparts in Dublin. Sumptuously appointed beds had been trundled down to Galway; in the capital, even greater attention was given to the fabrics which hung at the windows and around the best beds. John Savage, an upholsterer and embryonic interior decorator, was paid £40 for the blue Kidderminster bed and a matching set of window curtains, settee and chairs, which dominated the 'street room'.[83] The Frenches wished to impress both relations and visitors from the country. Yet there are also signs that they did not aspire, or could not afford, to be in the vanguard of fashion. Many of the materials and furnishings that they assembled resembled those that had embellished another, grander house in Mary Street back in 1731.[84] The same terms were applied: Kidderminster stuff; paragon; trip and spider tables. The descriptive continuities may obscure decisive shifts in style. Undeniably, the Frenches, members of the parliamentary gentry and of the newly ascendant Protestant elite, patronized leading suppliers, such as Edwin Thomas, 'the mahogany joiner on the [Blind] Quay'. Yet some of what they bought was second-hand, if not yet antique.[85] Also, when obliged to fit up a rented house in 1767, French also rented some of the furniture, like the dining-room table. Those wishing to be leaders of fashion disdained yesterday's wares. Not so French.

The boundary between ostentation and what convention required of families of the standing of the Frenches is often hard to define. Paintings were widely seen as essential accoutrements to the residences of squires. In 1750, Francis Bindon, already an architectural adviser on Monivea, was commissioned to portray French. He charged £18 4s. for the portrait, but painted Mrs French free.[86] Family portraits, either lately painted or inherited through his

---

[82] NLI, MS 4918; TCD, MS 5096. Cf. Barnard, *Making the grand figure*, pp 282–309; T. Mooney and F. White, 'The gentry's winter season' in D. Dickson (ed.), *The gorgeous mask: Dublin 1700–1850* (Dublin, 1987), pp 1–16. [83] NLI, MS 4918, p. 123; Barnard, *Making the grand figure*, p. 300; Desmond Fitzgerald, Knight of Glin, *A directory of the Dublin furniture trade* (Dublin, 1993), p. 12; Glin and Peill, *Irish furniture*, p. 277. [84] Inventories of Bp S. Digby's houses in Dublin, Lackan and Abert, 1720, NLI, French Mss, E/26; *A catalogue of the china ware and linen, of the late Henry Ingoldsby*. [85] NLI, MS 4918, pp 131, 134; A.K. Longfield, 'Old wall papers in Ireland', *JRSAI*, lxxviii (1948), p. 157; Glin and Peill, *Irish furniture*, p. 290. [86] NLI, MS 4918, p. 123; Glin, 'Bindon', pp 3–36; B. Ó Dálaigh, 'Portrait of Francis Bindon', *The Other Clare*, xvii (1993), pp 17–20.

mother from the Digbys, were the staple of collections like that of French. His own taste may have expressed itself with the purchasing of a painting of Vertumnus and Pomona or a 'print landscape'.[87] Aesthetic leanings were powerful in the family in which Bishop Digby had been celebrated more as a portraitist than as a pastor, and the bishop's daughter, French's mother, adept with the pencil, widened the son's artistic and mental horizons.[88] When a tourist in England in 1751, Robert French made a point of inspecting several famous collections, notably Lord Pomfret's at Easton Neston, Lord Pembroke's at Wilton and the Titian of the Cornaro family at Northumberland House in London.[89] These were standard excursions for the cultivated. French's comments may have been culled from the bluffers' guides of the day. But some of his reactions spoke of a well-developed and individualistic sensibility.[90] On arriving in London in 1751, he headed directly to Westminster Abbey to see the recently completed statues of Argyle and General Wade by Roubiliac, over which he enthused as showing 'to what perfection the moderns have brought the art of statuary'. A little earlier, his younger brother, Digby French, while still at Trinity College, had been instrumental in commissioning Roubiliac to sculpt Swift.[91]

French, in responding to buildings, may sometimes have mouthed the aesthetic platitudes of the age. On other occasions, he was prompted to struggle towards his own judgements.[92] The achievements of the moderns, especially the Palladians, pleased him. Accordingly, Burlington's villa at Chiswick could be praised as 'in miniature the model of a light beautiful building'; the chapel at Greenwich Hospital as 'the neatest finished modern building I have seen'. Wren's library at Trinity College Cambridge, though judged inferior to the newer library at Trinity College Dublin, was admired as a 'a very sumptuous modern building'. Additions in Oxford were generally liked, with the palm awarded to the Palladian Peckwater quadrangle at Christ Church (his brother's

---

87 Inventory of Abert, 1720, NLI, French Mss, E/26; ibid., MS 4918, pp 122, 125. **88** William Butler to Sir D. O'Brien, 2 May 1711, NLI, Inchiquin Mss, folder 2621; Barnard, *Making the grand figure*, p. 163. It is likely that some of Bishop Digby's paintings descended to Robert French. Memorandum, 13 March 1732[3], NLI, French Mss, E/26. **89** NLI, MS 7375. For an English visitor's comments on the same sights, see S. Markham, *John Loveday of Caversham, 1711–1789* (Salisbury, 1984), pp 93, 98–9, 500–2, 510–12, 524, 539–42. **90** For Wilton, there was R. Cowdry, *A description of the pictures, statues, busto's, basso-relievos, and other curiosities at the earl of Pembroke's house at Wilton* (London, 1751). For Westminster and Windsor there were more substantial compilations by Crull and Pote: I. Ousby, *The Englishman's England: taste, travel and the rise of tourism* (Cambridge, 1990), pp 79–80. **91** NLI, MS 4919, f. 102; 7375; D. French to R. French, 14 April 1747, NLI, French Mss, E/6; A. Crookshank and D.A. Webb, *Paintings and sculpture in Trinity College Dublin* (Dublin, 1990), p. 132; K.A. Esdaile, *The life and works of Louis François Roubiliac* (Oxford, 1928), pp 54–5, 61–4, 71. The statue of Wade is said not to have been set up until 1752. **92** Peter Kivy, *The seventh sense: a study of Francis Hutcheson's aesthetics and its influence on eighteenth-century Britain* (New York, 1976), pp 109–21; D. Summers, *The judgement of sense: renaissance naturalism and the rise of aesthetics* (Cambridge, 1987), pp 311–34.

college), regarded as 'the finest building of the kind that I have seen'. Apparently enslaved to the rule of taste, he responded subjectively to Westminster Abbey, 'a more awful building and becoming the dignity of the church even than St Paul's', and wondered at the virtuosity of the late gothic, displayed in Henry VII's fan-vaulted chapel at Westminster, King's College Chapel in Cambridge and Gloucester Cathedral. These deeply felt and considered responses are summed up in his love of the Raphael cartoons at Hampton Court: 'the oftener I have seen them, the more I admire them'. He relished the paradox that the disciples, although poor, were clothed in gay colours. 'Yet there is a gravity and dignity preserved even in the colours by a fine strength of shading. Our Saviour, which is most admirable figure I have seen in painting, is clothed in white, deeply shaded.'[93]

French's feeling for painting is attested in his will. He bequeathed to his eldest daughter and younger son, four of his 'watercoloured pictures' and two landscapes in oils. His 'cartoons' and other paintings were 'to go as heirlooms with the house of Monivea as long as the law will permit'. The Galway house, inherited by his grandson, not any rented pad in Dublin, was the proper setting for these visible celebrations of the family and its status.[94] French agreed with those in the eighteenth century who believed that the graphic arts communicated moral messages. As he toured England, he was instructed by pictures no less than by well-drained and richly dunged fields. All had possible application in the campaigns of improvement that he had inaugurated in the west of Ireland. As he rambled around England, he drew whatever caught his fancy: Stonehenge, the bulwark of Windsor Castle, and unfamiliar varieties of pump, gate or cart. At Wilton House, having viewed the sculpture and pictures, he bought seeds from the giant cedars in the hope that they might grow in Galway.[95] He frequently compared what he saw in England with what he knew at home. On reaching St Albans, for example, he wrote that they had not seen 'one plantation of potatoes since we landed'. The view from Richmond Hill, undeniably 'a sweet and pleasing prospect', 'wants the grandeur and wildness of nature which so often appears in the prospects in Ireland'.[96] French, schooled to approve the reasonable and regular, had stirrings of enthusiasm for the picturesque and untamed. The jaunt through England simultaneously stimulated and diverted. It put into practice the philosophy proclaimed by his uncle, John Digby.

[93] NLI, MS 7375. J. White and J. Shearman, 'Raphael's tapestries and their cartoons', *Art Bulletin*, xl (1958), p. 214. [94] Will of Robert French, 14 Feb. 1778, NLI, French Mss, E/128. [95] Cowdry, *Wilton*, p. 85. For early reactions to Stonehenge: C. Chippendale, *Stonehenge complete* (London, 1983), pp 66–99. He equipped himself with 'a book of painting' for 1s. 8d. in Dublin, perhaps some sort of teach-yourself manual. NLI, MS 7375. [96] NLI, MS 7375.

VI

French's encounters with England remind that the neighbouring island belonged to his world, as it did to those of so many others of his rank in eighteenth-century Ireland. The groups of the 'English in Ireland', populous in London and sizeable in Bath and Bristol, were the obvious points of entry for occasional visitors such as French.[97] On arrival in London in 1751, French, having travelled thither with his brother-in-law, the vicar of Athenry, headed straight for his brother's lodgings in Covent Garden. He was then reunited with a sister and her husband (a Persse from Spring Garden in County Galway). The Frenches shopped for their friends and neighbours back in the west. The inevitable lottery tickets had to be bought for the ever-hopeful. In Cambridge, he was guided by another Irish friend. At Bristol and Bath he met many whom he knew from Ireland. He also took up introductions provided by his father-in-law. Yet, in travelling around England, French did not simply move from one Irish ghetto to the next. Some whom he visited did belong to a shadowy group of kinsfolk and expatriate Irish; others did not. He was happy to call on his mother's grand relation, Lord Digby, whose seat at Coleshill was a favourite pull-in for respectable Irish itinerants.[98]

The ease and regularity with which Irish peers, gentlemen and professionals, such as the Frenches (and their spouses), travelled to England brought a mutual familiarity. Sometimes the visitors were ridiculed for their maladroitness. On their side, the Irish wanderers condemned some aspects of the English. So often lampooned as uncouth provincials, they prided themselves on belonging to a notionally sovereign state with a venerable history. Britain was an essential element in their world. So too, for many, was continental Europe, with which through culture and connections they were also strongly linked. The poor experienced these ties differently. For them, movements within Ireland and to England, Wales and Scotland were ruled by the seasons and economic imperatives. French, as has been seen, knew something of England. However, he was not one of those functionally Anglo-Irish who felt equally at home in either kingdom. He never absented himself for long from Galway. Content with his inheritance, he did not strive to build a career that would remove him for protracted spells, as, for example, an army commission would. Even his legal

---

97 For these groups, see Barnard, *Making the grand figure*, pp 326–37; D.M. Beaumont, 'An Irish gentleman in England – the travels of Pole Cosby, c.1730–1735', *Journal of the British Archaeological Association*, cxli (1996), pp 37–54. **98** R. French to W. Smythe, 6 Jan. 1712[13], NLI, PC 447/2; marriage articles of Jane French and Jeremy Marsh, 15 Aug. 1738, ibid., French Mss, E/116; marriage articles of Mary French and Patrick Persse, 2 Nov. 1747, ibid., E/118; ibid., MS 7375.

practice was discontinued once he decided to take the estate in hand. He did not own property in Britain that demanded his attendance. Furthermore, if a curious tourist, he was never a grand tourist. Relatively modest means and economy limited his travelling.

A life passed overwhelmingly either in the Irish provinces or capital shaped his outlook. Seeing the newly finished Westminster Bridge or confronted with the prospect of London from Greenwich Hill, he wrote excitedly of 'a noble building becoming the grandeur of the nation' and marvelled at 'the grandeur, wealth and power of the nation'.[99] In the end, while admiring of the achievements, he did not claim them as those of his own nation. Rather they offered a standard to which his own must aspire. At the same time, he could not overlook that the backwardness and poverty of Ireland arose from its subordination – both constitutional and economic – to Britain. On his own estate he could try to remedy the unhappy situation. In the end, though, the exertions of even the most strenuous and public-spirited could not overcome the structural deficiencies. French never advocated a separation, but he did plead for the reordering of the relationship between Ireland and England.[1]

In the seventeenth century, England still lacked an extended empire, and the Irish tended to liken their plight to that of the other subordinated kingdom, Scotland. The eighteenth-century expansion of a global empire, notably into North America and India, encouraged Ireland to be seen, and the aggrieved Irish to see themselves, as another, nearer colony. In 1770, French watched apprehensively as the ministry reacted to events in Boston, fearful that it might herald insensitive interference in Ireland.[2]

French, throughout his public life, bewailed the erosion of Irish liberty. He identified numerous causes: negligent peers; venal MPs: mercenary voters or a supine populace; the prevalence of Catholicism; the rapacity and vindictiveness of Britain. Such gloom, shared with patriots and country party members, stimulated a rediscovery and acknowledgment of Irishness. French reflected this development as he ruminated on Ireland's own ancient constitution and institutions. No measured reflections by French on the vexed issue of identity have survived. His fragmentary notes on these matters are cryptic and inconsistent.[3] When he wrote and spoke, he did so as a member of the Protestant ascendancy and of its parliament. In these utterances, he seemed to personify the total assimilation within two generations of the convert Frenches to the attitudes and

---

99 NLI, MS 7375. **1** Numerous drafts for parliamentary speeches, c.1768–1772, in NLI, French Mss, E/83; [Robert French], *The constitution of Ireland, and Poynings Law explained* (Dublin, 1770), pp 41–2, 44. **2** R. French to Sir L. O'Brien, 10 May 1772, NLI, Inchiquin Mss, folder 2789. **3** NLI, French Mss, E/83; French, *Constitution of Ireland*.

manners of the ruling Protestant order. The Frenches had come to Ireland as agents of the Anglo-Norman kings and there was a degree of consistency when French referred to the Catholics of Ireland as the 'conquered, and we the conquerors'.[4] At much the same time, having read the enquiries into the Irish language lately published by Charles Vallancey, he concluded that the author deserved the gratitude of 'every Irishman for the great pains he has taken to rescue their language from obscurity'. But, as French revealed, theirs was not his language. He did recant his own dismissal of a barbarous literature and conceded that some ancient Irish poems had been composed 'in an enlightened age', but he would not learn Irish himself.[5]

The assimilation of French into local Protestant society was acknowledged by a notable of Cromwellian origins, Lord Eyre, who unblushingly coupled himself and French as 'men of family and fortune'.[6] For contemporaries, the key to French's integration into the regional and national élites was his Protestantism. Others with backgrounds comparable to that of the Frenches also converted. To some, the reek of popery clung. Thus, Anthony Malone, more successful professionally and politically than French, remained 'a name extremely unpleasing to the protestant and Whig interest in Ireland', owing to residual doubts about the sincerity of his recantation. Even after Malone offered to rebuild the local church, at the end of the avenue to his seat and the ancient burial place of the family, suspicions persisted. As the local Protestant bishop remarked, 'we are to lead such gentlemen by the hand into our interests. Their private thoughts are known to Almighty God'.[7] The Frenches had indeed been led by the hand, and, as Protestant policy planned, what had perhaps begun as a nominal conformity ripened into a fervent commitment to the established Church of Ireland. Robert French's ardour for Protestantism as a tool as well as a consequence of improvement aligned him with the proponents of an aggressive evangelicalism. He patronized the charter schools, founded to wean the young from popery and inure them to industry. He also discriminated against tenants who married Catholics: a relapse into the prohibitions of the seventeenth-century plantations. In general, however, he preferred to guide not to goad. He was prepared to lift some of the disabilities from the Catholics, insisting that they had been disabled only because their political principles had

---

4 NLI, French Mss, E/83. 5 R. French to Sir L. O'Brien, c.1772, NLI, Inchiquin Mss, folder 2789. 6 Lord Eyre to R. French, 16 July 1773, NLI, French Mss, E/6. 7 H. Tuite to Bp H. Maule, 12 April 1745; Bp H. Maule to W. Smythe, 15 April 1745, NLI, PC 449; indenture of 27 Sep. 1721, ibid., French Mss, E/113; C.L. Falkiner (ed.), 'Correspondence of Archbishop Stone and the duke of Newcastle', *EHR*, xx (1905), p. 512. Robert French employed Malone professionally: opinion of 9 July 1747, NLI, French Mss, E/49.

become 'engrafted with their religion'. The seventeenth century proved the contention. Then they had fought not for their faith alone, but, under its cloak, for power. During recent emergencies, French agreed that the Catholics had shown docility. Economic self-interest and pragmatism justified an easing of their condition. Also, he begged fellow members of parliament to recall, 'that both they and we are men, and in preserving our rights remember that benevolence and humanity are due even to enemies'.[8]

Generous impulses were checked, both by a wish to preserve privilege and by a belief that Catholicism was inimical to the prosperity and liberties of Ireland. Everywhere French spotted threats to Irish freedom. Many originated in England; some among the self-indulgent and enervated beneficiaries of the ascendancy within Ireland; yet more were harboured by the Catholic population. Hostility to Catholicism, 'since the morals of that religion [are] incompatible with our constitution', limited what he would willingly grant to the papists.[9] He saw in Catholic doctrine and practices a set of political and social values at variance with his ideals of industry and civility. The evils which increasingly exercised him – an arbitrary executive, an insouciant legislature, corrupt electors and a slothful populace – arose from and perpetuated a moral malaise which Catholicism, if indulged, would only worsen. He lamented, but – except at Monivea – could not reverse the loss of primitive virtue. He approached the Catholic question from an essentially historical perspective, not on the basis of natural rights. He contemplated contemporary society with many of the same presuppositions as other critics – patriots, adherents of the country party, commonwealthsmen and 'true Whigs' – of British, Irish and American maladministration. French declared, 'our countrymen are strangers to those strict morals necessary to support civil liberty. Asiatic wealth is overturning the constitution of Great Britain as it formerly did those of Greece and Rome, and ours must fall with it'.[10]

For all that French's concept of virtue owed to classical and secular thinking, more derived from his own intense Protestantism. At root, he contended, the health, stability and prosperity of any state depended on the moral conduct of its inhabitants. Disciplined behaviour translated into a thriving nation and independent parliament. Protestantism instilled and promoted such virtues; Catholicism did not.[11] His own dedication to public duties, buffeted at the hustings, wavered. Aghast at the avarice of many voters and parliamentary col-

---

[8] Indenture of 23 Jan. 1753, French Mss, E/122. [9] Draft speech, NLI, French Mss, E/83. [10] Draft speech, NLI, French Mss, E/83. [11] R. French to Sir L. O'Brien, 10 May 1770, NLI, Inchiquin Mss, folder 2789; draft speeches, ibid., French Mss, E/83.

leagues, he championed a bill to regulate the running of elections, only to see it blocked by the English ministry. He had warned that unless electoral malpractices were eradicated, 'the honest man will in such case retire, rather than by his example countenance an evil which, like a cancer, eats into the vitals of the constitution'.[12] Accordingly, in 1772, he disengaged himself from national politics, passing the baton to his son-in-law, Sir Lucius O'Brien, whose attitudes usually mirrored French's.[13] A local notable appealed to the disillusioned French to resume the struggle. Revealingly this neighbour played on French's principal loyalty: to the *petit pays* of Galway, 'the county where your family live and have represented must kindle an *amor patriae* of a warmer nature'.[14]

French, neither colonial interloper nor *converso* fifth-columnist within the Protestant enclave, basked in the widespread approval of his independence, industry and public spirit.[15] His practical piety chimed with that of others who busied themselves in the voluntary groups forwarding improvements, such as the Incorporated Society and Dublin Society.[16] French was congratulated on creating a model settlement which could serve as a 'moral school' for his countrymen and successors. Yet his activism had sometimes taken unexpected forms. In 1777, he bequeathed to 'Winifred, the faithful mother of my children', £400, flax and linen yarn. This hardly matched the diamond earrings and paintings left to his favourite children and denoted the humbler status of the companion who had consoled him as a widower. Nevertheless, the legacies would at least save her from the habits of those unfortunates denounced earlier by Patrick French as 'idle, slutty gadding abroads who never spin a thread of woollen yarn'. Seven bastards of Robert French, ornamented with his patronymic, were set up with sixteen milk cows, 200 of his best sheep and dwellings in Monivea. Once more he had acted vigorously to enlarge the fragile Protestant colony in County Galway.[17] *Amor patriae* had indeed been focussed on the immediate vicinity, but public and private virtues had spectacularly diverged.

12 Heads of bill to regulate elections, NLI, French Mss, E/76; Sir L. O'Brien to Lady O'Brien, 26 May 1772, ibid., Inchiquin Mss, folder 2847; E.M. Johnston, *Great Britain and Ireland, 1760–1880* (Edinburgh and London, 1963), p. 125, n.2. **13** Heads of bill to regulate elections, NLI, French Mss, E/76; Sir L. O'Brien to Lady O'Brien, 12 Dec. 1775, 1 March 1776, ibid., Inchiquin Mss, folder 2849; Ainsworth (ed.), *Inchiquin manuscripts*, pp 496–7; Johnston-Liik, *HIP*, v, pp 372–5; O'Brien, *These my friends and forbears*, pp 80–9. **14** Lord Eyre to R. French, 16 July 1775, NLI, French Mss, E/6. **15** Address of Galway merchants, NLI, MS 2745; petition from Galway, ibid., French Mss, E/83; Lord Hertford to R. French, 12 Nov. 1766, ibid., MS 2745; M. Bodkin, 'Notes on the Irish parliament in 1773', *PRIA*, section C, xlviii (1942), p. 193; J. Hardiman, *The history of the town and county of Galway* (Dublin, 1820), p. 184; William Hunt, *The Irish parliament of 1775* (London, 1907), p. 22. **16** J. Liechty, 'Irish Evangelicalism, Trinity College Dublin and the mission of the Church of Ireland at the end of the eighteenth century', unpublished Ph.D. thesis, St Patrick's College, Maynooth (1987); K. Milne, *The Irish Charter Schools, 1730–1830* (Dublin, 1997). **17** Will of R. French, 14 Feb. 1778, NLI, French Mss, E/128; deeds of 15 Nov. 1774 and 14 Aug. 1777, ibid., E/130; E/132. Sir Lucius O'Brien also fathered a second family: O'Brien, *These my friends and forbears*, pp 89–90.

Appendix: Robert French's income and expenditure, 1744–74[18]

Year[19]	Income[20] £ sterling	Total spending £ sterling	Dublin spending £ sterling
1744–5		1494	
1745–6		3146	
1746–7	7414[21]	1879	668
1747–8		1539	341
1748–9	1066	1458	314
1749–50	1227	1361	355
1750–1	1090	1628	438
1751–2	1306	1474	227[22]
1752–3	1426	1450	173
1753–4	1452	1663	424
1754–5	1474	1246	68
1755–6	1422	1576	434
1756–7	1514	1117	140
1757–8	1426	1400	346
1758–9	1426	1232	104[23]
1759–60	1434	1126	196[24]
1760–1	1540	1124	
1761–2	1704	1236	236
1762–3	1727	1018	
1763–4	1679	1124	
1764–5	1783	1093	
1765–6	1687	1791	200
1766–7	1713	1217	
1767–8	1803	1919	307
1768–9	2384	1660	6[25]
1769–70	2333	1614	316
1770–1	2365	1572	10[26]
1771–2	2350	1862	179
1772–3	2440	1580	
1773–4	2332	1847	124

18 NLI, MS 4918. **19** The year for income ran from December to December; that for spending, from June to June. **20** Excluding profits from the demesne and legal practice. **21** The total from 3 June 1744 to 1 December 1748. **22** This includes a ten-week trip to England. **23** In Mallow, but not Dublin. **24** In Mallow and Dublin. **25** For a 'jaunt' to Dublin. **26** A payment for stables while French stayed with Sir Lucius O'Brien in Henrietta Street, Dublin.

CHAPTER SEVEN

Ireland improved?

BY MANY MEASURES, the Ireland of the 1760s and 1770s was much improved on what it had been a century earlier.[1] Population was rising. Prosperity not only seemed assured for the fortunate few who owned land, but was being diffused more widely among substantial tenants, traders, professionals and even the middling sorts of the capital, larger towns and countryside. Despite occasional and recent alarms, the kingdom remained peaceful. If placidity did not always betoken political tractability and docility, it nevertheless brought conditions that conduced to improvements. The visible signs ranged from roads and canals to the architectural splendours of Dublin, shops stocked with imported novelties and a busy associational life for civic activists. Ireland's place in the dynamic British Empire, albeit an ambivalent one – categorized variously as kingdom, province or colony – gave access to rewarding careers and commerce. It also encouraged reflection on how Ireland's condition compared with that of other dependencies in America and Asia. Concurrently, numerous factors – travel, work, correspondence and books – made the observant apply lessons learnt from continental Europe. These comparisons yielded, according to taste, conservative or radical conclusions. Although the ability to muse in these ways on the Irish situation could itself be seen as a sign of an improved Ireland, with a greater availability of print (and the means to buy and read it) and enlarged opportunities for more to travel, it seldom resulted in cheerful verdicts.

Material backwardness and moral malaise still alarmed the thoughtful. As has been noted, commentators in the 1760s and 1770s, while welcoming improvements, felt that much remained to be done. Moreover, the achievements seemed disturbingly vulnerable to reverses, as the recurrence of famines warned. Individual cases, such as the former Petty, now Petty-Fitzmaurice, estates in Kerry, reminded of how remoter regions could resist the standard prescriptions. Even a famed improver like Robert French of Monivea knew the

---

[1] For details of change, see: W.H. Crawford, *The impact of the domestic linen industry in Ulster* (Belfast, 2005); L.M. Cullen, *Anglo-Irish trade 1660–1800* (Manchester, 1968); L.M. Cullen, *An economic history of Ireland since 1660* (London, 1972), p. 54; D. Dickson, *Old world colony: Cork and south Munster, 1630–1830* (Cork, 2005).

fragility of the systems that he had adopted. By the 1770s – as has been noted – he was disillusioned. It may reasonably be argued that the subjective reservations of individual proprietors are no substitute for statistics. By such measures as exports and imports, income from rents and tax revenues, buoyancy not stagnation prevailed. Yet, the perceptions of contemporaries need to be considered. The persistence of pessimism at once reveals one mood of the times and its very persistence requires an explanation.

Dismay at what the sanguine regarded as a vastly improved situation took several forms. The first was to bewail the slow and uneven spread of improvements. Furthermore, impressive developments – for example, new canals and roads – were thought to accentuate the disparities between the separate regions. A similar, but even more pronounced bias arose from the one undeniable triumph: the making and sale of linen. This brought disproportionate benefits to Ulster, so aggravating an imbalance which had not only economic but political, confessional and social consequences not all of which were universally admired. Worryingly, not even the linen trade was immune to recession. Second, a few questioned the prevailing doctrine that equated these works with public spirit and civic-mindedness. Charles O'Hara believed that the rhetoric was at once flattering and self-deluding. Improvement catered to the self-regard of the improver, but the public good was exaggerated if not invented. The Catholic proprietor, Charles O'Conor, shared O'Hara's scepticism. O'Conor, through his own sustained exertions, modestly increased his rent rolls, but doubted whether poor tenants were any better off.[2]

Observers struck by the patchiness of progress frequently reverted to the traditional recipe. Much of what, during the 1770s, Lord Shelburne recommended to invigorate Kerry repeated what his forbear had suggested in the 1660s and 1670s. Belief in the largely untapped harvests of the lakes, rivers and seas of Ireland flowed from Petty through to Shelburne, Sir James Caldwell and William Burton Conyngham at the end of the eighteenth century.[3]

Self-interest recommended measures that might boost incomes. Sermons and tracts seconded this appeal. Assertive collectives promoted the cause. In the 1720s, a new and English bishop of Down and Connor, Francis Hutchinson, became the latest to plead for a 'good' natural history of Ireland. As in the 1650s and 1680s, its compilation was the prerequisite for full realisation of the country's assets. It fitted

---

2 R.J.S. Hoffman (ed.), *Edmund Burke, New York agent with his letters to the New York Assembly and intimate correspondence with Charles O'Hara*, Memoirs of the American Philosophical Society, 41 (Philadelphia, 1956), pp 281–2; R.E. Ward, J.F. Wrynn and C.C. Ward (eds), *Letters of Charles O'Conor of Belangare* (Washington, DC, 1988), pp 10, 59, 68, 106, 160–1, 205–6, 213, 232, 238, 378, 475. 3 See above, pp 50–72.

into a vision in which useful information was amassed and then, like an intellectual dung, spread. Also, it envisaged a Protestant Ireland. Hutchinson, fresh from the reprobate but tractable people of Bury St Edmunds, would punish the wilfully lazy, relieve the weak, teach the ignorant, curb luxury and excess, and create jobs. He reminded how God, in creating land and sea, bestowed on humans 'a gift well worth his [sic] acceptance'. The bishop sought to shepherd his unruly flock into the proper development of the resources. Like so many before him (and after), he wondered why the fish in Irish rivers and seas did not enrich more.[4] Hutchinson, as a substantial landowner, bobbed along in the wake of Cork, Petty, and even the Catholic Darcy. He too imagined that he had discovered the elixir for an enfeebled Ireland. Novelties were, in practice, rare. Radical remedies were constrained by geography, ecology and demography. Bishop Hutchinson, trying to ring the changes, hit one fresh note. Before accepting Irish preferment, he had established himself as an analyst of witchcraft. The north of Ireland offered unexpectedly few occasions to exhibit his expertise. It did at least provide him with an apt analogy as he urged improvements. 'Trade is like witchcraft and works wonders, and I should be glad to see our own people fonder of it.'[5] In so far as trade was gaining momentum in the north-east of Ireland, where Hutchinson was active, it was not through his passionate promotion of the fisheries, but through flax-growing and linen-weaving. The attendant commercial openings rather than well-meaning propaganda endeared the activities to locals.

Disappointment with the modest scale of changes encouraged other sorts of explanation. The structures in which the would-be improvers laboured were unhelpful, if not positively obstructive. It was easiest to blame unsympathetic officialdom, as Petty did, in the forms of the Dublin and London governments. The legal and economic subordination of Ireland to England was a concrete grievance that was readily adduced as a brake on profitable Irish developments. The ending of the dependency became a focus for campaigning. Until it was accomplished, many held back from investing in ventures that would never thrive so long as Ireland was discriminated against. Yet improvers, even if they involved themselves in the public campaigns to secure legislative independence from and commercial equality with Britain, did not always abstain from efforts to improve their own holdings.

To shift responsibility for slow progress onto others, especially such distant villains as the British parliament, preserved the self-esteem of the concerned in

---

4 J. Digby to W. Smythe, 14 Jan. 1744[5], NLI, PC 445; *Some thoughts on the general improvement of Ireland*, p 6; J. Kelly, 'William Burton Conyngham and the north-west fishery of the eighteenth century', *JRSAI*, cxv (1985), pp 64–85. **5** [F. Hutchinson], *A letter to a member of parliament, concerning the imploying and providing for the poor* (Dublin, 1723), p. 16.

Ireland. According to this reading of the situation, once the right framework was set in place, then the work could begin in earnest. Yet, not all who worried over the underdeveloped condition of Ireland put the blame of external forces. An obvious and local answer to the conundrum was that the population of Ireland remained overwhelmingly Catholic. Despite abundant evidence to the contrary – the improving activities of Catholics, such as Kenmare and O'Conor, who had hung onto lands, and the alarming successes of Catholic traders – there survived a strong belief that the confession stifled enterprise. Therefore, it continued to be an article of faith that Ireland would prosper only when it had become a predominantly Protestant country. The effective abandonment by the middle of the eighteenth century of any systematic attempts to suppress Catholicism was represented as a vital cause of the sluggish economy. Accordingly, the moral and evangelical elements of improvement, always present in the English and Protestant programme for Ireland, were rediscovered and given priority. They had never been altogether forgotten, as the manifestoes of the Incorporated Society, Physico-Historical Society and Dublin Society all demonstrated. But the assertively confessional or sectarian emphasis in both collective and individual projects had been submerged under more crudely utilitarian and sectarian arguments. The strongly Protestant ethos of the voluntary associations forwarding improvements was also apparent in energetic individuals, such as French or Lady Arbella Denny and Sir James Caldwell.

Fervent Protestants hoped to quicken torpid schemes to convert Catholics. Also, as so often in the past, it was much easier to look inwards than outwards. The introspective were hardly reassured. Protestants in Ireland had failed to use their advantages to promote the moral regime without which material changes would prove transitory. Little had been done to reach out towards the Catholic population; even less to woo them in their own tongue. Worse still, too many Protestants simply luxuriated in their good fortune, heedless of responsibilities towards the less fortunate. Poverty, endemic in Ireland, seemed to have worsened notwithstanding economic diversification. The visibility of the poor – mendicants, beggars, itinerants – offended and rebuked the well-to-do. It remained imperative to create jobs and relieve the impotent poor. Equally upsetting, but assumed to be a newer phenomenon, were the vicious rich. Alluring objects proliferated, and with them luxury. Once more a moral critique was devised to account for the unimproved state of Ireland.[6] Typical of this attitude, and apparently popular in quarters prone to self-flagellation, was a philippic delivered by the Reverend Philip Skelton from the pulpit of St

---

6 M.J. Powell, *The politics of consumption in eighteenth-century Ireland* (Basingstoke, 2005).

Andrew's church in 1776. The occasion was a day of prayer for the success of British arms against the American colonists. Skelton foretold the destruction of Britain. This ruin, he contended, was a necessary judgment from God on peoples sinking into luxury, vice and libertinism. He had no truck with the self-styled patriots in Protestant Ireland and suspected the volunteer movement of sinister motives. He approved 'the aloetic unction of adversity' as a necessary purgative of the ills – both national and individual – that had accumulated with peace and prosperity. Skelton's call for renewed efforts to reform manners prefigured a systematic campaign.[7]

By this time, the best organized institutional mechanism for improvement was the Dublin Society. It did not monopolize the work. As has been seen, two of the busiest improvers – Harris and Smith – did not join the Society, preferring to forward the cause through other groups. Nor did all improving landowners belong to the Dublin Society. Simple distance from the capital, where the society met, deterred some. An attempt in the 1730s to create a local equivalent for improvers in and around Limerick showed how the spirit might exist in the provinces but not connect up with the metropolitan organization.[8] Others, equally dedicated to furthering agriculture, rural industries and understanding of Ireland, abstained from the Society. Bishop Berkeley of Cloyne wished it and the Physico-Historical Society well, but subscribed to neither.[9]

Robert French personified the proprietor who found the Society, with its publications, premiums and ethos, helpful to his own projects. Three other examples must suffice to make the point that it was possible to promote improvements outside the ambit of the Society and its predecessors. Samuel Waring, a County Down squire, well-travelled, inquisitive and innovative, corresponded with the luminaries of the Dublin Philosophical Society, several of whom he would have been taught by or have known when an undergraduate at Trinity College in the 1680s. Waring served in parliament and as a trustee of the Linen Board. Yet, he was not recruited into the early Dublin Society. Perhaps this meant no more than that he was seldom in Dublin and that his health was declining.[10] Waring's zest for the kind of work beloved of the Society is demonstrated by a pamphlet that he published: on the culture of forest trees. The

---

7 P. Skelton, *A discourse preached at St Andrew's Church, Dublin: on Friday, the 13th of December, 1776*, 2nd edn (Dublin, 1777), p. 24. Cf. T. Leland, *A sermon preached before the University of Dublin, on Friday the 13th of December 1776* (Dublin, 1777), pp 8, 10–15. 8 *An essay to induce the gentlemen of the county of Lymerick to form a society for the improvement of tillage by English husbandry, and to encourage arts and manufactures* (Dublin, 1735). 9 A.A. Luce and T.E. Jessop (eds), *The works of George Berkeley, bishop of Cloyne*, 9 vols (London, 1948–57), viii, pp 285–6. 10 T.C. Barnard, 'What became of Waring? The making of an Ulster squire' in V. Carey and U. Lotz-Heumann (eds), *Taking sides? Colonial and confessional mentalités in early modern Ireland* (Dublin, 2003), reprinted in Barnard, *Ascents and descents*, pp 235–65

danger of equating the Dublin Society with the main thrust of improvements is illustrated by cases of non-members like Waring. The patchiness of information about what was being attempted, especially by individuals outside the well-known and reasonably documented groups, is also revealed by Waring. His tract seemingly survives only in a unique copy, fortuitously preserved outside Ireland, although it had been published there.[11]

A second enterprising and energetic landowner who was never recruited into the Dublin Society was William Smythe of Barbavilla in County Westmeath. Smythe's gradual ascent into the squirearchical élite of eighteenth-century provincial Ireland followed a familiar route. The established church enabled his father, successively bishop of Raphoe and Kilmore, to provide well for his progeny. Training for and practice at the bar, coupled with an advantageous marriage, helped William Smythe to establish himself at Barbavilla in the 1720s. There he adopted an orderly and impressive regime. A new mansion in the classical taste, albeit adjudged old-fashioned by some, was built and splendidly appointed. Smythe oversaw his estate attentively and experimented with new crops. Clover seed could be found in Dublin but superior hop seed had to be sent from England.[12] He also involved himself in schemes to improve inland navigation centring on the Shannon.[13] Particular efforts were directed into his own 'town' of Collinstown. In order to secure the grant of a market for Collinstown, protracted lobbying was required. Well-placed acquaintances in Dublin pleaded Smythe's case.[14] Once the patent was granted, the dates of the market and fair had to be advertised.[15]

For the venture to succeed, it had to compete successfully against rivals in the locality. To do this, facilities were provided by the landlord. A market house was constructed in which, on winter days, a fire was lit. Such comforts counted for little if there was not produce to be sold capable of attracting customers from a distance. Initially, the traders' fees payable to the patentee should be waived.[16] Like many contemporaries, Smythe was impressed by the success of the linen manufacture in the north and schemed to introduce it among his own

---

11 E.C. Nelson, 'A short treatise of firr-trees ... (Dubin, 1705) by Samuel Waring', *Archives of Natural History*, xix (1992), pp 305–6. This work is not included in the *English Short Title Catalogue*. **12** M. Clarke to W. Smythe, 17 June 1732, NLI, PC 447; W. Waller to same, 1 March 1745[6], ibid., PC 445. **13** T. Smythe to R. Smythe, 11 and 22 Nov. 1755, 15 Dec. 1755, 14 Feb. 1756, NLI, PC 448. Cf E. Magennis, 'Coal, corn and canals: parliament and the dispersal of public moneys, 1695–1772' in D.W. Hayton (ed.), *The Irish parliament in the eighteenth century: the long apprenticeship* (Edinburgh, 2001), pp 71–86. **14** D. Clarke to W. Smythe, 2 and 13 Feb. 1741[2], 16 May 1749, NLI, PC 447; R. Nugent to same, 16 Nov. 1749, NLI, PC 449. **15** R. Smythe to W. Smythe, 30 Oct. 1751, NLI, PC 436; W. Smythe to R. Smythe, [undated, Nov. 1751], 7 Nov. 1752, NLI, PC 445. **16** F. Thompson to W. Smythe, 18 Nov. 1749, NLI, PC 445; J. Cooley to W. Smythe, 3 and 24 Feb. 1750[1], NLI, PC 446.

tenants. Thomas Pakenham was one well-informed neighbour and ally who encouraged Smythe to try the expedient.[17] Smythe, like French at Monivea, appreciated the importance of expert instructors. As early as 1730, there was talk of establishing a school to teach spinning.[18] Several attempts were made to lure the proficient from Ulster. An intermediary at Dromore in County Down persuaded some from that area to see what Smythe and Westmeath might offer. The northerners disliked the strongly papist district and did not stay.[19] Later, connections in County Cavan were exploited to persuade operatives to try life in the midlands. Also, the Smythes advertised in Belfast for a manager of their linen mill.[20] By 1750, when Collinstown market eventually opened, linen yarn was the commodity that correspondents noted. In 1751, it seemed as if the enterprise was set fair for success because a dozen buyers had turned up.[21] How long the novelty lasted is unclear. In 1754, Smythe (according to his own account) had twenty-four looms at work.[22] Thanks to his good connections in high places, he had attracted subsidies. The Linen Board awarded equipment to Smythe's venture.[23] In times of agricultural plenty, the market thrived.[24] Yet, the smallness of scale, the volatility of the market and perhaps the variable quality of the product introduced uncertainties. Smythe himself admitted worries lest the young, for want of employment, lapse into sloth and idleness, despite coming of industrious and Protestant parents. Just as he had appealed for help through state aid for the nascent linen manufacture, so he looked for further assistance to the Incorporated Society. Also, he encouraged the establishment of a school to teach girls to read and needlework.[25]

Undoubtedly Smythe's gaze wandered beyond the demesne around Barbavilla that he had created and planted. His agreeable way of life depended on his rentals. Increasing them required investment and innovation. Smythe's paternalism need not have been altogether self-interested. His wife voiced alarm that the children of the poor would starve when the potato crop failed.[26] Notwithstanding the occasional expressions of humanity by the Smythes, the impact of their experiments is seen more easily in his and his successors' circumstances than in the lives of the tenants. Among the latter, the enterprising stressed what they had done, usually to second appeals for preferential treat-

17 T. Pakenham to W. Smythe, 5 Oct. 1739, 16 Feb 1741[2], 12 Feb. 1742[3], NLI, PC 447. **18** T. Doolittle to W. Smythe, 21 Dec. 1730, NLI, PC 448. **19** J. Brush to W. Smythe, 30 Nov. 1741, 7 and 19 April 1742, 22 May 1742, NLI, PC 449. **20** F. Thompson to W. Smythe, 4 March 1761; R. Smythe to M. Clarke, undated, NLI, PC 447. **21** M. Clarke to W. Smythe, 1 Dec. 1750, NLI, PC 447; J. Cooley to same, 3, 10, 20 and 24 Feb. 1750[1], 10 March 1750[1], 31 March 1751, NLI, PC 446. **22** W. Smythe to Linen Board, 12 Jan. 1754, NLI, PC 449. **23** M. Burgh to W. Smythe, 31 March 1747, NLI, PC 446. **24** W. Smythe to R. Smythe, 17 March 1753, NLI, PC 445. **25** W. Smythe to R. Smythe, 20 March 1753, NLI, PC 445. **26** B. Smythe to W. Smythe, 16 April [?1730], NLI, PC 448.

ment from the landlord. In this manner, a tenant living near Mullingar described the plantations of elm and oak in quincunx form, and suggested that his example should be copied by others, 'which would make a handsome figure in so naked a country'. This exemplar boasted that he had effected more improvements than any other of Smythe's tenants. 'Since you gave me a little beginning and by pinching myself and family a little', he had built up a stock of 130 sheep and twenty head of black cattle. The details prefaced a request for a tenancy of 100 acres.[27]

Smythe's township at Collinstown remained stubbornly puny. Moreover, agriculture and even the linen trade were susceptible to the vagaries of the weather and local, national and international oscillations. Contemporary comment indicated that one of the hoped-for changes, a drift away from Catholicism towards Protestantism, did not happen. Migrants from the north were deterred by the prevalent Catholicism. A change that was observed elsewhere was the emergence and growth of groups of tenants who, thanks to the generous terms of their tenures and their own exertions, raised themselves above the generality. This stratum, found in both the countryside and the towns, excited much hostility owing to its alleged rapacity, ruthlessness, parasitism and self-indulgences. Some of the denigration was envious and unfair. The middle-men, in thickening and complicating the hitherto simple and polarized social and economic structures of provincial Ireland, could be agents of improvement. Their tastes helped to stimulate local production and trade, and contributed to greater diversification in goods, services and ideas.[28] The final aspect was regarded as another unwelcome development, the implications of which had never been accurately foretold. The goods bought by the modestly prosperous included the books, newspapers and pamphlets which were circulating in greater quantities in provincial Ireland by the mid-eighteenth century. Reading and discussion led to a variety of opinions many of which help to explain the growing political volatility from the 1760s and, ultimately, the activism of the 1790s. Improvements, which had been predicted to sedate a contented population, instead excited expectations that neither the distant British nor the Dublin government seemed able or willing to satisfy.

So far as the Smythes at Barbavilla are concerned, personal responses are clearest. How far they were peculiar to the family (and others of their background) or more widely spread in later eighteenth-century Ireland remains to be established. There are strong parallels with – as well as differences from –

---

[27] F. Thompson to W. Smythe, 8 Nov. 1746, NLI, PC 445. [28] Barnard, *New anatomy*, pp 249–51; D. Dickson, 'Middlemen' in T. Bartlett and D.W. Hayton (eds), *Penal era or golden age: essays in Irish history, 1690–1800* (Belfast, 1979), pp 162–85.

French at Monivea. Squire Smythe did not moulder continuously in the midlands. He visited Dublin regularly and England occasionally. Through kindred and acquaintances he was abreast of events and experiments. He neither served in the House of Commons nor joined the Dublin Society. Again, then, he serves as a warning about overlooking those who do not appear in the records of the obvious agencies of improvement. Early in the century, the family's politics had inclined towards Toryism: an allegiance which faded into a discreet scepticism about successive administrations. Central to the behaviour of the family was its confessional affiliation. Despondency that the prescriptions recommended by expert analysts did not convert Ireland into a Protestant kingdom, together with the torpor of the economy, made the Smythes receptive to moves that might quicken the desired transformations. In particular, the established Church of Ireland, having made little headway against its twin competitors – the Catholics and Presbyterians – by the 1740s faced a new challenge from the Methodists. Calls for spiritual renewal among adherents of the state church resembled the periodic bouts of introspection in the wake of shocks and rebuffs, such as the 1641 uprising and the Jacobite *revanche* of 1685 to 1691. Billy Smythe, grandson and eventual heir of William Smythe, was carried along by the evangelical enthusiasm gathering momentum in Protestant Dublin.[29] His stated wish was to 'carry a conscience void of offence towards God and towards man'.[30]

Recourse to spiritual salves recurred regularly. This refuge was not of course unique to Ireland. Some of the same crises that turned Britain to authorized prayer and repentance, such as the war in America, affected Ireland. However, peculiar to Ireland were the sequence of natural disasters – famines – and disorders. In 1775, the owner of Barbavilla described how 'all the lower class of people within these last 30 years are become wild, uncivilized, untractable and ferocious'. Anguished Protestants, like Smythe, contemplated their shortcomings yet again. The situation in Westmeath was attributed to the partiality and corruption of the leading proprietors in the county.[31] The familiar plaint about the neglect of evangelizing among the ignorant and misguided was repeated. Spiritual sluggishness among the faithful was also berated. The carnal spirit that was always battling for ascendancy seemed to have become even stronger.

[29] The most thorough exploration remains, J. Liechty, 'Irish Evangelicalism, Trinity College Dublin and the mission of the Church of Ireland at the end of the eighteenth century', unpublished Ph.D. thesis, St Patrick's College, Maynooth (1987); K. Milne, *The Irish Charter Schools, 1730–1830* (Dublin, 1997); N. Yates, *The religious condition of Ireland, 1770–1850* (Oxford, 2006). On Presbyterian developments, see A.R. Holmes, *The shaping of Presbyterian belief and practice, 1770–1840* (Oxford, 2006); I. McBride, *Scripture politics: Ulster Presbyterians and Irish radicalism in the late eighteenth century* (Oxford, 1998).
[30] S.R. Penny, *Smythe of Barbavilla* ([Oxford], 1974), p. 79. [31] R. Smythe to L. Smythe, undated, after 14 Dec. 1775, NLI, MS 41,599/9; same to unknown, 1777, ibid., MS 41,599/11.

Prosperity bred materialism. Protestants in Ireland had long been familiar with poverty. Indeed, the familiarity made them ingenious and energetic in dealing with the poor. Outlets for practical piety proliferated: the parish vestry, voluntary organizations dedicated to schools, hospitals, work-houses, refuges and asylums. The consequences of wealth, although foreseen by the austere and disapproving like Richard Lawrence in the 1680s, were generally unexpected.[32] Faced with the phenomenon, it was easy enough for the anxious in Ireland to use the terminology and explanations popular elsewhere. So the concepts of luxury, corruption and oriental despotism were invoked. Nevertheless, the thoughtful hoped to introduce specifically Irish factors before devising remedies suited to the local circumstances.

Many of the solutions recalled earlier ones. Although they had been applied already and seemed to have failed, they were not totally discredited. Rather, it was contended that they had never been employed rigorously and systematically. Accordingly, faith was placed in the traditional blend of moral and material improvements. As early as 1758, a chaplain chided the members of the Dublin parliament over the enervating effects of luxury. He warned that noisy zeal for the Protestant cause, 'testified by a full glass and empty boastings', did not suffice. National guilt would provoke a national disaster, and could be prevented only by 'immediate reformation'. The preacher contrasted the insouciance of the Irish Protestants with the temperance, patience and fortitude of the Prussians.[33] Once more, societies were created to oversee initiatives. The Society for the Discountenancing of Vice seemed in its philosophy and programme reminiscent of the societies for the reformation of manners that had sprung up in the Dublin of the 1690s. The practical measures, proposed or tried – for example by Caldwell in Fermanagh or Shelburne in Kerry – merely redoubled what interventionist landlords and their agents had been recommending for a century or more.

II

A third figure, Sir James Caldwell, offers a different cautionary tale. Caldwell, bent on raising the rentals of his Fermanagh inheritance, followed many of the courses advocated by the Dublin Society. Indeed, so close was his thinking to its philosophy that he deluged it with his pet fancies.[34] A series of pamphlets

---

[32] See above, pp 73–88. [33] E. Bayly, *A Sermon, preached in St Andrew's Dublin. Before the Honourable House of Commons ... On Friday, the 17th of February, 1758* (Dublin, 1758); E. Bayly, *A sermon preached on the opening of the chapel of the Magdalen Asylum for female penitents* (Dublin, [1768]).   [34] S.

solicited support from the Society for his quirky innovations in fishing, iron-making, apiary, education and charity.[35] On his lands, Caldwell practised a benevolent and idiosyncratic regime.[36] In 1758 he congratulated himself that he never refused a supplicant a day's work and paid them promptly. He agitated to exploit the fishing on Lough Erne, the timber of the neighbourhood and other, hidden resources more intensively. He, too, grasped at the apparent wonder of the north – linen – not least because it would give paid labour to women and girls.[37] He was keen to publicize his achievements, and even keener to have visitors, notably Arthur Young, praise them in print.[38] However, Caldwell was too individualistic to work harmoniously with the Dublin Society. He quarrelled with its directors and pettishly ended his dealings with the body.[39] Candid friends warned Caldwell that his schemes, although undoubtedly welcome to his tenants, were frequently impracticable and unprofitable. At once idealistic and obsessive, Caldwell shows the complex, even contradictory motives of the improvers, and the mixed results of their efforts. A thorough analysis of the estate confirms the limited impact of Caldwell's grandiose schemes. Mixed husbandry with the raising of livestock for the local markets had not been displaced as the principal activity by the linen trade, although the latter supplemented farming very usefully.[40] Idiosyncratic ventures, such as supplying Dublin with preserved and barrelled eels, disappointed the innovator.[41]

Caldwell, an eccentric enthusiast, lurched from one project to the next. For a time, the novelty of his inheritance by Lough Erne absorbed him. But all too

---

Hutchinson to Sir J. Caldwell, 21 April 1767, JRL, B 3/10/709; Lord Arran to same, 22 April 1767, ibid., B 3/10/711; I. Mann to same, 25 April 1767, ibid., B 3/10/713–14; Lord Ranelagh to same, 1 May 1767, ibid., B 3/10/715; R. Woodward to same, 5 May 1767, ibid., B 3/10/716; J. Leigh to same, 20 June 1771, ibid., B 3/10/1151–2; Sir E. Loftus to same, 15 Nov. 1771, ibid., B 3/10/1153–5; T. Conolly to same, 11 May 1774, ibid., B 3/10, letter book 7/32. **35** Papers on salmon and other fisheries, JRL, B 3/26/83–91; Sir J. Caldwell, *A letter to the Dublin Society, from Sir James Caldwell, ... giving an account of the culture and quality of several kinds of grass* (Dublin, 1765); idem, *A proposal for the increase of apiaries in Ireland* (Dublin, 1764); idem, *Two letters to the Dublin Society. The first proposing the encouragement of a manufacture, and the second of a commerce* (Dublin, 1767). **36** T.C. Barnard, 'The artistic and cultural activities of the Caldwells of Castle Caldwell, 1750–1783', *IADS*, x (2007), pp 90–111; M. Busteed, *Castle Caldwell, County Fermanagh: life on a west Ulster estate, 1750–1800* (Dublin, 2006); J.B. Cunningham, *A history of Castle Caldwell and its families* (Monaghan, [1980]), pp 83–101. **37** Busteed, *Castle Caldwell*, p. 31. **38** Copies of an 'advertisement of the jubilee in print', 29 July 1773, JRL, B 3/26/115–17; O. Wynne to Sir J. Caldwell, 22 Oct. 1777, ibid., B 3/10, letter 509; W.H.G. Bagshawe, *The Bagshawes of Ford: a biographical pedigree* (London, 1886), pp 323–35; A. Young, *A tour in Ireland*, 2 vols (Dublin, 1780), i, pp 263–8. **39** Lord Westmeath to Sir J. Caldwell, 15 Nov. 1771, JRL, B 3/15/166; G.E. Howard to same, 14 Nov. 1771, ibid., B 3/16/169; Sir J. Caldwell to vice-president of the Dublin Society, 16 Feb. 1774, ibid., 3/16/415; R. Law to Sir J. Caldwell, 19 May 1774, ibid., B 3/10, letter books, 7, pp 37–40; M. Law, 6 May 1775, ibid., 3/6/203 **40** Busteed, *Castle Caldwell*, pp 31–3. **41** T. Dickson to Sir J. Caldwell, 3 Jan. 1756, JRL, B 3/20/91; R. Stanford to same, 12 March 1759, ibid., B 3/20/365; C. O'Neill to Sir J. Caldwell, 10 Nov. 1781, ibid., B 3/20/318; Caldwell, *Two letters to the Dublin Society*.

soon, he grew bored with rural routines and plunged anew into the society of Dublin, London and even Vienna.[42] Moreover, his country projects, although portrayed as public-spirited, were subordinated to one overriding obsession. Caldwell craved elevation to the Irish peerage: this honour would match the dignity that he had received in the Austrian imperial service. To qualify for the peerage required an annual income greater than his £2,300.[43] Improving his revenues, therefore, was the prerequisite for ennoblement. In addition, a reputation for public spiritedness would second his claims. Also, whether consciously or not, he applied the method extolled by Petty. Meticulous record-keeping, ensuring that each initiative was expressed in 'number, weight and measure', meant that the length of fish released into his pools and the tallies of eels netted were all noted.[44] Caldwell did indeed diversify the occupations available to his tenants and their dependants. The beneficiaries demonstrated their gratitude in pageants artfully choreographed by Caldwell himself. Victims of his despotism (benevolent or not) attracted less notice.[45]

Caldwell, like many in his station in eighteenth-century Ireland, linked improvement causally with Protestantism. Religious rituals bulked large in the celebrations on the estate. Special prayers and anthems were composed, in which the God-given duties to labour, obedience and hierarchy were stressed.[46] Caldwell also subscribed to the orthodox doctrine that wherever possible Protestants were to be preferred as tenants. In public, too, he argued against even moderate relaxation of the legal inhibitions on Catholics.[47] The intransigence is the odder when it is remembered that Caldwell had prospered as a Protestant in the army of a Catholic sovereign, and had benefited from a more tolerant policy than he was now prepared to support in Ireland.[48] On his own holdings, he was obliged to grant leases, *faute de mieux*, to Catholics. In practice, he behaved generously towards the local Catholic communities, assisting in the building of their chapels, and maintaining friendly relations with the bishops of the region.[49]

---

42 Lord Fitzmaurice to Sir J. Caldwell, 8 April 1755, JRL, B 3/14/45; Sir J. Caldwell to Lord Fitzmaurice, undated [spring 1755 or 1756], JRL, B 3/14/46; Sir J. Hort to Lady Caldwell, 4 March 1758, PRONI, D 1634/2/15; same to Sir J. Caldwell, 14 March 1758, ibid., D 1634/2/16; Lady Caldwell to Sir J. Caldwell, 2 Feb. 1773, JRL, B 3/29/58. **43** Busteed, *Castle Caldwell*, p. 31. **44** Caldwell account book, openings 31, 33, 73, 100–6, JRL, B 3/28/2; Lady Caldwell, account book, s.d. 5 Nov. 1762, ibid., B 3/28/3. **45** Bagshawe, *The Bagshawes of Ford*, pp 335–7. **46** *Anthems, to be sung in the Chapel of Castle Caldwell*, JRL, B 3/26/55; prayers composed by Dr John Hawkesworth at request of Caldwell, 25 May 1771 and undated, ibid., B 3/26/56, 59, 65; 'Advertisement of the jubilee in print', ibid., B/ 3/26/115; T. Barnard to Sir J. Caldwell, 27 Aug. 1777, ibid., B 3/17/4. **47** W. Maxwell to Sir J. Caldwell, 17 Feb. 1763; Lord Mount Florence to same, 4 Jan. 1764; Sir John Hort to same, 15 March 1764, JRL, B 3/10, Caldwell letter books, 3, pp 425–6, 467–9, 471; Sir James Caldwell, *A brief examination of the question whether it is expedient either in a religious or political view to pass an act to enable papists to take real securities for money which they may lend* (Dublin, 1764). **48** *A few remarks on a pamphlet* [written by Sir James Caldwell] (Dublin, 1764), p. 3. **49** Dr Peter

The practical accommodations sit awkwardly with Caldwell's public stance, and arouse the suspicion of hypocrisy. Like so many other Protestant proprietors, Caldwell's position rested on the seventeenth-century dispossession of Catholics. This fact was inescapable and obliged defence of the skewed system of landownership throughout Ireland. However, the feeling was growing that inherited privilege carried obligations, and these Caldwell – like French and Smythe – certainly strove to fulfil. The political need to uphold Protestantism obscures the private beliefs of members of the élite. In Caldwell's case, he was on the fringes of, if not more deeply immersed in, the worlds of pious Protestantism. His wife was a bishop's daughter, and, though that background did not guarantee strong religious feelings, she seems to have been sympathetic towards the practical piety favoured by a section of prospering Dublin society.[50] Similar attitudes can be discerned in Caldwell's mother. These influences were fortified by others within the extended circle of kin and acquaintances. Visiting George Rochfort at Rochfort (later Tudenham) in Westmeath during 1773, Caldwell approved a household marked by 'regularity and religion'.[51] This sober tone echoed his own domestic arrangements.[52]

The worthy and reprobate were distinguished at all levels. Caldwell, hardened by years in the saddle, was easy in raffish and sporting company. He fought duels and laid extravagant wagers. Yet he was readily welcomed into the society of *literati* and the ingenious, whether in Dublin or London. He seems too to have shared some of the attitudes of devoted Protestants. Lady Arbella Denny, a distant connection by marriage, was pre-eminent in this company. Caldwell agreed with the common estimation of her as the best contemporary personification in Ireland of Christian virtue and civic activism: 'I know of no such woman either with respect to piety, virtue or understanding'. Her letters conveyed 'sentiment, politeness & elegance; ... piety without enthusiasm and virtue without ostentation'. A Dubliner described her hyperbolically as the 'most angelic being here'.[53] In an unusually strong form, Lady Arbella embodied an important but often neglected strain in eighteenth-century Ireland. Her interests extended over many areas, but focussed sharply on philanthropy. She

---

Kelly to Sir J. Caldwell, 21 Sep. 1765, JRL, B 3/17/40; Dr Denis Maguire to same, 20 June 1765; Lord Taaffe to same, Dublin, 29 June 1765, 2 July 1765, JRL, B 3/10, Caldwell letter books, 3, pp 548–52, 553–6, 557–8, 565–71. **50** Abp J. Hort to E. Hort, 12 July 1748, JRL, 3/30/105. **51** Sir J. Caldwell to Lady Caldwell, 11 Feb. 1773, JRL, B 3/29/58; Bagshawe, *The Bagshawes of Ford*, p. 334. **52** Owen Wynne to Sir J. Caldwell, 20 Nov. 1777, JRL, B 3/10/445–9. **53** P. Magran to Lady Caldwell, 4 Jan. 1770, JRL, B 3/32/30; Sir J. Caldwell to unknown, April 1769, ibid., B 3/10, pp 303–5; Northumberland to Lady A. Denny, 15 Oct. 1763, PRONI, T 2872/35; E.G.P. Fitzmaurice (ed.), *Life of William, earl of Shelburne ... with extracts from his papers and correspondence*, 3 vols (London, 1875–6), i, pp 7, 11–15; M.P. O'Malley, *Lios-an-Uisce: the history of a house and its occupants from 1753 to the present day* ([Dublin], 1982), p. 18.

addressed the endemic problems of poverty and some of the less familiar ones arising from wealth. Steely in her principles, she seldom condemned even the most inveterate sinner. So, when in 1787 the lord lieutenant, Rutland, died prematurely of his dissipations, she merely observed that his death 'has made many of his associates shrink back a little towards regularity of hours and sobriety'.[54]

Rather than judge, she preferred to devise remedies for the unfortunates who abounded in later eighteenth-century Dublin. Three institutions were especially dear to her: the Lying-In Hospital; the Foundling Hospital; and the Magdalen Asylum. She cooperated with the like-minded to raise and spend funds for the refuges. Other similar charities had sprung up, both within the capital and the provinces. Each attested to the severe problems of poverty and ignorance and a wish on the part of the fortunate to rectify the situation. Oversight of the schools, hospitals and workhouses fell to a small number of activists who wished to translate their dismay into help. Clergymen and professionals predominated. The Madgalen Asylum sheltered and aimed to rehabilitate destitute women, some of whom had resorted to prostitution. Admissions were on the basis of recommendations from a few clergymen, whom Lady Arbella evidently knew and trusted.[55] Another in the same circle intended to raise money for the charity through a collected edition of his writings.[56] He – Philip Skelton – was a Church of Ireland incumbent of a conservative and pessimistic outlook.[57] However, like his patron, Lady Arbella, and indeed like his former pupil, Caldwell, Skelton knew that it was not enough to lament and figuratively rend garments, even if of foreign manufacture. Instruction, both practical and ethical, was vital. So, too, was the provision of food in the dire emergencies that overwhelmed his poor parishioners in the north-west.[58]

Skelton put his popularity as a preacher at the disposal of Lady Arbella Denny's favourite charities. Other clergymen drawn into her ambit thanks to their shared values included William Henry and Edward Bayley.[59] Henry had

---

[54] Lady A. Denny to Dowager Lady Shelburne, 1 March 1788, Bowood House, Shelburne Mss, 6/67. [55] Register, Magdalen Asylum, Representative Church Body Library, Dublin, MS 551/1.1; Barnard, *New anatomy*, p. 322. [56] P. Skelton to W. Knox, 14 Sep. 1766, 16 Oct. 1769, Clements Library, Ann Arbor, Knox Mss; Lady A. Denny to Dowager countess of Shelburne, 8 Oct. 1770, Bodleian, Lyell empt. 36, f. 13v; same to Lady Shelburne, 15 May 1784, Bowood House, Shelburne MSS 6/48; proposal for volume 6 of P. Skelton's collected works, ibid., MSS 6/50; *The works of the Rev. Philip Skelton*, 6 vols (Dublin, 1770–84), i, pp i–viii; vi, dedication. [57] P. Skelton to W. Knox, 5 Dec. 1769, Ann Arbor, Knox Mss; S. Burdy, *The life of Philip Skelton*, ed. N. Moore (Oxford, 1914), pp 109, 183–4; 'Mundanus' [Philip Skelton], *The candid reader, or a modest, yet unanswerable apology for all books that ever were, or possibly can be wrote* (Dublin, 1744); [P. Skelton], *Ophiamaches: or Deism revealed* (London, 1749); [P. Skelton], *Some proposals for the revival of Christianity* (Dublin and London, 1736); P. Skelton, *A discourse preached at St Andrew's Church, Dublin: on Friday, the 13th of December, 1776*, 2nd edn (Dublin, 1777). [58] P. Skelton to Sir James Caldwell, 27 April 1757, JRL, B 3/17/65; Burdy, *Life of Philip Skelton*, ed. Moore, pp 134–5. [59] For Bayley: T. Barnard, 'Almoners of

long championed the interconnected causes of physical and moral improvement. He had contributed to the task of surveying natural resources and composed a lengthy description, based on his own travels, of the physical changes wrought by improvers in the north west of Ireland.[60] On his own account, he promoted a Protestant colony at Ballymote with spiritual and martial weapons.[61] He took his spiritual duties seriously. Yet, he was regarded by Catholics as a Protestant bigot, moving from the fierce Presbyterianism of his father into the episcopal church only because there had been no Presbyterian minister in his district when he was growing up. Henry, 'that little prattling pulpit orator', was derided as an apologist in the pay of the Dublin government.[62]

Lady Arbella Denny won loud acclaim for her steadfastness in adhering to her principles. Widowed early, she turned her homes – in Dublin itself and a nearby suburban seaside villa – into models of civility and disciplined conviviality.[63] Much more than her showy and attention-seeking neighbour, the duchess of Leinster, Lady Arbella showed how the benevolent could advance material and moral reform. Left with a generous competence – probably at least £1500 p.a. – she moved easily in the most elevated social and political circles. From this position she mordantly observed passing crazes. She recognized that charities, if they were to succeed in creating work for the indigent, had to catch contemporary fancies. Accordingly she watched closely the changing fashions in dress, furnishings and sociability.[64] She devoted much of her income to her favourite causes. At the same time, she prodded others into giving. The Christian dimension to her concerns, if seldom obtruded, nevertheless dominated her activities. This same polite, but resolutely committed Protestantism bound together others who shared her attitudes. These firm religious beliefs drew strength from developments in Britain and continental Europe.[65] They were also necessary responses to the worrying challenges within Ireland: from a more visible and sometimes militant Catholicism, from Methodism and the older but tenacious varieties of Protestant dissent, and from the restlessness of

---

Providence: the clergy, 1647–1780' in T. Barnard and W.G. Neely, *The clergy of the Church of Ireland, 1000–2000: messengers, watchmen and stewards* (Dublin, 2006), p. 103. **60** W. Henry, 'A natural and typographical [*sic*] history', NA, Dublin, M 2533; W. Henry, *An account of Lough Lheichs in the county of Cavan* ([Dublin], 1736); C.S. King (ed.), *Henry's Upper Lough Erne in 1739* (Dublin, 1892); Magennis, '"A land of milk and honey"', pp 209, 215–16. **61** Calendar of miscellaneous papers and letters prior to 1760, s.d. 15 March 1758, NA; Barnard, *New anatomy*, pp 100, 291, 365 n.92. **62** W. Henry to F. Lyne, 20 July 1761, NLI, MS 20,601; Ward, Wrynn and Ward (eds), *Letters of Charles O'Connor of Belangare*, pp 117–18. **63** B.B. Butler, 'Lady Arbella Denny, 1707–1792', *Dublin Historical Record*, ix (1946–7), pp 1–20; O'Malley, *Lios-an-Uisce*, pp 10–25, 61–7. **64** Barnard, 'The artistic and cultural activities of the Caldwells of Castle Caldwell'. **65** W.R. Ward, *The Protestant evangelical awakening* (Cambridge, 1992). Lady Arbella Denny had earlier travelled to the continent of Europe. At Bowood House in Wiltshire, she met Richard Price and Joseph Priestley. Lady A. Denny to Lord Fitzmaurice, 29 July 1780, Bodleian, MS Lyell empt. 36, f. 41.

sections of the population, both in Dublin and the countryside. By the 1770s, Ireland might have been untroubled by open rebellion for eighty years. In one vital sense, this placidity realised the prognostications of the projectors of the seventeenth century. However, in many other details, the kingdom was very far from conforming to the hopeful scheme – of prosperity and Protestantism – that had been conjured by the prophets of the previous age. Lady Arbella Denny, accepting that much remained to be done, set an example.

Lineage gave Lady Arbella Denny an *entrée* to the smart and wealthy. She was related to the Petty-Fitzmaurices, earls of Shelburne. Possessed of vast estates in County Kerry, elsewhere in Ireland and in England, the Shelburnes had through marriage improved on the flying start provided by Sir William Petty, founder of the family fortunes in Ireland. Through upbringing and then her brief marriage, Lady Arbella knew Kerry intimately, and the contrasts between its developed and undeveloped districts. Furthermore, she was familiar with piquant contrasts between its remoteness and backwardness and the modes that prevailed in metropolitan Dublin and London and in the elegant country houses of the Shelburnes in Buckinghamshire and Wiltshire. The women of the Shelburne family displayed something of the same Protestant pietism as Lady Arbella. They discharged some of the responsibilities to the areas from which they derived ample revenues through conventional giving: to the Incorporated Society to finance charter schools; and in the distribution of exhortatory tracts.[66] Otherwise, the successive wives and widows devoted themselves to the strenuous routines of the high life in St Stephen's Green, Berkeley Square, High Wycombe and Bowood. The heir to the enviable patrimony, the second earl of Shelburne (advanced to be first marquess of Lansdowne in 1784), acknowledged the kindness and practical interest in his upbringing of his aunt, Lady Arbella Denny. She continued to see and exert influence over him. At his table, she met the assortment of guests with whom he diverted himself. They included philosophers, scientists, writers and men of affairs, radicals and reactionaries, visitors from continental Europe and Ireland. How greatly these conversations affected Lady Arbella's strategies in Ireland and Shelburne's thinking on Ireland has yet to be established.

Shelburne, possessed of vast but scattered lands across Ireland, although often an absentee was not habitually so. Moreover, both in his private capacity, drawing a substantial proportion of his £40,000 p.a. from Ireland, and in his public responsibilities (a cabinet minister and briefly prime minister between 1783 and 1784) he was interested in Ireland and its continuing problems. On periodic visits, he

---

[66] Lady Mary Coghill [formerly Cremer] to Lady Caldwell, 4 March 1776, JRL, B 3/30/55; William Sleator to Sir J. Caldwell, 7 June 1776, ibid., B 3/20/353.

inspected his holdings. Both in Dublin and England, he consulted those apparently expert on Irish affairs: not just his aunt, but also, for example, another family connection, Sir James Caldwell.[67] In turn, it was Shelburne who recommended that arch exponent of the doctrine of improvement, Arthur Young, to Caldwell.[68] Shelburne received contradictory advice. It reflected not only the strikingly divergent conditions in the regions where his informants owned land, but also varied presuppositions. Yet, if not always convergent, the schemes of Lady Arbella Denny, Caldwell and the Revd William Henry (another adviser of Shelburne)[69] focussed on the universal nostrum of improvement. These commentators shook up the familiar ingredients – schooling, devotional and practical manuals, financial incentives and the *noblesse oblige* of the grandees – so that the exact flavour was unfamiliar. The essence, however, remained the same.

III

The continuities are particularly apparent when Shelburne toured his southwestern estates. Undoubtedly they had undergone some changes in the century since they had come into the family. Yet, no less than Petty before him, Shelburne was at once dismayed and exhilarated by what he saw. In particular, the unrealised potential and the mistakes of his predecessors struck him. In Kerry Shelburne also viewed the holdings of the most celebrated improver in the locality, Lord Kenmare, who, as a Catholic, defied inhibitions to keep his estate and expectations by improving it.[70]

Another contemporary who contradicted Protestant presuppositions about Catholic unwillingness or inability to improve was Charles O'Conor of Belanagare. O'Conor, one of the best documented Catholic proprietors to survive on part of his family estate in County Roscommon, enthusiastically endorsed the current doctrine of improvement.[71] He recognized that it was the key to raising his own income and providing adequately for two sons. He prided himself on the steady progress that he made, with land reclaimed, cleared and cultivated. In addition, he was keen to introduce the linen manufacture into his district.[72] Yet, in 1786, as he surveyed the modest improvements that he had

---

67 Lord Shelburne to Sir J. Caldwell, 18 June 1764, JRL, B 3/10, pp 483–4; Sir J. Caldwell to Dowager Lady Shelburne, 10 Aug. 1764, ibid., B 3/10, pp 494–7; Sir J. Caldwell to Lord Shelburne, 3 Feb. 1768, ibid., B 3/10, pp 293–8; same to same, undated [?1770], ibid., B 3/14/128; same to Lady Caldwell, 29 April 1766, 22 Oct. 1772, 3 and 12 Nov. 1772, 10 and 15 Dec. 1772, ibid., B 3/29/24, 33, 34, 37, 44, 45. **68** Lord Shelburne to Sir J. Caldwell, 1 June 1776, JRL, B 3/16/411. **69** Lord Shelburne to Sir J. Caldwell, 21 Feb. 1759, JRL, B 3/14/124; P. Magran to same, 9 April 1759, ibid., B 3/20/241. **70** Lord Kenmare's observations, PRONI, D 4151/S/5/1; E. MacLysaght (ed.), *The Kenmare manuscripts* (Dublin, 1942), pp 450–4. **71** Ward, Wrynn and Ward (eds), *Letters of Charles O'Conor of Belanagare*, pp 7, 158, 167, 340, 423, 497. **72** Ibid., p. 207.

achieved, if he acknowledged that he had profited, he doubted that the poor tenants had. Better housing, for example, simply exposed them to the hearth tax.[73] Despite this gloomy conclusion, O'Conor approved the steps taken by parliament to encourage developments, such as inland navigation, road building and bounties for growing corn. Furthermore, he enthused over individual initiatives such as those of William Burton Conyngham with the fisheries in Donegal. At the same time, he conceded that much remained to be done.[74]

Travelling through the north west, he was struck by the dramatic terrain and expressed a perhaps conventional wonder at the 'romantic prospects'. However, stronger than this sensibility was O'Conor's regret that the places slumbered 'in the state of nature', with stores of iron and coal still not exploited. He acknowledged the problems – distance from markets and poor transport – that had thwarted so many of the earlier ventures.[75] But these insights did not stifle his belief that the potential of the created world could and should be realised. Like many improvers, O'Conor had faith in printed manuals, especially on agriculture.[76] Indeed, he wrote one himself: on mining. Less usual, but nevertheless – as has been suggested above – a theme in improvement, was O'Conor's view that clearer understanding of the past was a key to a better future. Joining in collective explorations of Irish antiquities, he contended that uncovering 'latent treasures under and over ground would excite a spirit of improvement throughout the whole kingdom'.[77] This belief linked him with the utopians and investigators of the Cromwellian interregnum.

Where O'Conor diverged from the optimistic assessors of Ireland's potential was in blaming the present retardation less on indolence, ignorance and infrastructural weaknesses, and more on the political and legal systems. He contended that the laws which prevented Catholics from acquiring freehold land or renting it on long leases explained the shift in the eighteenth century to the most immediately profitable types of cultivation. Grazing not arable husbandry was the result.[78] Only when the discriminatory laws were repealed would the majority of the population have an incentive to work for the betterment of the island. Accordingly, while O'Conor innovated on his own holdings, he was politically active – through pressure groups like the Catholic Association – to accomplish political change. Only Petty, of the propagandists and projectors considered above, contemplated that particular re-drawing of the map of Ireland, and then only during the exceptional times under the Catholic King James.

73 Ibid., pp 10, 59, 68, 106, 160–1, 205–6, 213, 232, 238, 378, 475.   74 Ibid., pp 114, 399, 428, 453.   75 Ibid., pp 171, 426, 453–4, 471.   76 Ibid., pp 9–10, 175–6, 180, 205.   77 Ibid., p. 460.   78 Ibid., pp 33–4, 40, 125, 142–3, 174–5, 187–8, 239, 242, 244, 246, 262–3, 268, 356, 358,

Index

Abert, Co. Galway, 144
absenteeism, 15, 31, 33, 38, 56, 66, 68, 73, 74, 77, 79, 122, 136, 140, 142, 161–2, 182–3
Acheson, Sir Arthur, 149, 152
acts of parliament: Declaratory Act (1720), 101
Adam, Robert, 72
Addison, Joseph, 148
adventurers, for lands in Ireland, 19, 48, 50
agriculture, 13, 15, 19, 25, 27–8, 29, 30–1, 33–6, 39–40, 56–7, 65, 71, 116, 119, 120, 134, 146, 147, 149, 151, 152, 160, 165, 172–3, 174, 184
Alemand, Louis-Augustin, 100–1, 110; *plate 1*
America, 34, 55, 162, 167, 171, 175
Anderson, James, 124, 126, 128, 130, 133, 141
Anne, queen, 89, 112
Aristotle, 18
Armagh, county, 152
Argyll, duke of, *see* Campbell, Archibald
Asia, 164, 167
Assyria, 88
atheism, 51, 62
Athenry, Co. Galway, 154
Aughrim, Co. Galway, 146
Augustine, saint, 18
Augustinians, religious order, 102
Austria, 178

Babylon, 92
Bacon, Francis, 19, 23, 30, 34, 41, 46–7, 92
Ballymote, Co. Sligo, 38, 181
Ballynacregg, Co. Galway, 153
Banagher, Co. Offaly, 146
banks, 60, 86–7
Baptists, 75–6, 79, 82–4
Barbavilla, Co. Westmeath, 152, 172–3
Barry, James, 4th earl of Barrymore, 125, 133
Barrymore, earl of, *see* Barry, James
Bath, 105, 161
Bayley, Revd Edward, 176, 180
Belfast, 151, 173
Berkeley, George, bishop of Cloyne, 126, 135, 139, 141, 171
Berkeley, John, 1st Baron Berkeley of Stratton, 78
Berkeley, William, 126
Berwick, duke of, *see* Fitzjames, James
Bible, 21, 38, 40, 95
Bindon, Francis, 146, 151, 155, 158
Blake, family, 145, 154
Blaymires, Jonas, 117–18; *plates 4, 5*
Blondel, François, 132
Blundell, family, 125
Boate, Arnold, 20–33, 35–6, 40, 93, 94
Boate, Gerard, 20–33, 35–6, 40, 93
bogs, draining, 36, 147, 151, 154
Bolton, Theophilus, archbishop of Cashel, 118
Borlase, Edmund, 110
Boston, Massachusetts, 162
Bowood, Wiltshire, 72, 182
Boyle, family, earls of Cork and Burlington, 22, 25, 28, 51, 56, 66, 107, 121, 125, 136, 159
Boyle, family, earls of Orrery, 107
Boyle, Richard, first earl of Cork, 22, 23, 25, 28, 32, 36, 40, 44, 50–1, 54, 56, 63, 132, 169
Boyle, Richard, second earl of Cork and first earl of Burlington, 32, 33–4, 44–5, 66
Boyle, Robert, 47
Boyle, Roger, first earl of Orrery, 33–4, 52, 66, 77, 87, 128; his *Art of War*, 134
Brereton, Captain George, 138, 139, 140
Brereton, Revd Robert, 127, 138, 139
Brewster, Sir Francis, 75, 87
Brian Boru, 107
Bristol, 161
Browne, family, Viscounts Kenmare, 16, 17, 170, 183
Browne, Thomas, 4th Viscount Kenmare, 16, 17, 170, 183
Brydges, James, first duke of Chandos, 113, 115
Buckinghamshire, 182
Buckworth, Theophilus, bishop of Dromore, 22, 27
Burke, family, 145, 154
Burke, Edmund, 127
Burton House, Co. Cork, 127, 138; *plate 7*
Bury St Edmunds, Suffolk, 169
Butler, James, 1st duke of Ormond, 28, 29–30, 52, 54–5, 60, 67, 75, 78, 79, 85, 87, 94, 103–4

INDEX

Butler, James, earl of Ossory and 2nd duke of Ormonde, 75, 79, 101, 103
Butler, Sarah, 102–4

Caldwell, Elizabeth, *née* Hort, 179
Caldwell, Sir James, 168, 170, 176–9, 183
Callan, Co. Kilkenny, 78
Cambrensis, Giraldus, 104
Cambridge, 105, 161; King's College, 159; Trinity College, 159
Camden, William, 92, 93
Campbell, Archibald, 3rd duke of Argyll, 159
canals, 37, 38, 40, 71, 131, 139, 168, 184; *plate 16*
Capel, Arthur, earl of Essex, 60–1, 78
Capuchin order, 62
Carlow, town, 105
Carolan, Turlough, 105
Carr, Charles, bishop of Killaloe, 118
Carrick-on-Shannon, Co. Leitrim, 156
Carrick-on-Suir, Co. Tipperary, 78
Carte, Thomas, 103–4
Carter, Cornelius, 99
Carteret, Sir George, 55–7
Carton, Co. Kildare, 145
Cashel, archbishop of, *see* Bolton, Theophilus
Cashel: cathedral, 118; Cormac's chapel, 118
Castlecomer, Co. Kilkenny, 26
Castlelyons, Co. Cork, 125, 133
catechism, 40
Catherine of Braganza, queen, 100
Catholic Association, 184
Catholicism, 13–14, 16, 19, 22, 26–9, 71, 81–2, 84, 88, 91, 95, 101, 104–5, 162–4, 174, 178, 181
Catholics, 62, 76, 81, 88, 90, 99, 109, 132–4, 154, 155: clergy, 62, 101, 111, 133, 134, 162–4, 178, 181, *plate 1*; exiled, 48; landowners, 16, 17, 30, 35–6, 39, 42, 45–9, 54, 58, 80, 144–5, 147, 170, 179, 183–4; lobby, 48–9; in London, 106; tenants, 32, 36, 46, 71, 132–3, 135, 138–9, 153, 163–4, 174, 178, 184
Cavan, county, 173
Cecil, family, earls of Salisbury, 125, 129, 131, 136, 138
Cecil, Lady Catherine, Viscountess Perceval and countess of Egmont, 125, 129, 131, 136, 138
Cecilstown, Co. Cork, 137–8; *plate 15*
census, 69
Chamberlayne, Edward, 110
Channel Islands, 55
Chapelizod, Co. Dublin, 75, 77, 78, 85–6, 88
Charlemagne, 123
Charles I, king, 18, 19, 21, 48
Charles II, king, 30, 42, 43, 45–6, 47–9, 52, 59, 60, 70, 75, 81, 82, 87, 100

Charles V, Holy Roman Emperor, 101
Charles Edward, prince, 'the younger pretender', 132, 134
Charlton, Kent, 142
Child, Robert, 24, 30–1, 33, 36
Chiswick House, Middlesex, 159
chivalry, 135–6
Church of Ireland, 35, 50, 76, 82, 85, 91, 96, 112, 113, 144, 155, 163, 175: its bishops, 19, 36–7, 113, 117–18; its clergy, 37, 40, 62, 96, 108, 110, 115, 117–18, 146, 176, 180–1; conversions to, 163
Churchtown, Co. Cork, 127
Clahisy, Patrick, 138
Clare, County, 46, 69, 75, 80, 154, 156
Clarendon, earl of, *see* Hyde, Edward and Hyde, Henry
Clonfert, Co. Galway, 117
Clonmacnoise, Co. Offaly, 117
Clontarf, battle of (1014), 103
Cluer, Thomas, 107
Cobb, Thomas, 107
Colchester, Essex, 83
Coleshill, Warwickshire, 161
Colgan, Fr John, 101
Collins, Anthony, 131
Collinstown, Co. Westmeath, 172–4
Comenius, Jan, 19, 22–3
Compton, family, earls of Northampton, 136
Compton, Lady Catherine, countess of Egmont and Baroness Arden of Lohort Castle, 136; *plate 14*
Connacht, province, 46, 69, 73, 75, 80, 100, 149, 155
Conry, John, historian, 109
Constans, Christopher, 150
Conyngham, William Burton, 168, 184
Cooley, William, 130–5, 137–42; his wife, 130, 139
Cooltragh, Co. Galway, 146
Coote, family, earls of Mountrath, 22, 31, 107, 125
Coote, Sir Charles, 23, 25, 31
Cork: city, 36, 64, 138; county, 52, 89, 113, 116, 117, 121–5, 128, 134, 141–2
Cornaro family, 159
Corrondoe, Co. Galway, 155
Court of Claims, 48–9, 52–5
Coventry, 83
Cox, Sir Richard, the elder, 79, 89, 97, 98, 101, 104, 110
Cox, Sir Richard, the younger, 89–90, 114, 116
Creake, Benjamin, 105, 106
Cregboy, Co. Galway, 153
Crespin, Jean, 21
Cromwell, Henry, 42, 51, 52, 67
Cromwell, Oliver, 21, 24, 47, 52

Crossly, Aaron, 107, 110, 124
Culloden, battle of, 134
Cumberland, Prince William Augustus, duke of, 134

Daly, family, 145
Daly, Charles, 156
Darcy, Patrick, 17, 27, 169
Dartmouth, earl of, *see* Legge, George
Davies, Sir John, 18, 23, 80, 93, 94
Deane, Sir Matthew, 140, note
Denny, Lady Arbella, 170, 179–80, 182–3
Denton, Thomas, 'galloping topographer', 93
Derry, bishopric of, 97
Derryglissane, Co. Galway, 153
Descartes, René, 41
Devereux, Robert, earl of Essex, 111
diet, 13, 33
Digby, John, 147–8, 160
Digby, Simon, bishop of Elphin, 144, 159
Digby, Robert, Baron Digby of Geashill, 161
Dineley, Thomas, 94
Dingle, Co. Kerry, 122
Dobbs, Arthur, 24
Dobson, Eliphal, 110
Donegal, county, 184
Doneraile, Co. Cork, 125, 130, 137
Donnellan, family, 154
Dopping, Anthony, bishop of Meath, 97
Dorchester, 83
Dorset, duke of, *see* Sackville-Cranfield, Lionel
Down, County, 30, 77, 85, 113, 171, 173
Down Survey, 41, 44–5, 51, 58, 65, 69, 70, 72
dress, 13, 43, 78, 80, 181
Dromore, Co. Down, 173; bishop of: *see* Buckworth, Theophilus
Dublin, 14, 29, 35, 37, 47–8, 52, 56, 64, 66, 67, 68, 72, 74, 75, 81, 88, 93, 97, 100, 110, 112, 113, 121, 124, 144, 145, 146, 149, 156, 160, 167, 172, 175, 177, 179, 182; St Andrew's church, 171; Blind Quay, 158; booksellers, 102, 118; Bull Head Club, 157; charity in, 83–4; corporation, 113; costs of living, 157, 166; Foundling Hospital, 180; government in, 15, 42; Henrietta St, 166; King's Inns, 147; Lying–In Hospital, 180; Magdalen Asylum, 180; Mary St, 157, 158; newspapers, 102; Protestant élite, 116; Ross St, 157; St Patrick's cathedral, *plate 5*; St Stephen's Green, 182; Skinner Row, 157; Smithfield, 72, 77
Dublin, archbishopric of, 97
Dublin, county, 77, 113
Dublin: Trinity College, 34, 95, 96, 98, 109, 110, 115, 116, 147, 171; proposed second college, 34

Dublin Bay, 65
Dublin Castle, 60, 75, 133
Dublin Philosophical Society, 15, 24, 35, 41, 43, 61, 94–6, 98, 99, 106, 109
Dublin Society, 24, 25, 31, 38, 40, 74, 83, 115, 117, 119, 140, 154, 165, 170, 171–2, 177
Dugdale, Sir William, 101
Duhallow, Co. Cork, 124
Duncan, James, 138
Dungarvan, Co. Waterford, 116
Dury, John, 20, 22

Easton Neston, Northants, 159
Edinburgh, 105
Egypt, 37, 92
Elizabeth I, queen, 89, 111, 124
Elphin, bishop of, *see* Digby, Simon; Howard, Robert
empire, British, 162, 164, 167
England, 13, 18, 19, 25, 50, 56, 72, 73, 75–6, 83, 85, 90, 123, 134, 152; antiquarianism in, 92, 94, 104, 105, 120, 129–30, 150, 158–62, 165, 172, 175; army, 21, 24; commonwealth of (1649), 18, 21, 42, 73, 144; government of, 43, 48, 78, 162; king of, 13, 21; land in, 39; parliament of, 21, 28, 31, 43, 49, 52, 122, 169; privy council, 48, 58, 59, 67; revolution in, 18; settlers from, 26, 57, 69–70, 91, 94, 143, 161; Treasury, 59, 132
Enmore, Somerset, 129, 138, 142
Enniscorthy, Co. Wexford, 63
Erasmus, Desiderius, 18
Essex, earl of, *see* Capel, Arthur; Devereux, Robert
Europe, 14, 18, 20, 22, 23, 30, 34, 38–9, 50, 67, 92, 94, 96, 97, 98, 102, 103, 108, 123, 125, 136, 138, 150, 161, 167, 181
Eyre, John, Baron Eyre of Eyrecourt, 163, 165
Eyre Court, Co. Galway, 152

famine, 37, 132, 141, 173, 175
fashion, 15, 31, 50, 88, 115–16, 135, 141–2, 149–51, 181
Faulkner, George, 74, 100
Fermanagh, county, 176–7
Fermor, Thomas, 1st earl of Pomfret, 159
Fisher, Jonathan, plate 16
fishing, 16, 17, 37, 53, 57, 63, 64–5, 69, 83, 168–9, 177, 178, 184
Fitzgerald, Emily, *née* Lennox, duchess of Leinster, 181
Fitzjames, James, 1st duke of Berwick, 112
Fitzjames, James Stuart-, 2nd duke of Berwick and duke of Liria, 112
Fitzmaurice, family, earls of Kerry, 67

INDEX

Fitzroy, Henry, 2nd duke of Grafton, 107
flax, growing, 16, 137, 139, 151, 154, 168, 169; *see also* Linen Board; textiles
Fleetwood, Charles, 51, 75
Forest of Dean, 63
Forman, Charles, 102
Fornenbergh, Alexander van, 86
Fowkes, Ann, 83
Foxe, John, 21
Foy, Nathaniel, bishop of Waterford, 82
France, 44, 100, 101, 132
Franciscan order, *plate 1*
Freeman, William, 140 note
freemasonry, 124, 130, 135
French, family (French Park), 147
French, family (Monivea), 143–66
French, Revd Digby, 159
French, Jane, *née* Digby, 145, 147, 149, 157, 159
French, Nicola, *née* Acheson, 149, 153, 157, 158
French, Patrick, 144, 145, 146, 151, 156
French, Robert, 143–66, 167–8, 170, 171, 173, 175; income, 148–9, 166
furnishings, 128, 130, 131, 136, 149–50, 157–8, 181; *plate 14*

Gaelic: customs, 13, 23, 25, 26, 53, 62–3, 80, 90–2, 93, 95–7, 98, 109, 120, 126, 155, 163, 175
Gale, Roger, 104
Galileo, 41
Galway: city, 17, 99, 100, 143–4, 145, 154, 156; commission of the peace, 156; county, 143–66; electoral politics, 156
gardens and gardening, 128–31, 139, 145, 148, 160; plates 12, 13
garrison, 30
genealogy, 93–4, 106–8, 116, 123–5, 136–7
George I, king, 125
George, prince of Wales, later king George II, 106, 123; his daughter, 123
Germany, 56
Gildon, Charles, 103
Glasgow, 71
Gloucester, 83; cathedral, 160
Gobelins, 85
Gookin, Vincent, 73
Gothic, 120, 126, 129, 130, 136, 142
Gough, Richard, 104, 105
Goulart, Simon, 21
Grafton, duke of, *see* Fitzroy, Henry
Greece, 92, 164
Greenwich, Hill, 162; Hospital, 159

Hamner, Meredith, 110

Hampton Court, palace, 160
Handel, G.F., 157; his *Messiah*, 157
Harris, Walter, 24, 89–90, 98, 101, 110, 113–19, 171; plate 4
Hartlib, Samuel, 19–21, 22–4, 28, 30–4, 36, 38, 47, 74, 77, 93, 111, 112
Harwich, Suffolk, 122
Hay, Charles, 129, 130, 132, 139; plates 12, 13
Headfort, Co. Meath, 72
Henry II, 14
Henry VII, 160
Henry VIII, 14
Henry, Revd William, 'prattling pulpit orator', 38, 180–1, 183
heraldry, 93, 107, 123–4, 125, 129, 135–6, 137, 138
Herbert, family (County Kerry), 71
Herbert, Henry, 10th earl of Pembroke, 159
Heylin, Peter, 110
Higgins, Winifred, mistress of Robert French, 165
High Wycombe, Bucks, 182
Hill, Col. Arthur, 30–1
Hobbes, Thomas, 41, 82
Holy Cross Abbey, Co. Tipperary, 118
hospitality, 128, 149–50, 182
hospitals, 15, 83, 176, 180
housing, 13, 29, 33, 50, 52, 66, 77, 80, 94, 126, 128, 130, 132, 137, 138, 142, 145, 153, 154–5, 156–8, 172, 184
Howard, Robert, bishop of Elphin, 35–7
Huntington, Robert, 95, 96, 110
Hutchinson, Francis, bishop of Down and Connor, 37–8, 73–4, 83, 168–9
Hyde, Edward, first earl of Clarendon, 91
Hyde, Henry, second earl of Clarendon, 100–1

Inchiquin, earl of, *see* O'Brien, William
Incorporated Society, 40, 155, 165, 170, 173, 182
Independents, religious, 62
India, 162
Ireland, 19: army in, 30, 51, 73, 75, 78, 100; coinage, 74, 78, 79, 86–7; Council of Trade, 43, 74, 75, 78, 85, 87; Danes in, 95, 97, 103; government of, 19, 28, 30, 49, 54, 57, 60, 69–70, 75–6, 92, 97, 101, 132–3, 162–3, 181; exiles from, 20–2, 25, 27–9, 30, 161–2; histories of, 21–3, 28, 71, 89–119; House of Lords, 66; land in, 16–17, 18, 39–40; landscape of, 36, 72, 118, 119, 120, 123, 126–30, 135, 142, 160, 184; monasteries in, 118; natural history of, 20, 34–6, 41, 94, 97–8, 110, 113, 115, 168–9; Old English in, 26–7; parliament, 31, 37–8, 40, 43, 48–50, 51, 83, 89, 99, 116, 120, 121, 122, 155–6, 162–3, 164–5, 175, 176, 184; population, 24, 40, 41, 69, 167; privy council, 28, 42, 48, 58, 60, 67, 68, 78, 85, 121; revenues, 59, 167;

INDEX

settlement of, 13–15, 18–22, 35–6, 39–40, 42, 44, 46, 47–8, 51, 69–70, 73, 76–7, 80, 82, 87–8, 93, 95; war in, 18–19, 28, 29, 35, 39–40, 42, 93, 95, 100, 109, 115, 127, 130, 132–4
Ireton, Henry, 24
Italy, 56, 86, 106

Jacobites, 103, 126, 132, 145
James VI and I, king, 18, 89, 124
James VII and II, king, formerly duke of York, 35, 42, 45–6, 49, 57, 61, 62, 67, 70, 81, 82, 98, 99, 112, 121, 144, 184
Jesuit order, 44, 62, 81
Jocelyn, Robert, 1st Baron Newport and Viscount Jocelyn, 114
Johnson, Benjamin, 154
Jones, Richard, 1st earl of Ranelagh, 87

Kanturk, Co. Cork, 123, 125, 128, 132, 138; *plate 8*
Keating, Geoffrey, 103–8, 110–11, 117; *plates 2, 3*
Kells, Book of, 95
Kelly, Daniel, 153
Kenmare, river, 53, 63
Kenmare, Viscount, *see* Browne, Thomas
Kent, 127
Kerry, county, 16, 46, 53–8, 61, 62–5, 68, 70–1, 113, 167, 176, 182, 183
Kerry, earls of, *see* Fitzmaurice
Kilcolman, Co. Cork, 127
Kilconnel, Co. Galway, 146
Kilkenny: city, 105; round tower, 118; St Canice's cathedral, 118
Kilkenny, Confederation of, 26
Kilkenny Castle, 60
Killaloe, bishop of, *see* Carr, Charles
Killaloe, cathedral, 118
Killarney, Co. Kerry, plate 16
King, William, successively bishop of Derry and archbishop of Dublin, 91, 97–8, 109, 112, 117; *plate 3*
Kinsale, Co. Cork, 67
Knight, James, 84
Knight, Revd Nicholas, 109–10
Knockaniver, Co. Galway, 154

Landenstown, Co. Kildare, 147
Lane, Sir George, 1st earl of Lanesborough, 87
Langley, Batty, 129
language, 13, 37, 80, 105, 108, 163, 170
latin, 98, 100
law: admiralty court, 67; assizes, 115; courts of, 13, 30, 48–9, 58–9, 149; grand jury, 16, 114–15; records of, 95, 98; systems of, 13, 93, 98, 184

Lawrence, Richard, 73–88, 112, 176
lawyers, 18, 21, 50, 95, 105, 144, 146, 149, 156
leases, 16, 32, 153
Legge, George, 2nd earl of Dartmouth, 47
Leicester, 83
Leinster, duchess of, *see* Fitzgerald, Emily
Leinster, province, 27
Leipzig, 34, 96
Leitrim, county, 156
Le Neve, Peter, 104
Levant, 94, 95–6
libraries, 98, 102, 109–11, 113, 115, 116–17, 131, 150, 159
Limerick, 52, 64, 140, 171; cathedral, *plate 4*
Linen Board, 85, 137, 140, 151–2, 171, 173
Liria, duke of, *see* Fitzjames, James Stuart
Liscarroll, Co. Cork, 123, 125, 128, 129; *plate 9*
Lismore, Co. Waterford, 56
Liverpool, 150
Lodge, John, 110, 124
Lohort Castle, Co. Cork, 123, 125–42; *plates 10–13*
London, 22, 29, 34, 47, 48, 51, 56, 58, 66, 103, 132, 138, 144, 145: Berkeley Square, 182; British Library, 41; Covent Garden, 161; government in, 14; 'Invisible College' in, 22, 47; Irish in, 106, 108, 122, 161, 177, 179; Middle Temple, 144, 147; Northumberland House, 159; Royal Society, 41, 43, 61, 96; St Paul's cathedral, 160
Longfield, John, 138
Longford, County, 37
Longueville, Co. Cork, 138
Lough Corrib, 146
Lough Erne, 29, 177
Loughreagh, Co. Galway, 145, 146
luxury, 15, 39, 73, 84, 88, 164, 170, 176
Lynegar, Charles, 93
Lysaght, John, 140 note

Macale, James, 154
Macale, Richard, 154
MacCurtin, Hugh, 104
McFinin, Donough, 54, 62
McGilllicuddy, Donough, 54, 62
Machiavelli, Nicolai, 18
Mackenzie, Sir George, 99
Madden, Samuel, 24
Mallow, Co. Cork, 136, 138, 157, 166
Manners, Charles, 4th duke of Rutland, 180
manufactures, 13, 15, 16, 25, 33, 35–6, 37, 38, 40, 53, 57, 63–5, 71, 78, 85, 119, 120, 123, 154–5, 163, 174, 184: of glass, 25, 29; extractive, 25–6, 33, 65, 184; of iron, 22, 23, 25, 33, 53, 63–5, 69, 71, 177, 184; metallurgical, 25–6, 65, 71; *see also* textiles

Malone, Anthony, 163
maps, 20, 34, 35, 41, 69, 94, 101, 118, 184
Market Hill, Co. Armagh, 149
markets, 29, 30, 146, 155, 172–3, 177, 184
Marsh, Narcissus, archbishop of Armagh, 95, 96, 110
Mary II, queen, 97
Massingham, Thomas, 110
mathematics, 37, 87–8, 151
Maule, Henry, bishop of Meath, 163
Meath: county, 17
medicine, profession of, 27, 44, 51, 67, 157
Melton Constable, Norfolk, 131
Methodists, 175, 181
Michelangelo, 132
militia, 133, 135
millenarianism, 18–19, 23
Miller, Philip, 131
Mitchell, Thomas, 126
Mizen Head, 53
Moll, Herman, 101
Molyneux, Dr Samuel, 98–9, 105, 106
Molyneux, Thomas, 95, 98
Molyneux, William, 24, 94, 95, 98, 110, 111, 114
Monivea, Co. Galway, 143–66, 167, 173
Montagu, John, 2nd duke of Montagu, 107; *plate 2*
Montfauçon, Bernard de, 96
Mortlake, 85
Mount Hillary, 129
Mount Pleasant, Kent (*alias* Tunbridge Castle), 142
Mountrath, Co. Offaly, 23, 25
Mulkiran, Edward, 106
Mullingar, Co. Westmeath, 174
Munster, 14, 120, 134, 140; plantation of, 27–8, 31, 33, 120–1, 126, 132

Naples, 106
Navan, Co. Meath, 140
Netherlands, Spanish, 86
Newport, Baron, *see* Jocelyn, Robert
Nicolson, William, successively bishop of Carlisle and of Derry, 99, 109
Normans, 125: and Ireland, 13, 91, 97, 143–4, 163
Northampton, earls of, *see* Compton

O'Brien, Sir Lucius, 148, 154, 156, 165, 166
O'Brien, William, 4th earl of Inchiquin, 105, 107
O'Carroll, family, 106
O'Connor, family, 106
O'Connor, Dermod, 98, 104–8, 110–11
O'Connor, Maurice, 106

O'Conor, Charles, 16, 17, 93, 100, 106, 117, 168, 170, 183–4
O'Dwyer, Count, 106
O'Flaherty, Roderick, 98–100, 107, 110, 115; his *Ogygia*, 98–9; *Ogygia Vindicated*, 99–100, 106
office, 66, 67–8, 113, 121, 125
O'Hara, Charles, 168
O'Mulchonry, family, 109
O'Mulrian, Thady, major, 106
Ormsby, William, 157
Ousley, William, 111
Oxford, 105: Christ Church, 159–60; university, 44, 47, 51, 67, 147, 159–60

painting, 43, 146, 150, 158–9, 160
Pakenham, Thomas, 173
Pale, the, 14, 144
Paris, 34, 96, 100, 118
Parsons, Sir Laurence, 30
Parsons, Richard, 22, 29
Parsons, Richard, first Viscount Rosse, 29–30
Parsons, Sir William, 22, 28–9, 30
Parsonstown (Birr), King's County (Offaly), 29–30
Patrick, saint, 91
patriotism, 37–8, 40, 79, 88, 126, 165, 171
peace, 14, 167, 182
peerage, 66, 72, 79–80, 107, 110, 123–4, 125, 131, 136, 161, 162, 178, 183
Pembroke, earl of, *see* Herbert, Henry
Pepys, Samuel, 61
Perceval, family, earls of Egmont, 66, 120, 132, 136, 139–42; income, 122
Perceval, Sir John, Viscount Perceval and 1st earl of Egmont, 122–33
Perceval, John, Viscount Perceval and 2nd earl of Egmont 122–3, 129, 130, 132, 135, 136–40, 142; *plate 14*
Perceval, Revd Kane, 140
Perceval, Sir Philip, 132, 133
Perceval, William, 139
Persia, 111
Persse, family, 161
Pett, Peter, 61
Petty, family, 121, 136, 167, 182
Petty, Anne, countess of Kerry, 67
Petty, Charles, 2nd Baron Shelburne, 68
Petty, Elizabeth, *née* Waller, sometime Lady Fenton and subsequently Baroness Shelburne, 52, 55, 68
Petty, John, 1st earl of Shelburne, 70
Petty, Sir William, 20, 24, 30, 34–5, 41–72, 73–5, 79, 84, 87, 88, 94, 112, 168, 177, 182, 184; income, 53,

72, 84; his *Political Anatomy*, 61, 68–9, 93; religious opinions, 61–2
Petty-Fitzmaurice, William, 2nd earl of Shelburne and 1st marquess of Lansdowne, 71–2, 168, 176, 182–3
Phillips, Richard, mayor of Kilkenny, 105
Phillips, Thomas, 128
Phipps, Sir Constantine, 105
Physico-Historical Society, 24, 74, 83, 113–16, 117, 132, 140–1, 170, 171
Physiocrats, 18
Piers, Sir Henry, 110–11
Pitt, Moses, 94
plague, 24
playwright, 79
Plot, Robert, 24
Plunkett, Nicholas, 17, 27, 90
Poland, 37
Pomfret, earl of, *see* Fermor, Thomas, 159
Poor Clares, order of nuns, *plate 1*
Portugal, 87, 100
Portumna, Co. Galway, 145
poverty, 15, 30, 37, 39, 40, 83–5, 170, 176, 180–1
Powell, Samuel, 114
Presbyterianism, 62, 175, 181
printing, 21, 31, 33, 34, 35, 38, 85, 89–91, 96, 111, 167, 171, 174, 180, 182; in Dublin, 91, 99, 100, 102, 105, 107, 111, 112–13, 115, 118, 171; in London, 91, 100, 103–7, 111, 118
Prior, Thomas, 126
prosperity, 13, 16, 33, 39, 50, 83, 167, 176, 182
Protestantism, 13, 19, 20, 22–3, 170, 175, 178, 181
Protestants: in Ireland, 15–16, 20–1, 27–9, 35, 48–9, 76–7, 101, 109, 116, 132–5, 147, 158, 176; as landlords, 30–1, 36–7, 39, 40, 45–7, 50, 52–3, 58, 66, 68–70, 80, 87–8, 124–6, 132, 141, 148, 155, 175, 176; legends among, 21, 83, 90–2, 97, 109, 111–12, 124–5, 133–4; as tenants, 40, 56–7, 68–70, 71, 126, 137, 138–9, 153, 172–4, 178
Protestant interest, 32, 57, 137, 141, 155, 162–3
Prussia, 176
Purcell, Richard, 122–3, 132, 134–5, 137, 138

Quakers, 88, 112

Ranelagh, earl of, *see* Jones, Richard
Raphael, 160
Raymond, Revd Anthony, 98, 108
Reilly, Alice, 114
republicanism 70, 75
Rhames, Aaron, 99
Rhineland, 86
Richmond, Surrey, 160

Rider, Ebenezer, 102
roads, 37, 38, 40, 71, 168, 184
Robartes, John, 2nd Baron Robartes of Truro and 1st earl of Radnor, 78
Rochfort, George, 179
Rokeby, Yorkshire, 131
Romans, 13, 96–7
Rome, 81, 132, 164
Romsey, Hampshire, 84
Roscommon: county, 16, 17, 37, 183–4
Rota Club, 43
Roubiliac, Louis François, 159
Rouen, 150
Rundle, Thomas, bishop of Derry, 37
Rutland, duke of, *see* Manners, Charles
Rycaut, Sir Paul, 94
Rye House Plot, 75

St Albans, Herts, 160
St George, a herald, 125
St Leger, family, 125
St Leger, Hayes, 137
Sackville-Cranfield, Lionel, duke of Dorset, 156
Salisbury, 83
Salisbury, earls of, *see* Cecil family
Sankey, Sir Hierome, 51
Sardanapalus, 88
Savage, John, 158
Saxons, 97, 120
schools, 15, 29, 34, 37–40, 83, 84, 137, 155, 163, 173, 176, 177, 182, 183
Scotland, 13, 18, 22, 44, 45, 46, 73, 78, 91, 99, 105, 120, 133, 161, 162
Selborne, Hampshire, 119
servant: 145, 149, 155, 156–7; fat, 139
Seville, 106
Shaw, garden designer, 132, 138
Shelburne, Baron, Baroness and earls of, *see* Petty and Petty-Fitzmaurice
Skelton, Revd Philip, 170–1, 180
Smith, Charles, 115, 116, 119, 128, 132, 134, 141, 171; *plate 6*
Smith, Hugh, hatter, 105
Smythe, family, 152
Smythe, Revd James, 110–11
Smythe, William, successively bishop of Raphoe and Kilmore, 172
Smythe, William, 111, 172–5
Smythe, William ('Billy'), 175
Society for Discountenancing of Vice, 83, 176
soldiers: from Ireland, 71, 102, 106; in Ireland, 19, 22, 30, 48, 50, 52, 69, 73, 146, 178
Somerset, 127, 129

INDEX

Southampton, earl of, *see* Wriothesley, Henry
Southwell: family, 66, 120, 121, 125, 136; Robert, 67; Sir Robert, 61, 67
Southwell, Thomas, 2nd Baron Southwell, 124
Spain, 87, 100, 106, 132
Spenser, Edmund, 18, 80, 110, 127
Spottiswood, James, bishop of Clogher, 29
Spring Garden, Co. Galway, 161
Stearne, John, bishop of Clogher, 109
Stevens, John, 98, 100–2, 110, 117, 118; *plate 1*
Stillingfleet, Edward, bishop of Worcester, 99
Stone, George, archbishop of Armagh, 155, 156
Stonehenge, 160
Story, Revd George, 97
Stukeley, William, 104
surveys, 20, 34, 69, 120, 154
Swift, Jonathan, 159
Symner, Miles, 24, 34
Synge, Revd Richard, 88

Talbot, Richard, earl of Tyrconnell, 49
Tarrant, Samuel, 138
Taylor, Thomas, 72, 77
Taylor, Sir Thomas, 72
Taylour, Thomas, 1st earl of Bective, 72
Taylour, Thomas, 2nd earl of Bective and 1st marquess of Headfort, 72
taxation, 20, 43, 57–8, 61, 63, 69, 140, 168, 184
Temple, family, viscounts Palmerston, 66, 125, 136
Temple, Sir John, 21, 22, 23, 26, 90–1, 110, 111, 117
Temple, Sir William, 75, 87
tenants, 16, 25, 31, 32, 34, 40, 137, 145, 146, 153, 163–4, 165, 168, 169, 173–4, 175, 178, 183–5
textiles, 13, 16, 23, 25, 29, 33, 40, 71, 75, 77, 85, 123, 137, 149, 151–2, 165, 168, 172–3, 177, 183
Thomas, Edwin, 157
Titian, 159
Tobberbracken, Co. Galway, 146
Toland, John, 105
Toms, W.H., 128; *plate 10*
towns, 13, 23, 29, 134, 137–8, 149, 167, 172
trade, 13, 16, 19, 25, 29, 38, 39, 40, 65, 67, 77–8, 82–3, 86–7, 123, 149, 167–9, 170, 172–4, 177, 184
Traill, James, bishop of Down and Connor, 38–9
travel, 14, 67, 86, 87, 93, 153, 159–62, 167, 171, 175, 181
Trim, Co. Meath, 108
Tudenham, Co. Westmeath, 179

Ulster, 14, 27–8, 30–1, 36, 46, 151–2, 168, 169, 180–1

United Provinces, 19, 20, 30, 36, 75, 86, 87, 123
Ussher, James, archbishop of Armagh, 101, 110

Vallancey, Charles, 163
Vauban, Sébastien Le Prestre, Maréchal, 128
Venice, 131
Vienna, 178
Vikings, 95, 103
Virgil, 148
Vistula, river, 37

Wade, General George, 159
Wake, William, archbishop of Canterbury, 106
Wales, 45, 83, 92, 94, 120, 161; Geoffrey of, 104; settlers from, 26, 44, 71, 73, 78, 91
Waller, Sir Hardress, 130, 133
Walpole, Horace, 130
Walsh, Fr Peter, 104, 110
Wandesforde, family, 26
Ware, family, 113
Ware, Sir James, 23, 89, 101, 102, 110, 112–19
Ware, Robert, 112
Waring, Samuel, 86, 171–2
Waring, William, 85–6
Waterford, county, 113, 116, 117
Wentworth, Sir Thomas, 1st earl of Strafford, 28
Westmeath, county, 172, 175; history of, 110–11
Westminster, 105: abbey, 131, 159; bridge, 162
Wetenhall, Edward, bishop of Cork, 88
White, Revd Gilbert, 119
Wibault, Jacques, 128
Wicklow, County, 40
Willes, Edward, 15–16
William I, king, 125
William III, king, 97, 113
William of Orange, prince, 123
Williams, Revd Daniel, 84
Williamson, Sir Joseph, 61
Wilton House, Wiltshire, 159, 160
Windsor, Berkshire, 136, 160
witchcraft, 169
Wood, Robert, 24, 34, 77
Wootton, Sir Henry, 131
Worsley, Benjamin, 20, 24, 30, 33, 34, 51, 87
Wren, Sir Christopher, 159–60
Wriothesley, Henry, earl of Southampton, 111

Youghal, Co. Cork, 56, 136
Young, Arthur, 119, 155, 177, 183
Yvery, 124, 128, 133, 134, 141